JESSICA JONES

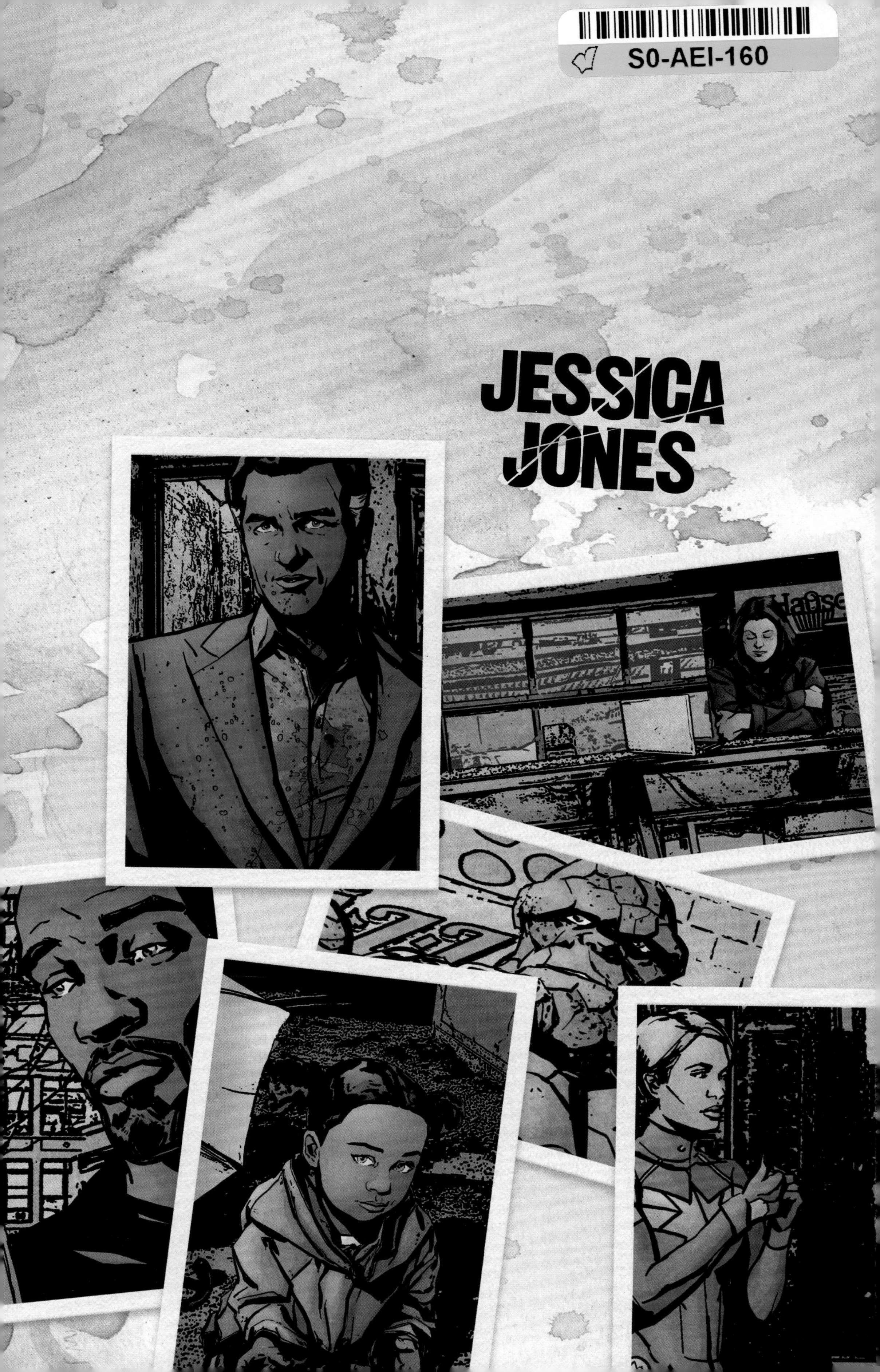

Jessica Jones, a former costumed super hero, is now the owner and sole employee of Alias Investigations — a small private investigative firm.

Not long ago, the nefarious Purple Man used his persuasive powers to destroy Jessica's life. Jessica was eventually able to overcome his control and defeat him, and he was taken into S.H.I.E.L.D. custody.

But after the rise and fall of the Hydra Empire, S.H.I.E.L.D. no longer exists — and according to former S.H.I.E.L.D. director Maria Hill, no one knows where Purple Man is...and no one is looking.

JESSICA JONES

Return of the Purple Man

Writer: **Brian Michael Bendis**
Artist: **Michael Gaydos**
Color Artist: **Matt Hollingsworth**

Letterer: **VC's Cory Petit**
Cover Art: **David Mack**

Assistant Editor: **Alanna Smith**
Editor: **Tom Brevoort**

Based on characters created by **Brian Michael Bendis** & **Michael Gaydos**

Collection Editor: **Jennifer Grünwald** • Assistant Editor: **Caitlin O'Connell**
Associate Managing Editor: **Kateri Woody** • Editor, Special Projects: **Mark D. Beazley**
VP Production & Special Projects: **Jeff Youngquist** • SVP Print, Sales & Marketing: **David Gabriel**
Book Designer: **Jay Bowen**

Editor in Chief: **C.B. Cebulski** • Chief Creative Officer: **Joe Quesada**
President: **Dan Buckley** • Executive Producer: **Alan Fine**

JESSICA JONES VOL. 3: RETURN OF THE PURPLE MAN. Contains material originally published in magazine form as JESSICA JONES #13-18. First printing 2018. ISBN 978-1-302-90637-5. Published by MARVEL WORLDWIDE, INC., a subsidiary of MARVEL ENTERTAINMENT, LLC. OFFICE OF PUBLICATION: 135 West 50th Street, New York, NY 10020.

Printed in Canada. DAN BUCKLEY, President, Marvel Entertainment; JOHN NEE, Publisher; JOE QUESADA, Chief Creative Officer; TOM BREVOORT, SVP of Publishing; DAVID BOGART, SVP of Business Affairs & Operations, Publishing & Partnership; DAVID GABRIEL, SVP of Sales & Marketing, Publishing; JEFF YOUNGQUIST, VP of Production & Special Projects; DAN CARR, Executive Director of Publishing Technology; ALEX MORALES, Director of Publishing Operations; SUSAN CRESPI, Production Manager; STAN LEE, Chairman Emeritus. For information regarding advertising in Marvel Comics or on Marvel.com, please contact Vit DeBellis, Custom Solutions & Integrated Advertising Manager, at vdebellis@marvel.com. For Marvel subscription inquiries, please call 888-511-5480. **Manufactured between 3/2/2018 and 4/3/2018 by SOLISCO PRINTERS, SCOTT, QC, CANADA.**

10 9 8 7 6 5 4 3 2 1

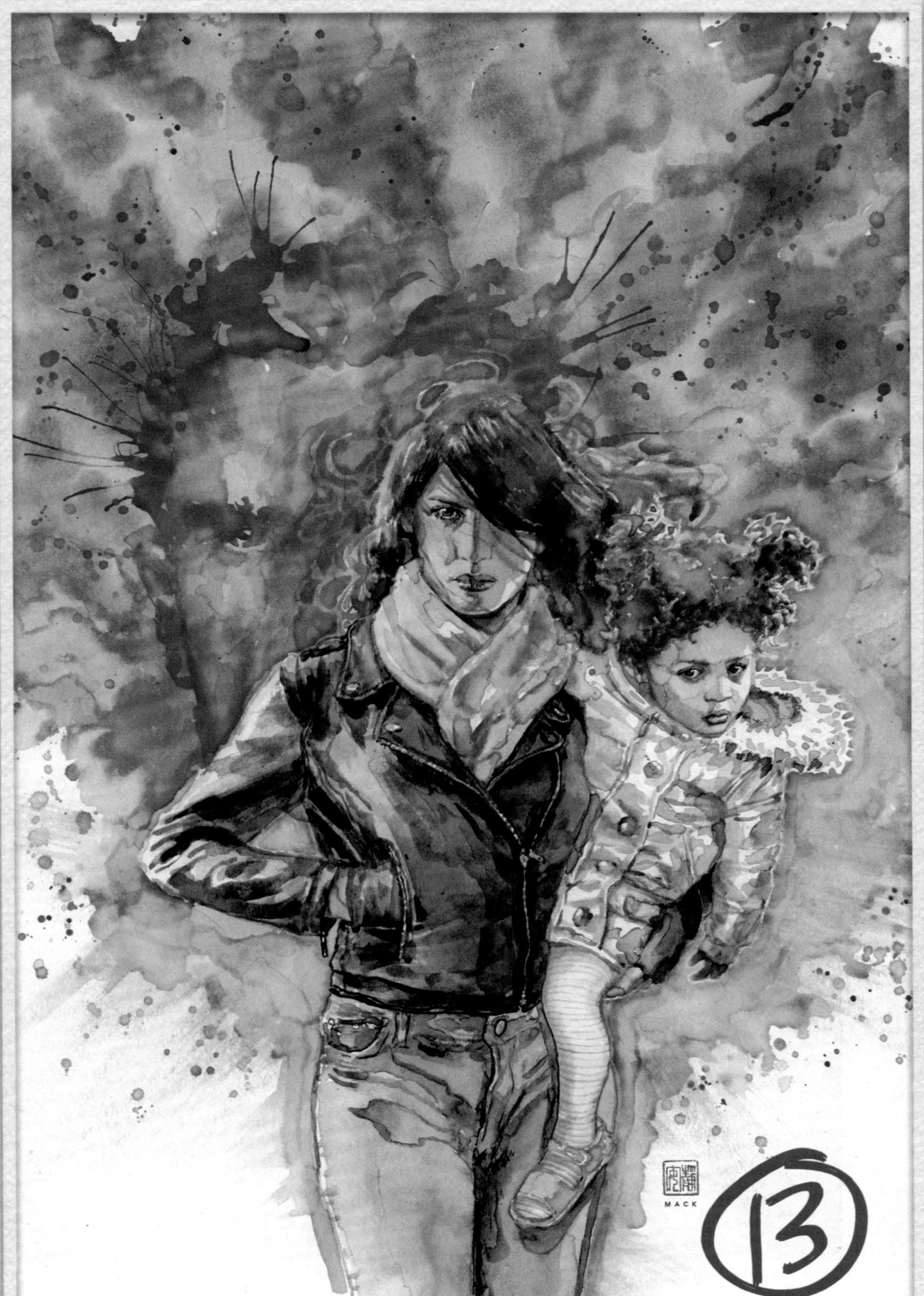
MACK
13

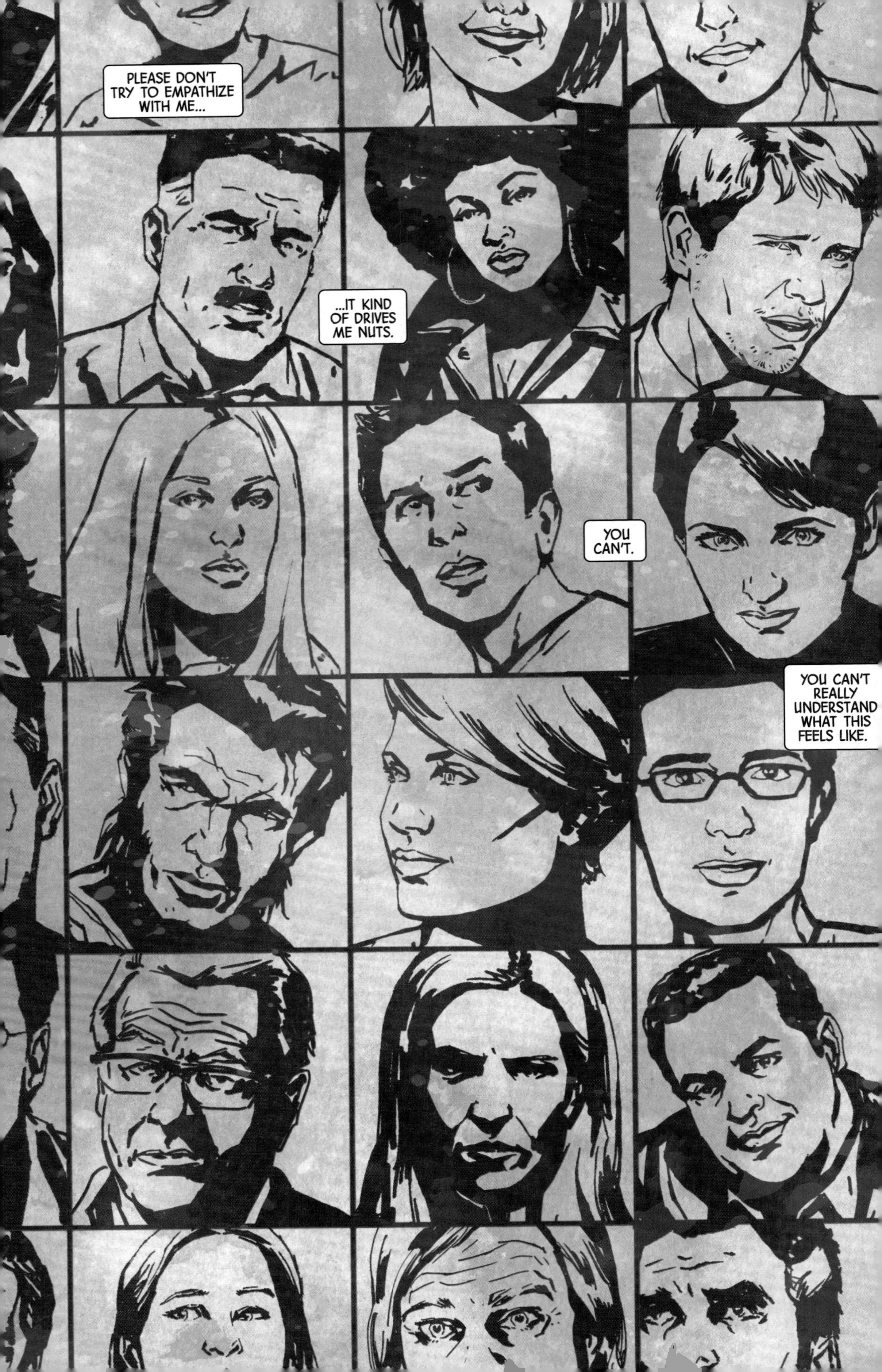
PLEASE DON'T TRY TO EMPATHIZE WITH ME...
...IT KIND OF DRIVES ME NUTS.
YOU CAN'T.
YOU CAN'T REALLY UNDERSTAND WHAT THIS FEELS LIKE.

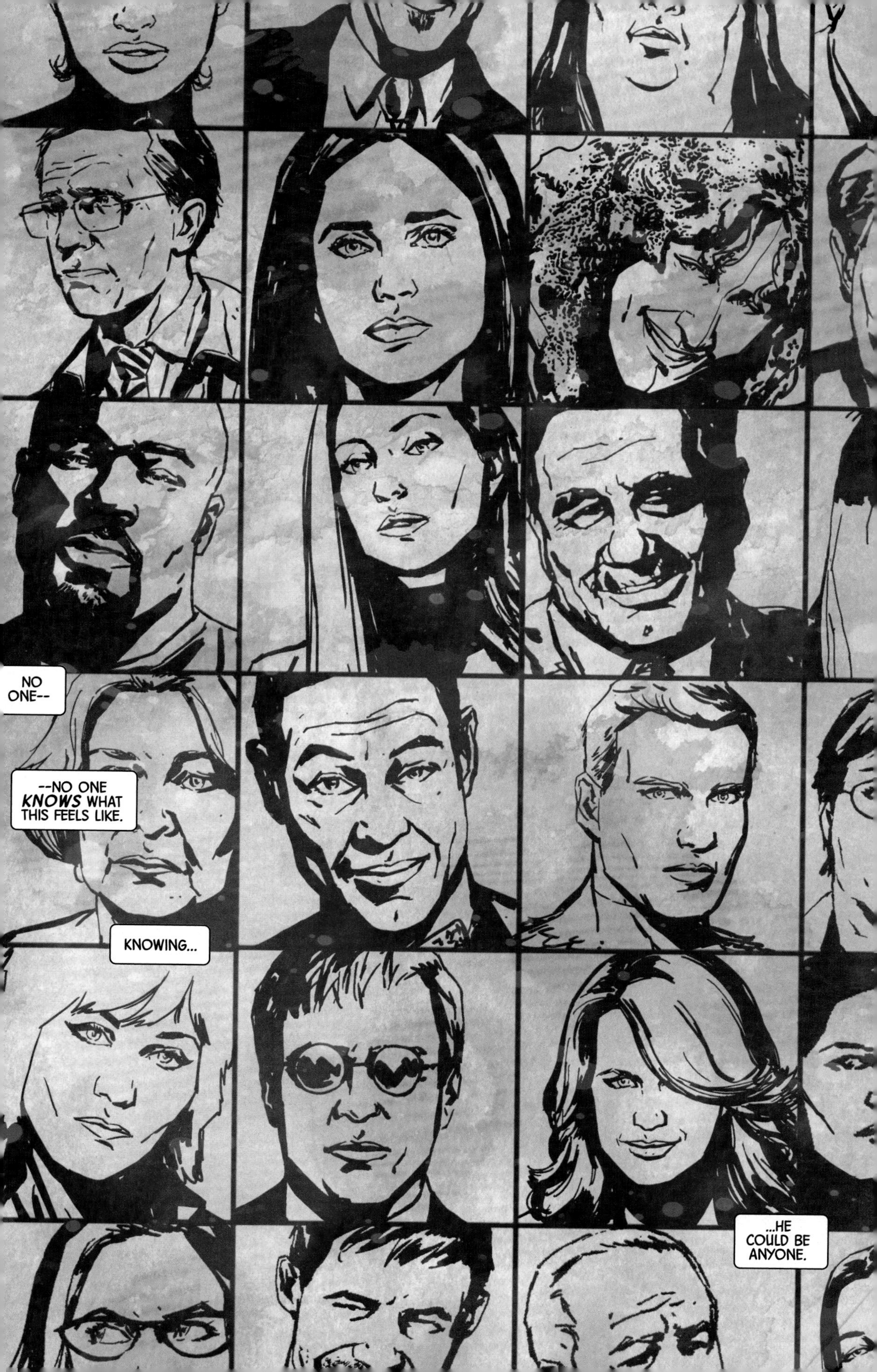
NO ONE--
--NO ONE KNOWS WHAT THIS FEELS LIKE.
KNOWING...
...HE COULD BE ANYONE.

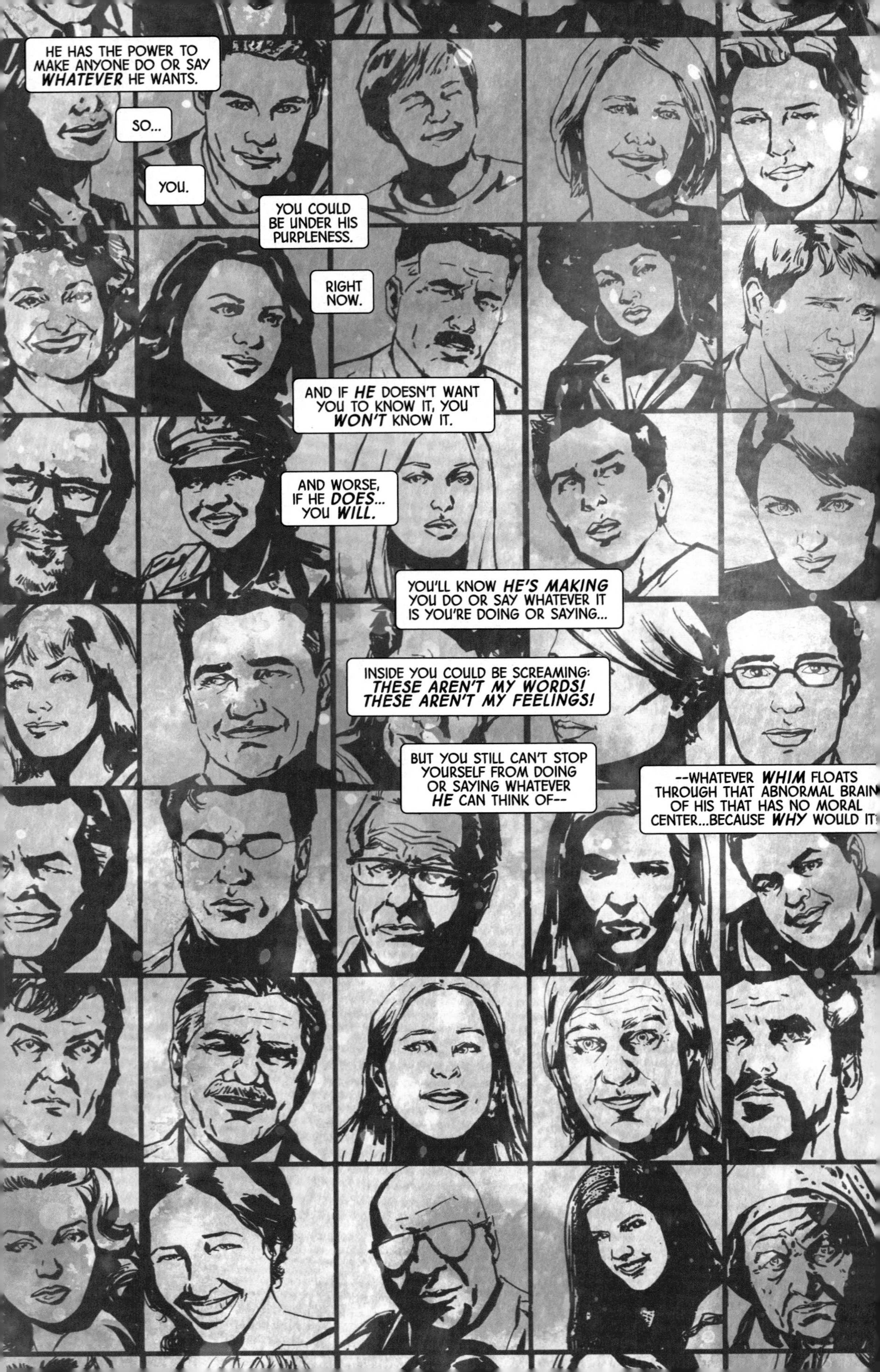
HE HAS THE POWER TO MAKE ANYONE DO OR SAY WHATEVER HE WANTS.
SO...
YOU.
YOU COULD BE UNDER HIS PURPLENESS.
RIGHT NOW.
AND IF HE DOESN'T WANT YOU TO KNOW IT, YOU WON'T KNOW IT.
AND WORSE, IF HE DOES... YOU WILL.
YOU'LL KNOW HE'S MAKING YOU DO OR SAY WHATEVER IT IS YOU'RE DOING OR SAYING...
INSIDE YOU COULD BE SCREAMING: THESE AREN'T MY WORDS! THESE AREN'T MY FEELINGS!
BUT YOU STILL CAN'T STOP YOURSELF FROM DOING OR SAYING WHATEVER HE CAN THINK OF--
--WHATEVER WHIM FLOATS THROUGH THAT ABNORMAL BRAIN OF HIS THAT HAS NO MORAL CENTER...BECAUSE WHY WOULD IT?

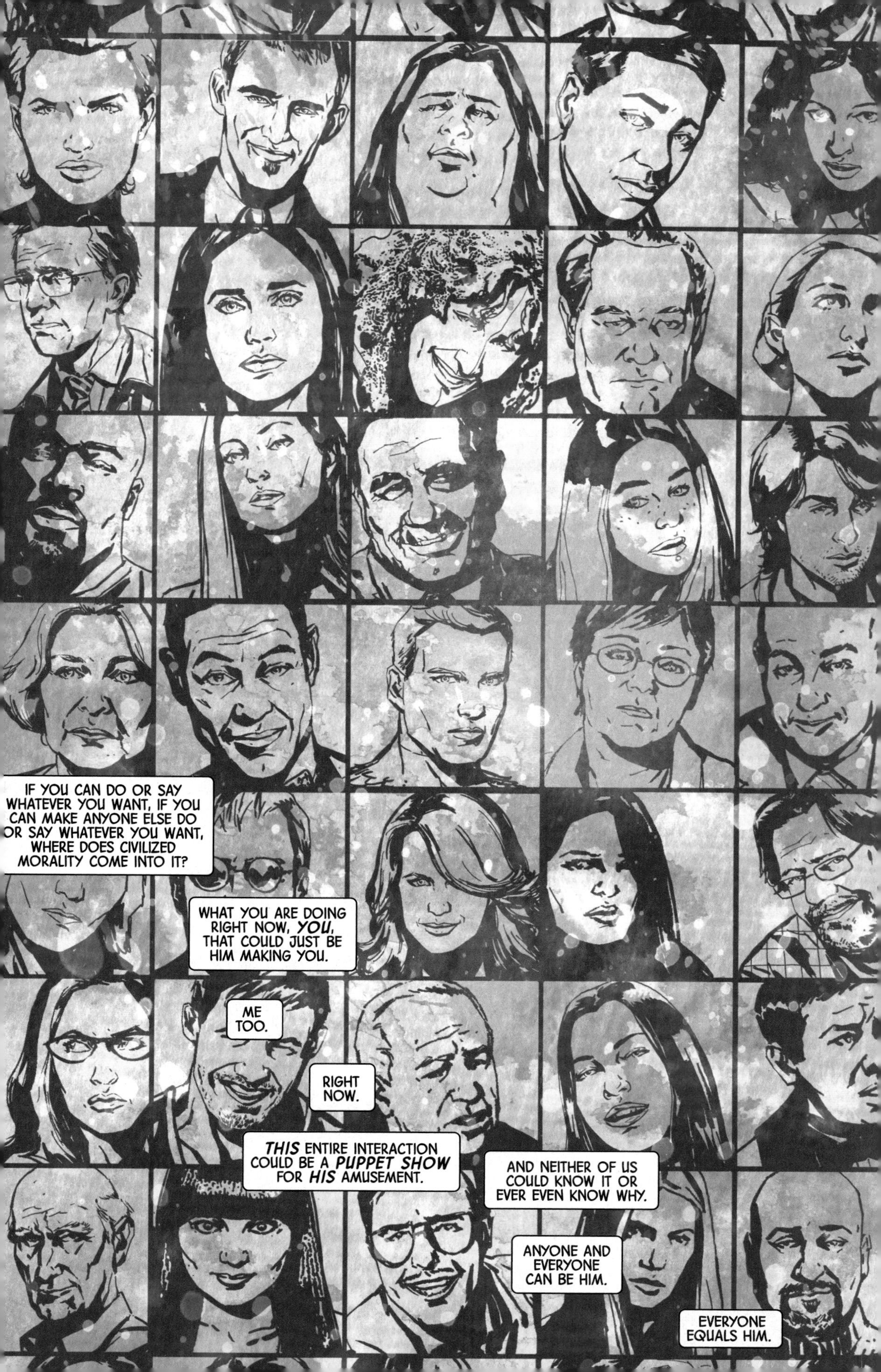
IF YOU CAN DO OR SAY WHATEVER YOU WANT, IF YOU CAN MAKE ANYONE ELSE DO OR SAY WHATEVER YOU WANT, WHERE DOES CIVILIZED MORALITY COME INTO IT?
WHAT YOU ARE DOING RIGHT NOW, *YOU*, THAT COULD JUST BE HIM MAKING YOU.
ME TOO.
RIGHT NOW.
THIS ENTIRE INTERACTION COULD BE A *PUPPET SHOW* FOR *HIS* AMUSEMENT.
AND NEITHER OF US COULD KNOW IT OR EVER EVEN KNOW WHY.
ANYONE AND EVERYONE CAN BE HIM.
EVERYONE EQUALS HIM.

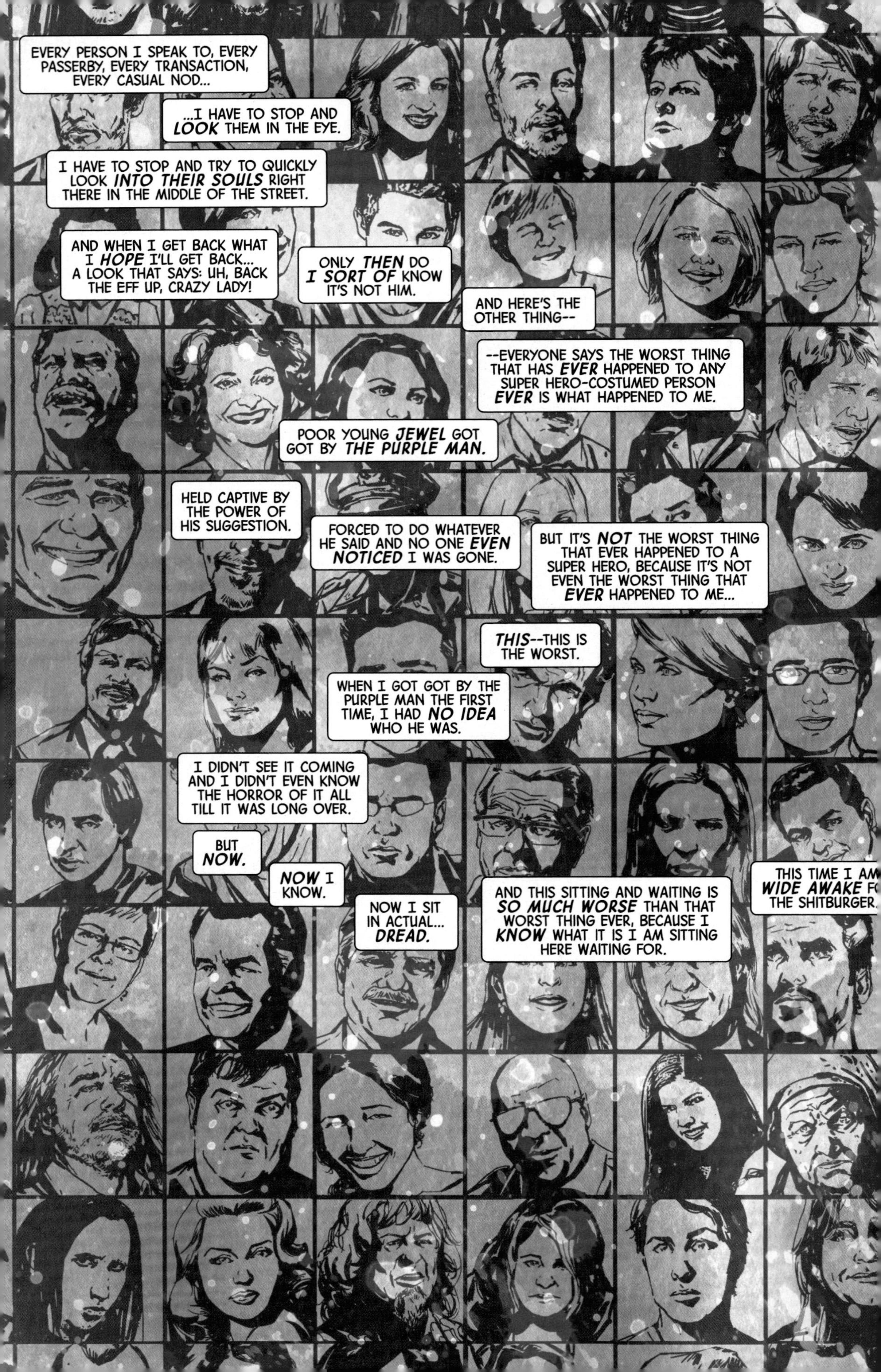
EVERY PERSON I SPEAK TO, EVERY PASSERBY, EVERY TRANSACTION, EVERY CASUAL NOD...
...I HAVE TO STOP AND LOOK THEM IN THE EYE.
I HAVE TO STOP AND TRY TO QUICKLY LOOK INTO THEIR SOULS RIGHT THERE IN THE MIDDLE OF THE STREET.
AND WHEN I GET BACK WHAT I HOPE I'LL GET BACK... A LOOK THAT SAYS: UH, BACK THE EFF UP, CRAZY LADY!
ONLY THEN DO I SORT OF KNOW IT'S NOT HIM.
AND HERE'S THE OTHER THING--
--EVERYONE SAYS THE WORST THING THAT HAS EVER HAPPENED TO ANY SUPER HERO-COSTUMED PERSON EVER IS WHAT HAPPENED TO ME.
POOR YOUNG JEWEL GOT GOT BY THE PURPLE MAN.
HELD CAPTIVE BY THE POWER OF HIS SUGGESTION.
FORCED TO DO WHATEVER HE SAID AND NO ONE EVEN NOTICED I WAS GONE.
BUT IT'S NOT THE WORST THING THAT EVER HAPPENED TO A SUPER HERO, BECAUSE IT'S NOT EVEN THE WORST THING THAT EVER HAPPENED TO ME...
THIS--THIS IS THE WORST.
WHEN I GOT GOT BY THE PURPLE MAN THE FIRST TIME, I HAD NO IDEA WHO HE WAS.
I DIDN'T SEE IT COMING AND I DIDN'T EVEN KNOW THE HORROR OF IT ALL TILL IT WAS LONG OVER.
BUT NOW.
NOW I KNOW.
NOW I SIT IN ACTUAL... DREAD.
AND THIS SITTING AND WAITING IS SO MUCH WORSE THAN THAT WORST THING EVER, BECAUSE I KNOW WHAT IT IS I AM SITTING HERE WAITING FOR.
THIS TIME I AM WIDE AWAKE FO THE SHITBURGER.

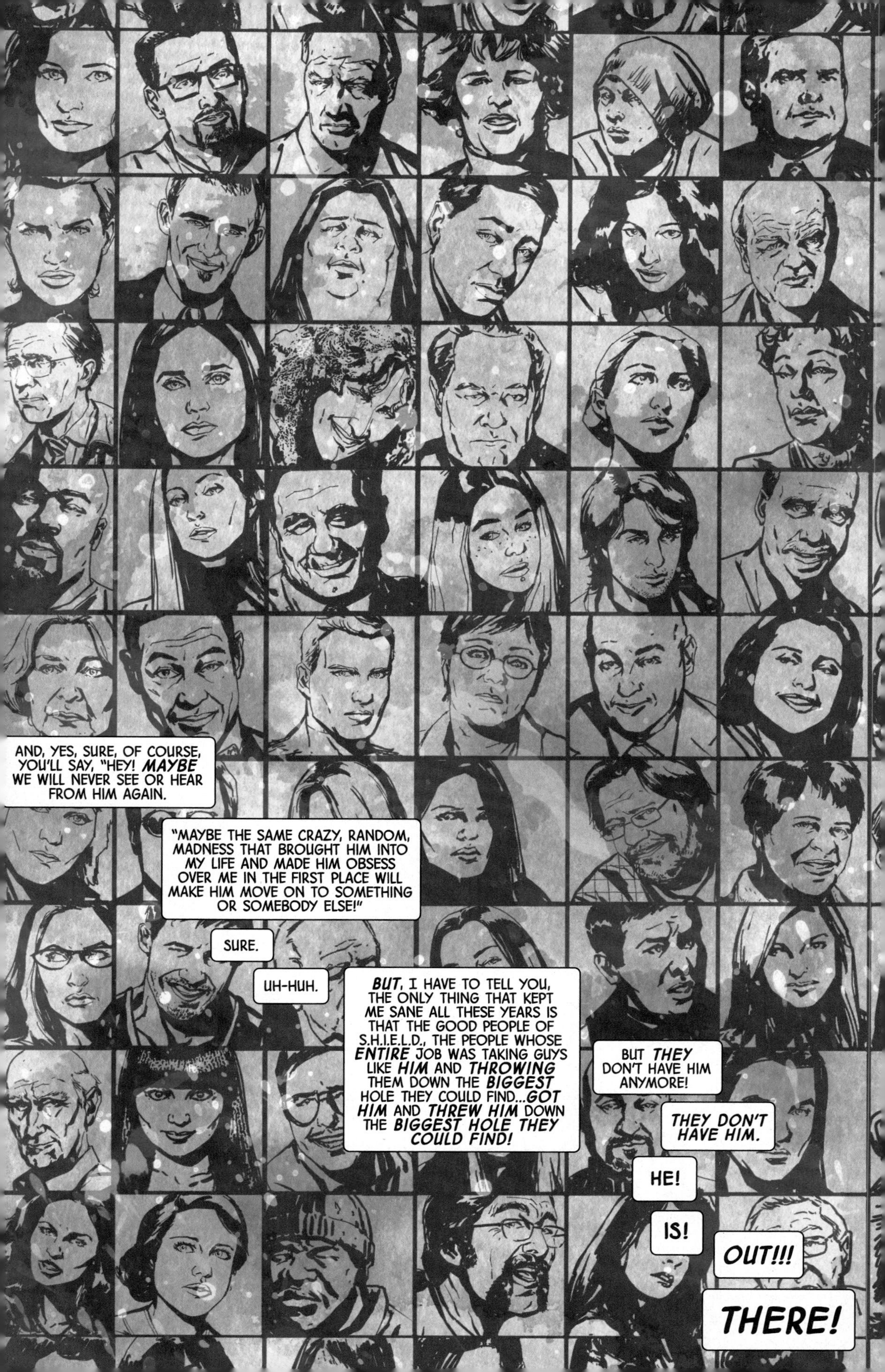
AND, YES, SURE, OF COURSE, YOU'LL SAY, "HEY! MAYBE WE WILL NEVER SEE OR HEAR FROM HIM AGAIN.
"MAYBE THE SAME CRAZY, RANDOM, MADNESS THAT BROUGHT HIM INTO MY LIFE AND MADE HIM OBSESS OVER ME IN THE FIRST PLACE WILL MAKE HIM MOVE ON TO SOMETHING OR SOMEBODY ELSE!"
SURE.
UH-HUH.
BUT, I HAVE TO TELL YOU, THE ONLY THING THAT KEPT ME SANE ALL THESE YEARS IS THAT THE GOOD PEOPLE OF S.H.I.E.L.D., THE PEOPLE WHOSE ENTIRE JOB WAS TAKING GUYS LIKE HIM AND THROWING THEM DOWN THE BIGGEST HOLE THEY COULD FIND...GOT HIM AND THREW HIM DOWN THE BIGGEST HOLE THEY COULD FIND!
BUT THEY DON'T HAVE HIM ANYMORE!
THEY DON'T HAVE HIM.
HE!
IS!
OUT!!!
THERE!

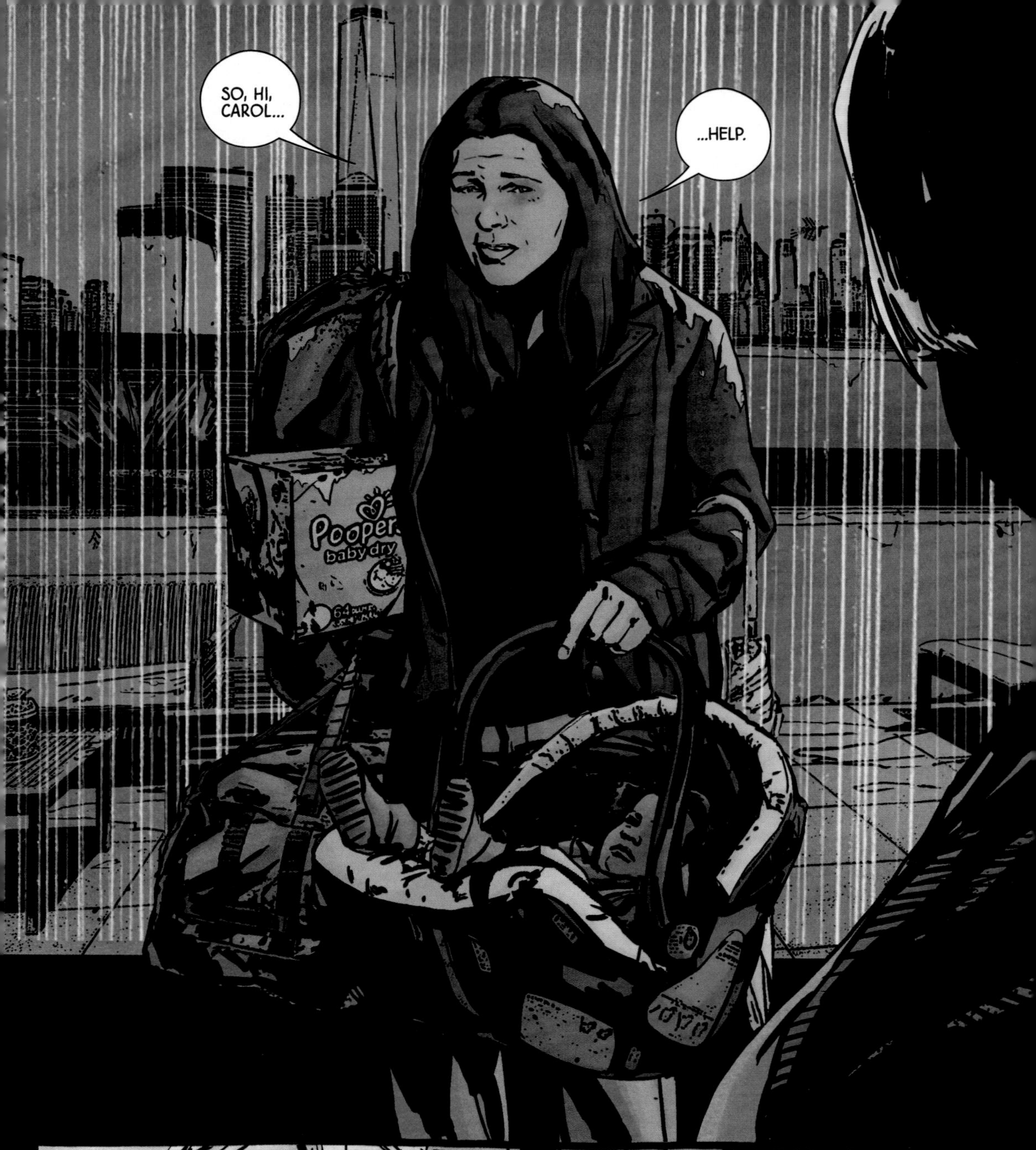
SO, HI, CAROL...
...HELP.
Poopers baby dry

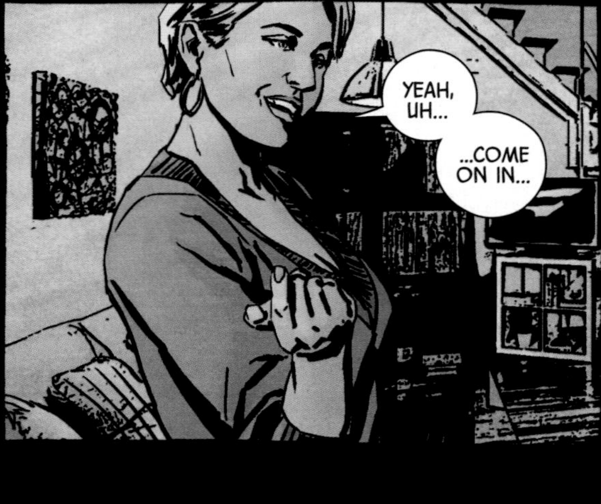
YEAH, UH...
...COME ON IN...

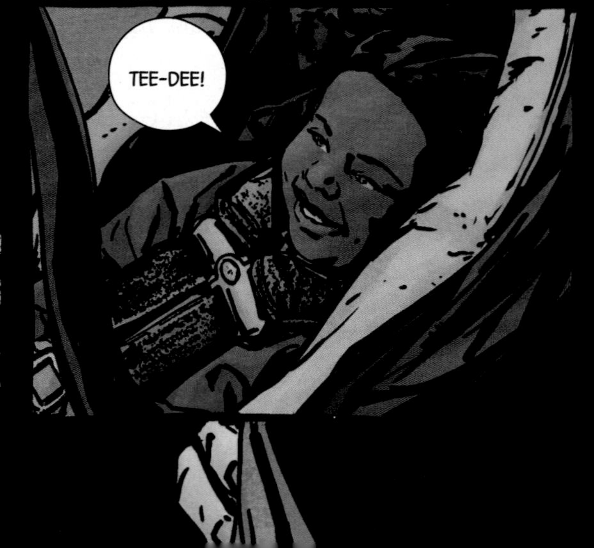
TEE-DEE!

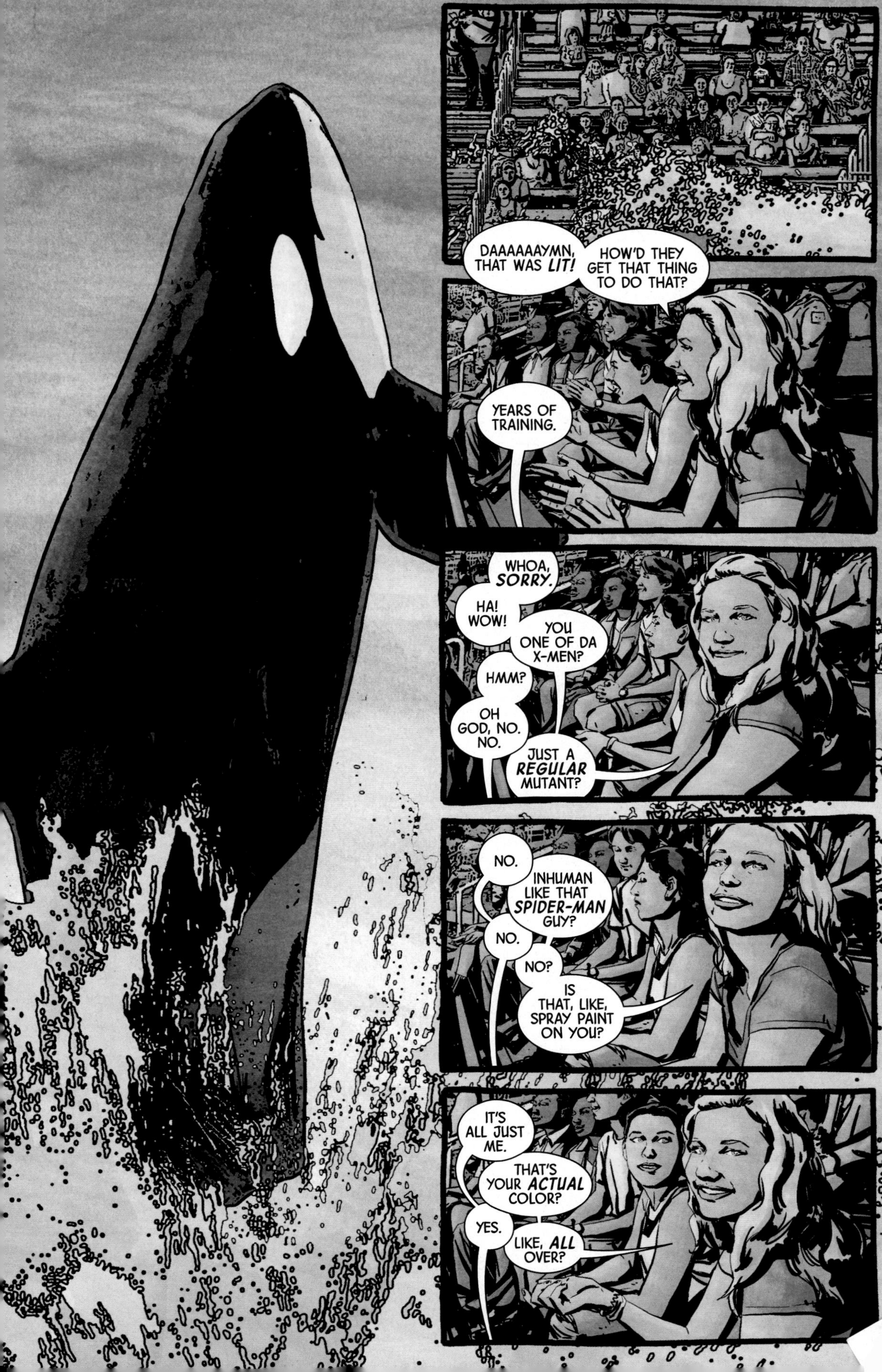

DAAAAAAYMN, THAT WAS LIT!
HOW'D THEY GET THAT THING TO DO THAT?
YEARS OF TRAINING.
WHOA, SORRY.
HA! WOW!
YOU ONE OF DA X-MEN?
HMM?
OH GOD, NO. NO.
JUST A REGULAR MUTANT?
NO.
INHUMAN LIKE THAT SPIDER-MAN GUY?
NO.
NO?
IS THAT, LIKE, SPRAY PAINT ON YOU?
IT'S ALL JUST ME.
THAT'S YOUR ACTUAL COLOR?
YES.
LIKE, ALL OVER?

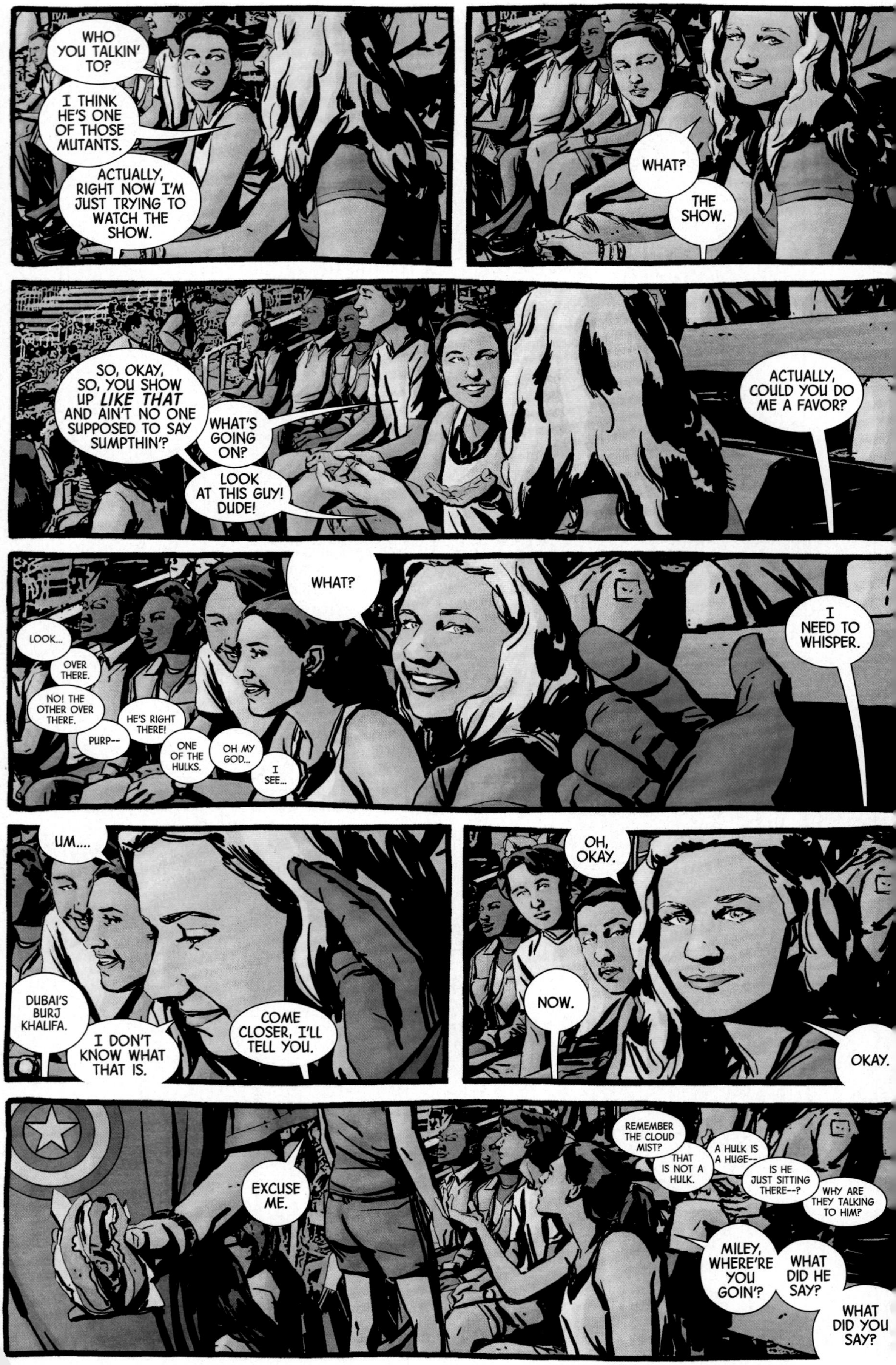

WHO YOU TALKIN' TO?
I THINK HE'S ONE OF THOSE MUTANTS.
ACTUALLY, RIGHT NOW I'M JUST TRYING TO WATCH THE SHOW.
WHAT?
THE SHOW.
SO, OKAY, SO, YOU SHOW UP *LIKE THAT* AND AIN'T NO ONE SUPPOSED TO SAY SUMPTHIN'?
WHAT'S GOING ON?
LOOK AT THIS GUY! DUDE!
ACTUALLY, COULD YOU DO ME A FAVOR?
WHAT?
LOOK...
OVER THERE.
NO! THE OTHER OVER THERE.
PURP--
HE'S RIGHT THERE!
ONE OF THE HULKS.
OH MY GOD...
I SEE...
I NEED TO WHISPER.
UM....
DUBAI'S BURJ KHALIFA.
I DON'T KNOW WHAT THAT IS.
COME CLOSER, I'LL TELL YOU.
OH, OKAY.
NOW.
OKAY.
EXCUSE ME.
REMEMBER THE CLOUD MIST?
THAT IS NOT A HULK.
A HULK IS A HUGE--
IS HE JUST SITTING THERE--?
WHY ARE THEY TALKING TO HIM?
MILEY, WHERE'RE YOU GOIN'?
WHAT DID HE SAY?
WHAT DID YOU SAY?

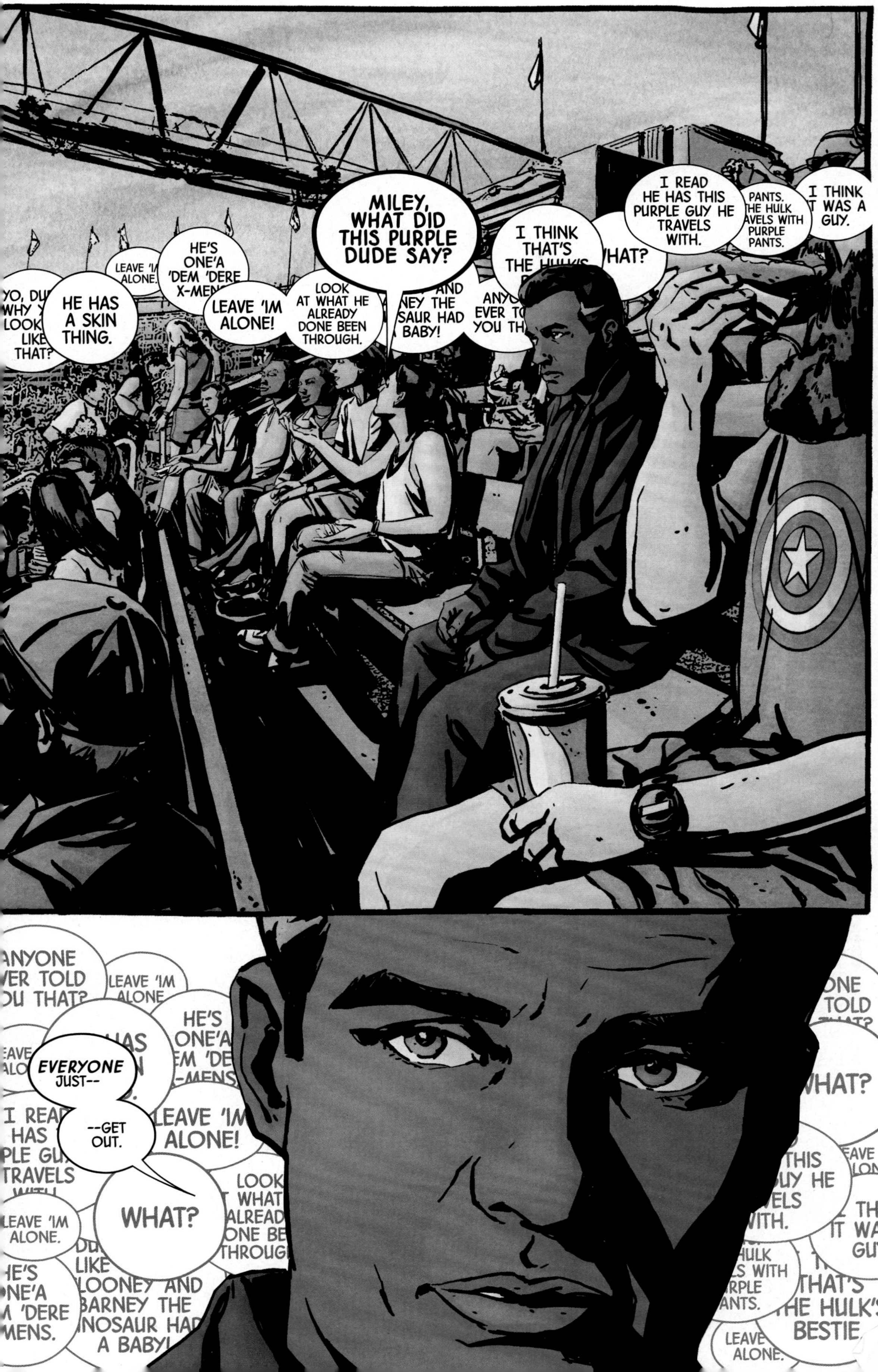

LEAVE 'IM ALONE.
HE'S ONE'A 'DEM 'DERE X-MENS
HE HAS A SKIN THING.
LEAVE 'IM ALONE!
LOOK AT WHAT HE ALREADY DONE BEEN THROUGH.
MILEY, WHAT DID THIS PURPLE DUDE SAY?
I READ HE HAS THIS PURPLE GUY HE TRAVELS WITH.
I THINK THAT'S
EVERYONE JUST--
--GET OUT.
LEAVE 'IM ALONE!
WHAT?
LEAVE 'IM ALONE.

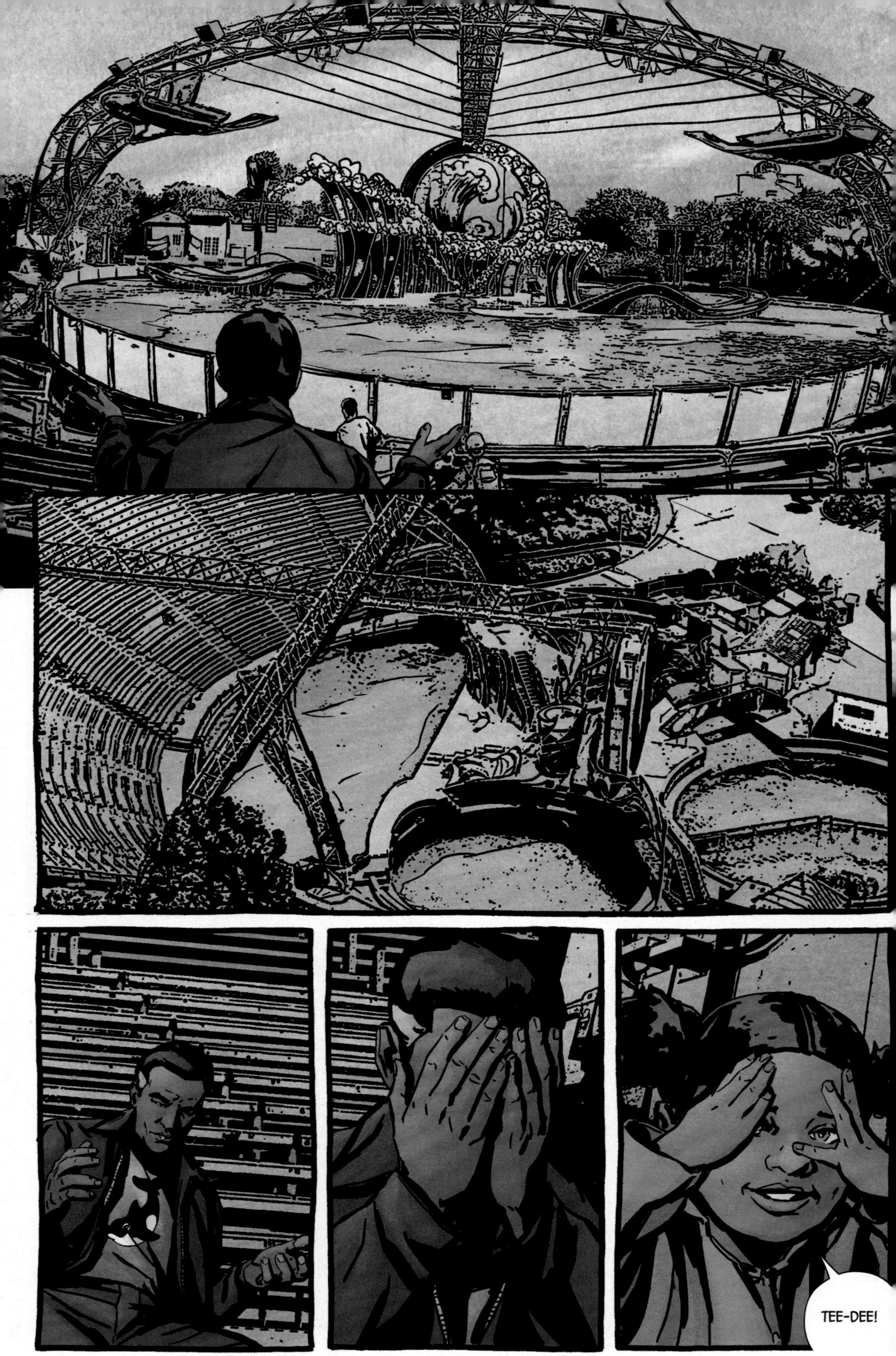
TEE-DEE!

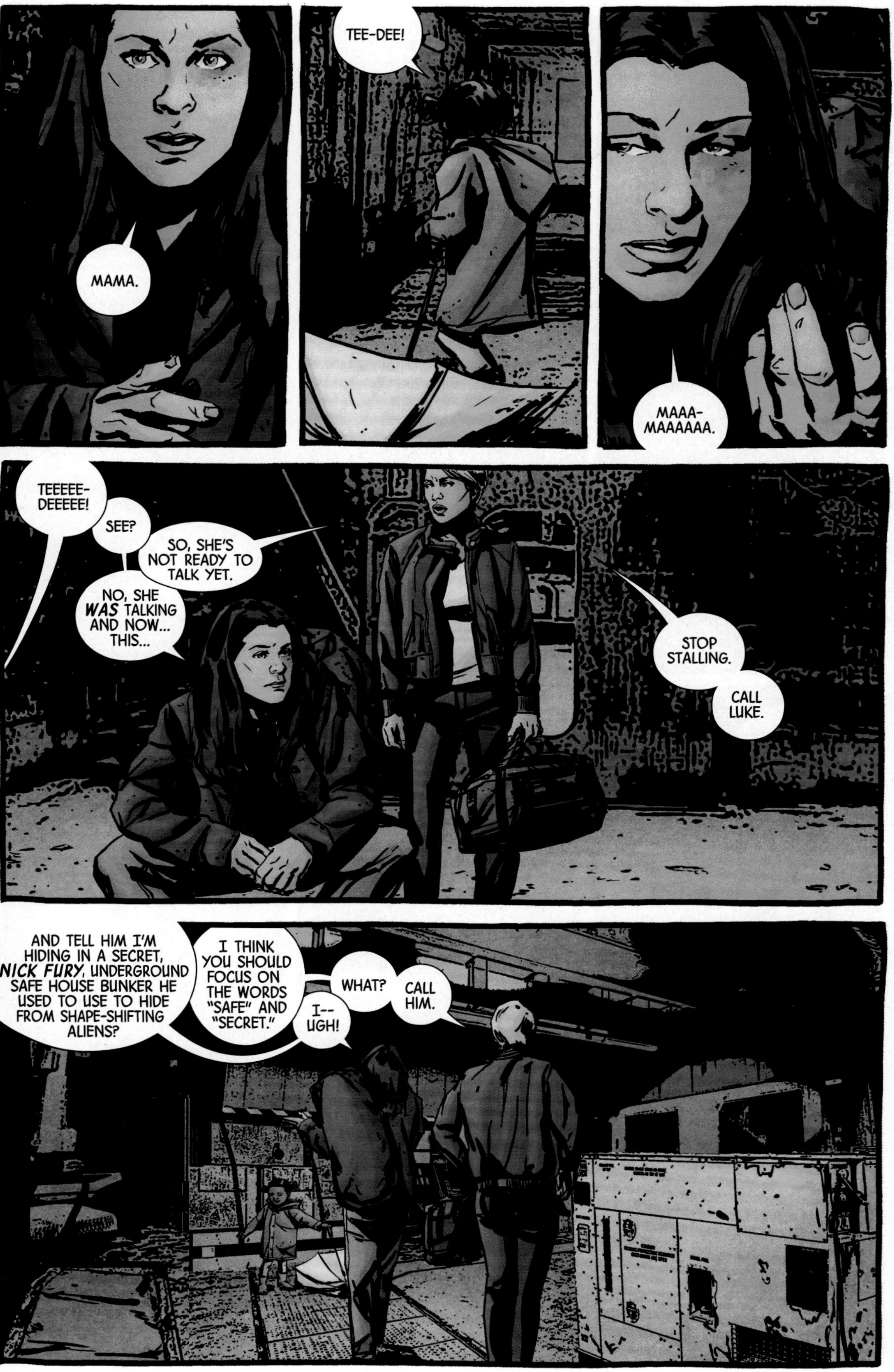
MAMA.
TEE-DEE!
MAAA-MAAAAAA.
TEEEEE-DEEEEE!
SEE?
SO, SHE'S NOT READY TO TALK YET.
NO, SHE *WAS* TALKING AND NOW... THIS...
STOP STALLING.
CALL LUKE.
AND TELL HIM I'M HIDING IN A SECRET, *NICK FURY*, UNDERGROUND SAFE HOUSE BUNKER HE USED TO USE TO HIDE FROM SHAPE-SHIFTING ALIENS?
I THINK YOU SHOULD FOCUS ON THE WORDS "SAFE" AND "SECRET."
WHAT?
CALL HIM.
I-- UGH!

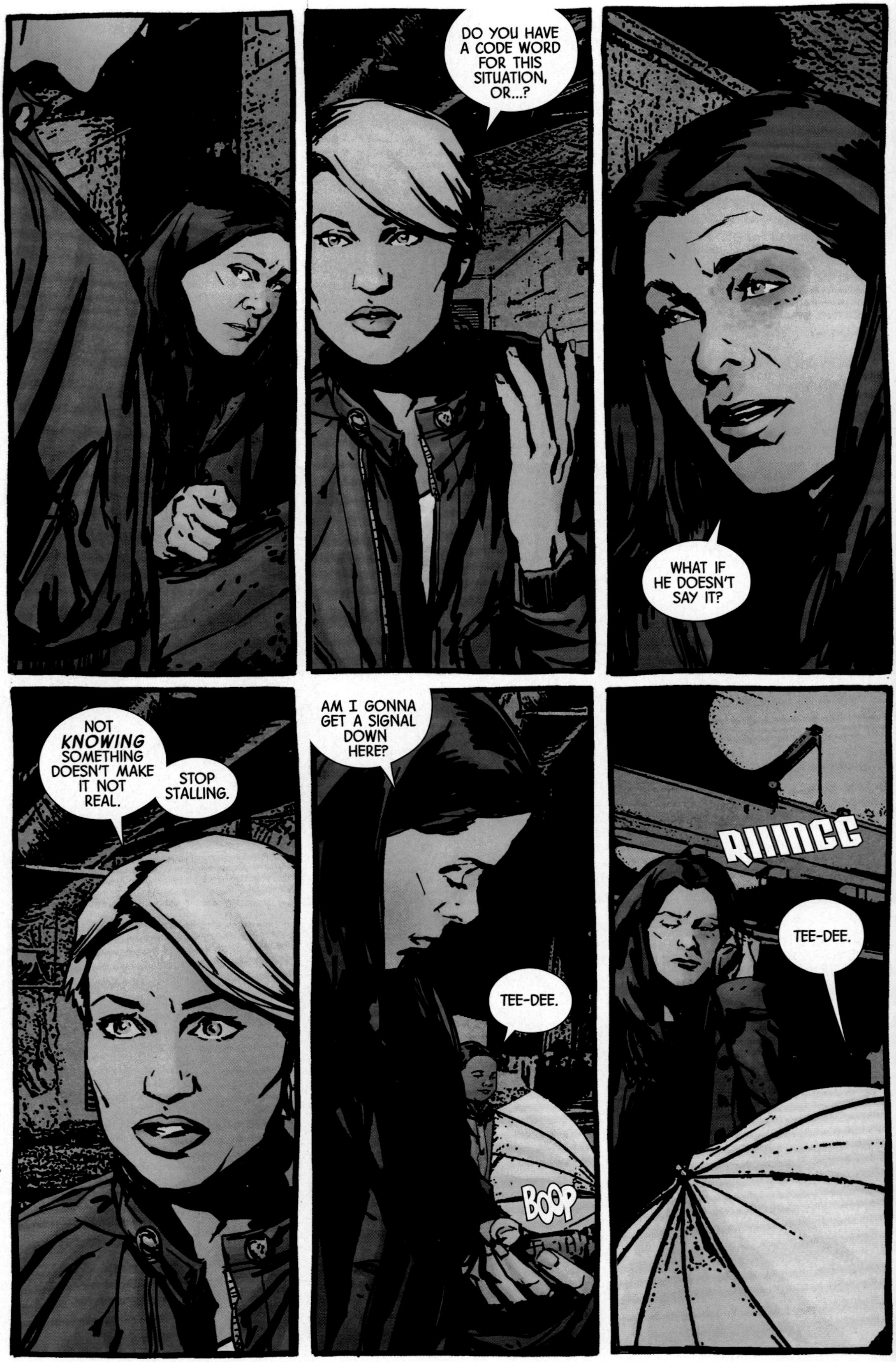
DO YOU HAVE A CODE WORD FOR THIS SITUATION, OR...?
WHAT IF HE DOESN'T SAY IT?
NOT *KNOWING* SOMETHING DOESN'T MAKE IT NOT REAL.
STOP STALLING.
AM I GONNA GET A SIGNAL DOWN HERE?
TEE-DEE.
BOOP
RIIINGG
TEE-DEE.

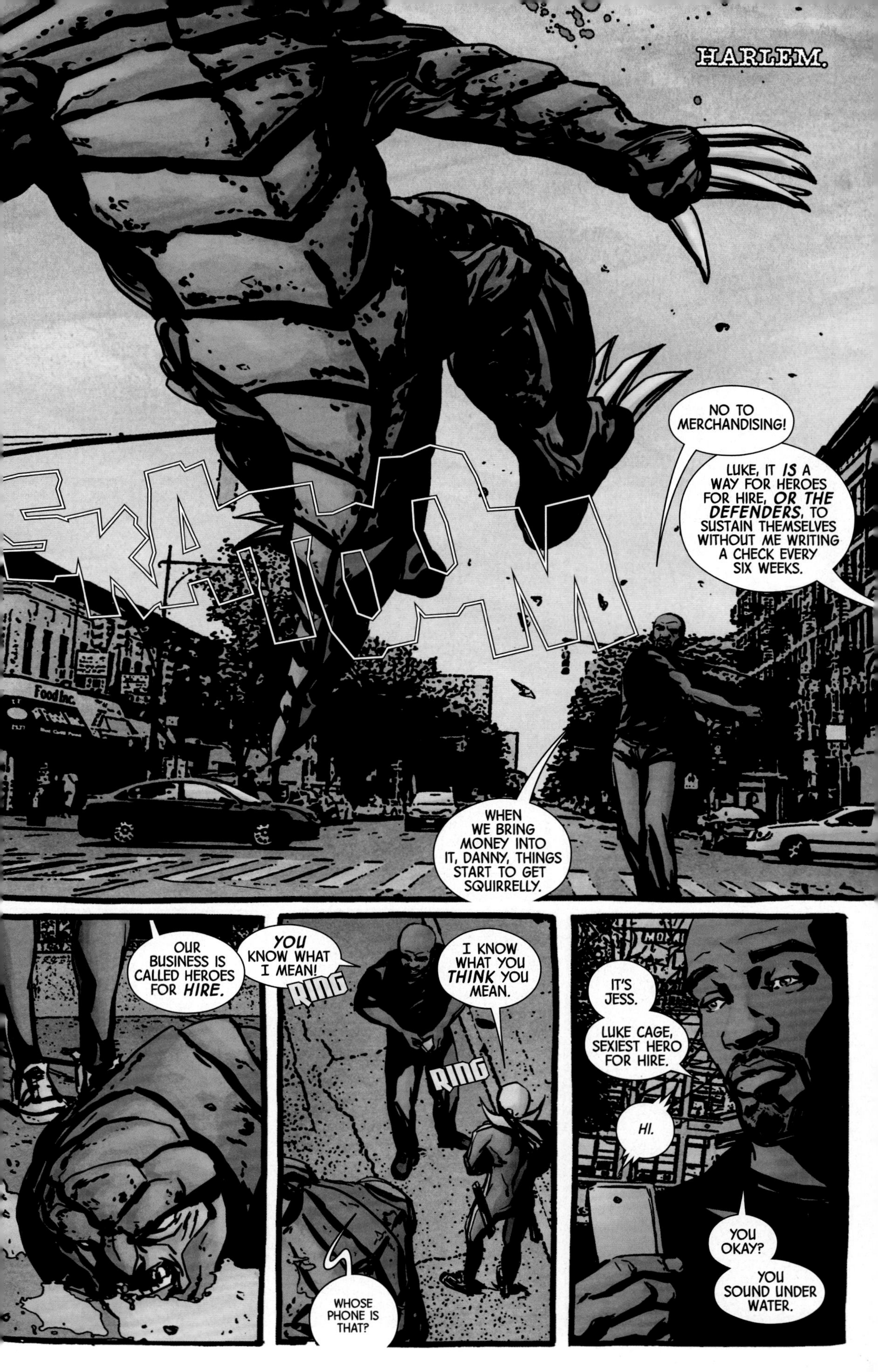
HARLEM.
KRAKOOM
NO TO MERCHANDISING!
LUKE, IT *IS* A WAY FOR HEROES FOR HIRE, *OR THE DEFENDERS*, TO SUSTAIN THEMSELVES WITHOUT ME WRITING A CHECK EVERY SIX WEEKS.
WHEN WE BRING MONEY INTO IT, DANNY, THINGS START TO GET SQUIRRELLY.
Food Inc.
OUR BUSINESS IS CALLED HEROES FOR *HIRE.*
YOU KNOW WHAT I MEAN!
RING
I KNOW WHAT YOU *THINK* YOU MEAN.
RING
WHOSE PHONE IS THAT?
IT'S JESS.
LUKE CAGE, SEXIEST HERO FOR HIRE.
HI.
YOU OKAY?
YOU SOUND UNDER WATER.

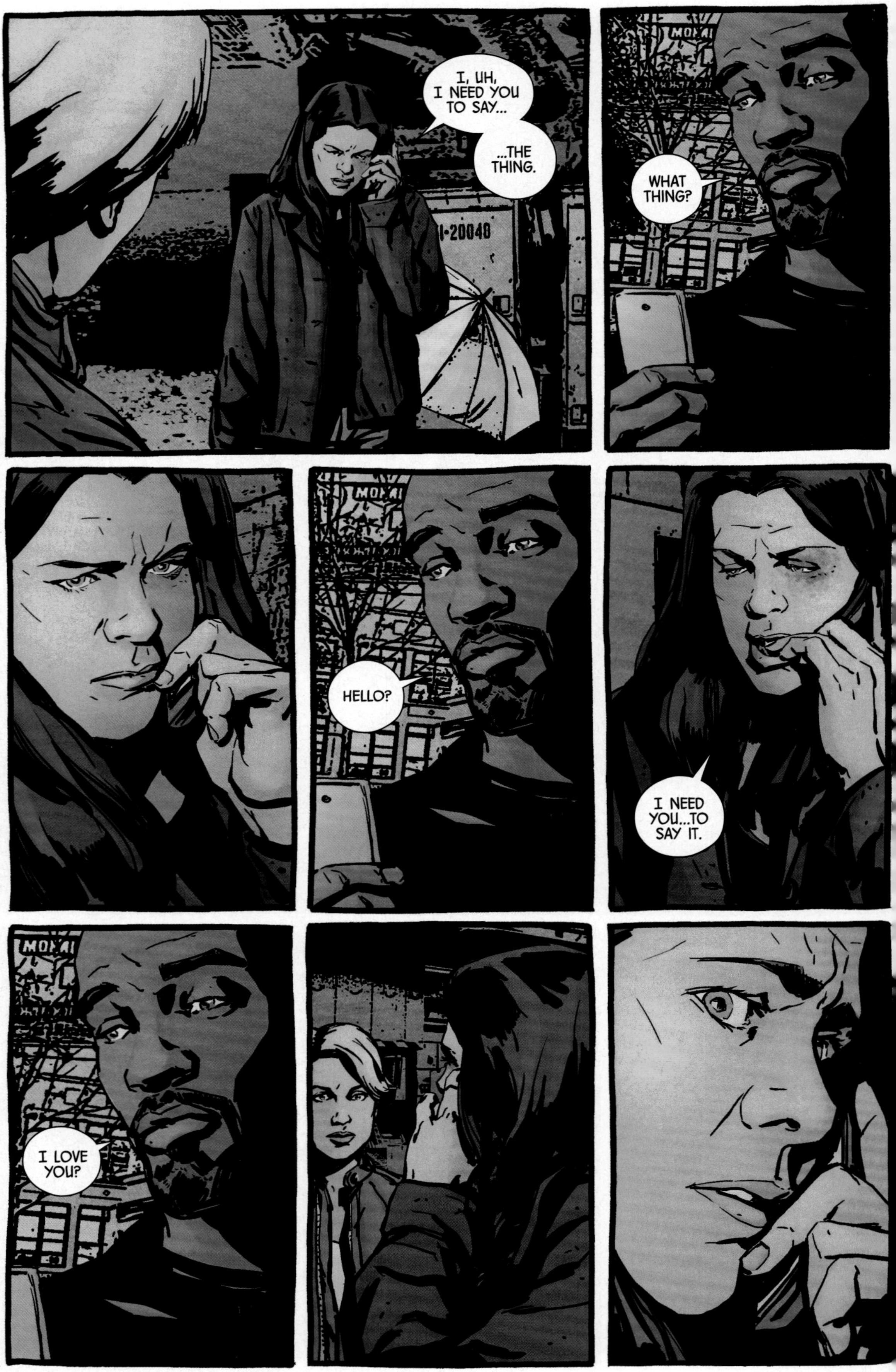
I, UH, I NEED YOU TO SAY...
...THE THING.
WHAT THING?
HELLO?
I NEED YOU...TO SAY IT.
I LOVE YOU?

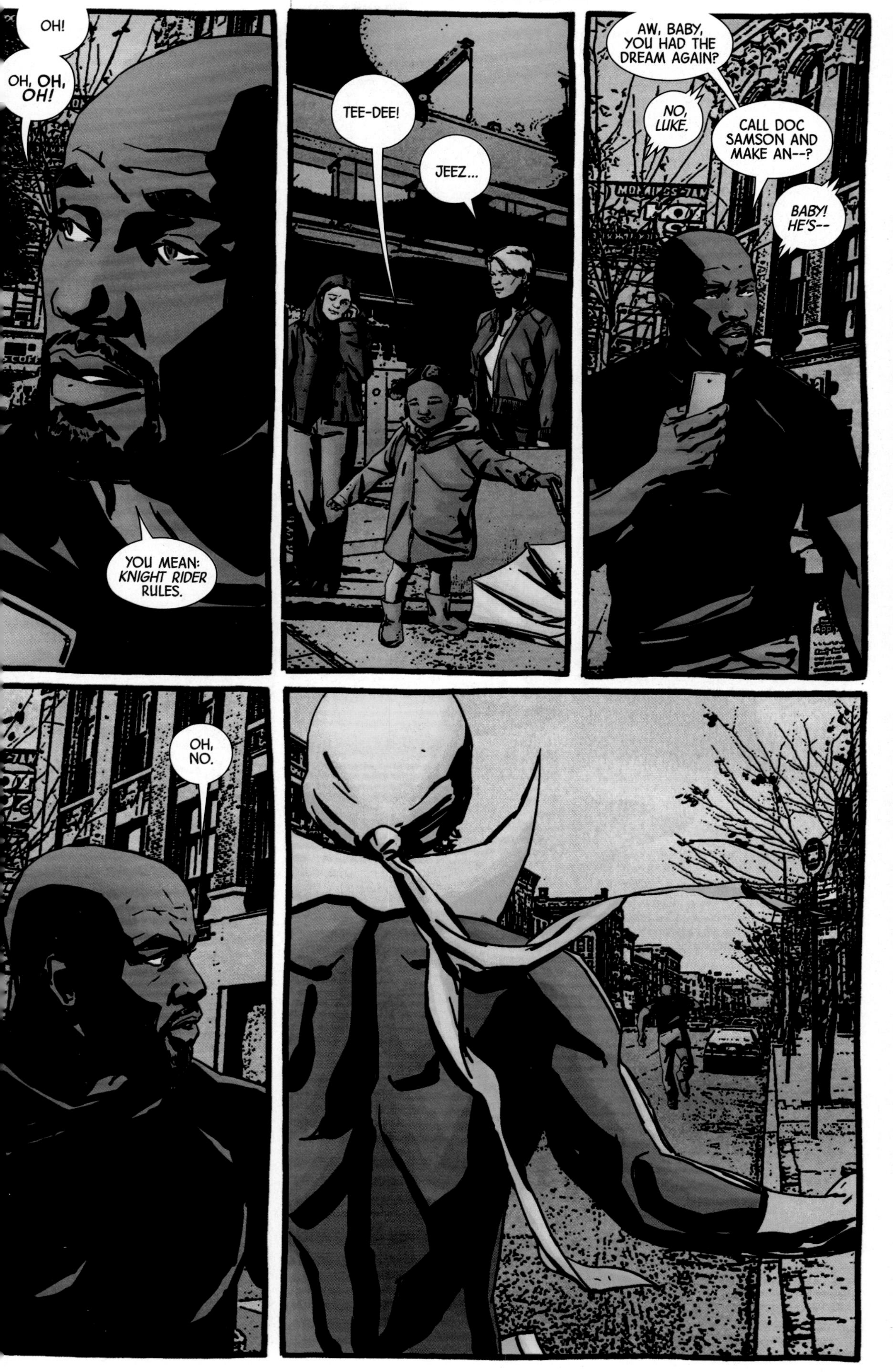
OH!
OH, OH, OH!
YOU MEAN: KNIGHT RIDER RULES.
TEE-DEE!
JEEZ...
AW, BABY, YOU HAD THE DREAM AGAIN?
NO, LUKE.
CALL DOC SAMSON AND MAKE AN--?
BABY! HE'S--
OH, NO.

HAS HE CONTACTED YOU?

BABY, YOU NEED TO GET TO SOMEPLACE SAFE AND--

HE HUNG UP.

WHAT IS HE GOING TO DO?

JUMP ALL THE WAY TO RYKER'S ISLAND PRISON AND BEAT UP THE WARDEN.

NO, REALLY, WHAT IS HE GOING TO--

I HAVE TO GO OUT THERE AND FIND KILLGRAVE.

NO.

I LIKE THIS THING YOU'RE DOING NOW.

REACHING OUT FOR HELP. BEING PROACTIVE.

IT SHOWS GROWTH. YOU'RE NOT THE SAME LITTLE GIRL HE KIDNAPPED.

YOU'RE A GROWN WOMAN NOW. YOU'RE A MOM. YOU'RE A DEFENDER. AN *AVENGER*.

A WOMAN WITH ACTUAL THINGS TO LOSE.

SO *YOU* DO THE THING WHERE YOU'RE ONE OF THOSE PEOPLE THAT HAVE BABIES.

YOU STAY PUT. YOU PROTECT THE BABY.

LET ME GET OUR FRIENDS AND GO BEAT KILLGRAVE UP AND--

THROW HIM INTO THE SUN.

SURE.

OR WE BEAT HIM A FAR DARKER PURPLE.

IT HAS TO BE ME.

YOU KNOW HIM...

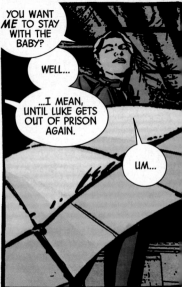

YOU WANT *ME* TO STAY WITH THE BABY?

WELL...

...I MEAN, UNTIL LUKE GETS OUT OF PRISON AGAIN.

UM...

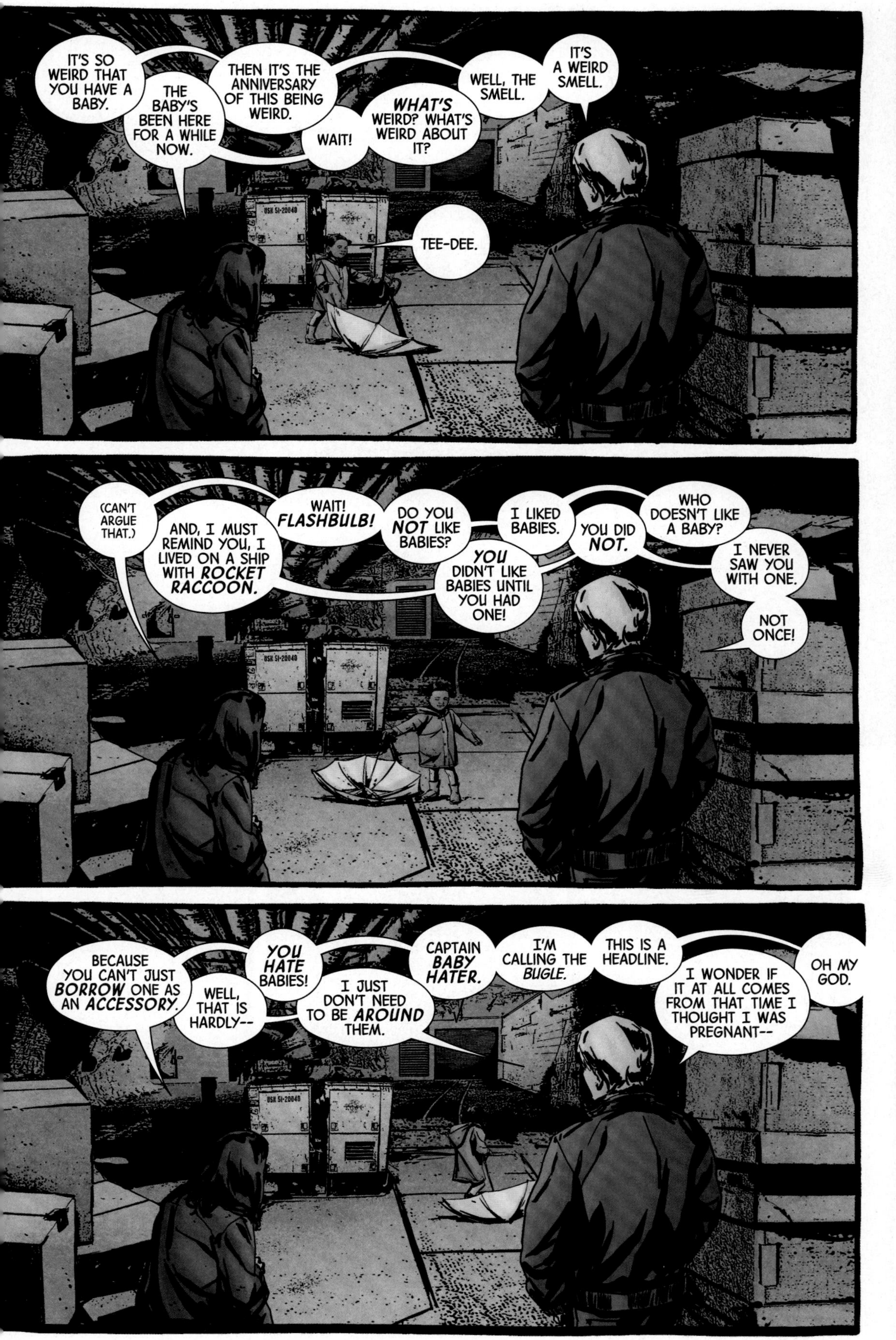
IT'S SO WEIRD THAT YOU HAVE A BABY.
THE BABY'S BEEN HERE FOR A WHILE NOW.
THEN IT'S THE ANNIVERSARY OF THIS BEING WEIRD.
WAIT!
WHAT'S WEIRD? WHAT'S WEIRD ABOUT IT?
WELL, THE SMELL.
IT'S A WEIRD SMELL.
USK 51-20040
TEE-DEE.
(CAN'T ARGUE THAT.)
AND, I MUST REMIND YOU, I LIVED ON A SHIP WITH ROCKET RACCOON.
WAIT! FLASHBULB!
DO YOU NOT LIKE BABIES?
YOU DIDN'T LIKE BABIES UNTIL YOU HAD ONE!
I LIKED BABIES.
YOU DID NOT.
WHO DOESN'T LIKE A BABY?
I NEVER SAW YOU WITH ONE.
NOT ONCE!
USK 51-20040
BECAUSE YOU CAN'T JUST BORROW ONE AS AN ACCESSORY.
WELL, THAT IS HARDLY--
YOU HATE BABIES!
I JUST DON'T NEED TO BE AROUND THEM.
CAPTAIN BABY HATER.
I'M CALLING THE BUGLE.
THIS IS A HEADLINE.
I WONDER IF IT AT ALL COMES FROM THAT TIME I THOUGHT I WAS PREGNANT--
OH MY GOD.
USK 51-20040

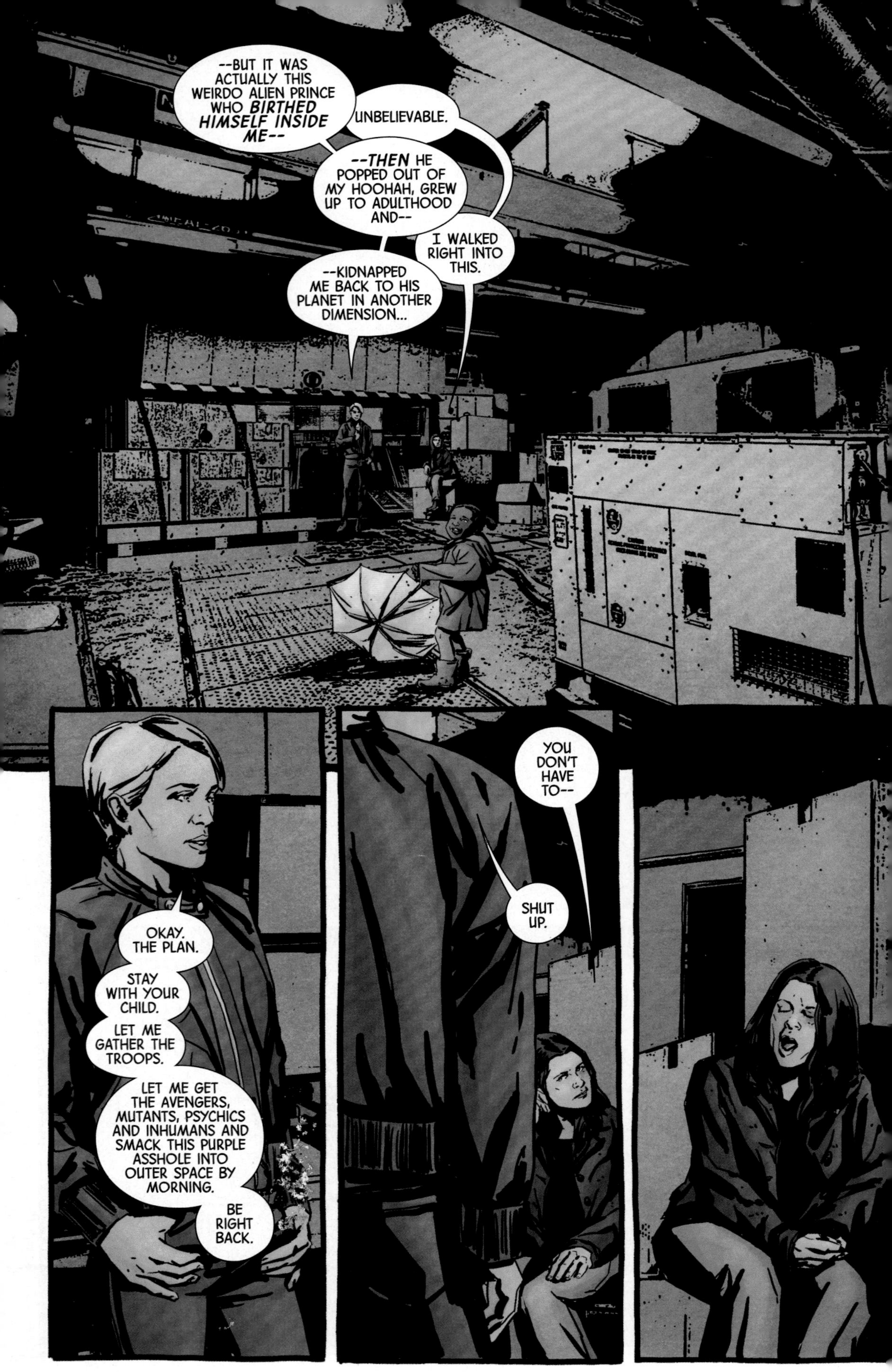
--BUT IT WAS ACTUALLY THIS WEIRDO ALIEN PRINCE WHO BIRTHED HIMSELF INSIDE ME--
UNBELIEVABLE.
--THEN HE POPPED OUT OF MY HOOHAH, GREW UP TO ADULTHOOD AND--
I WALKED RIGHT INTO THIS.
--KIDNAPPED ME BACK TO HIS PLANET IN ANOTHER DIMENSION...
OKAY. THE PLAN.
STAY WITH YOUR CHILD.
LET ME GATHER THE TROOPS.
LET ME GET THE AVENGERS, MUTANTS, PSYCHICS AND INHUMANS AND SMACK THIS PURPLE ASSHOLE INTO OUTER SPACE BY MORNING.
BE RIGHT BACK.
YOU DON'T HAVE TO--
SHUT UP.

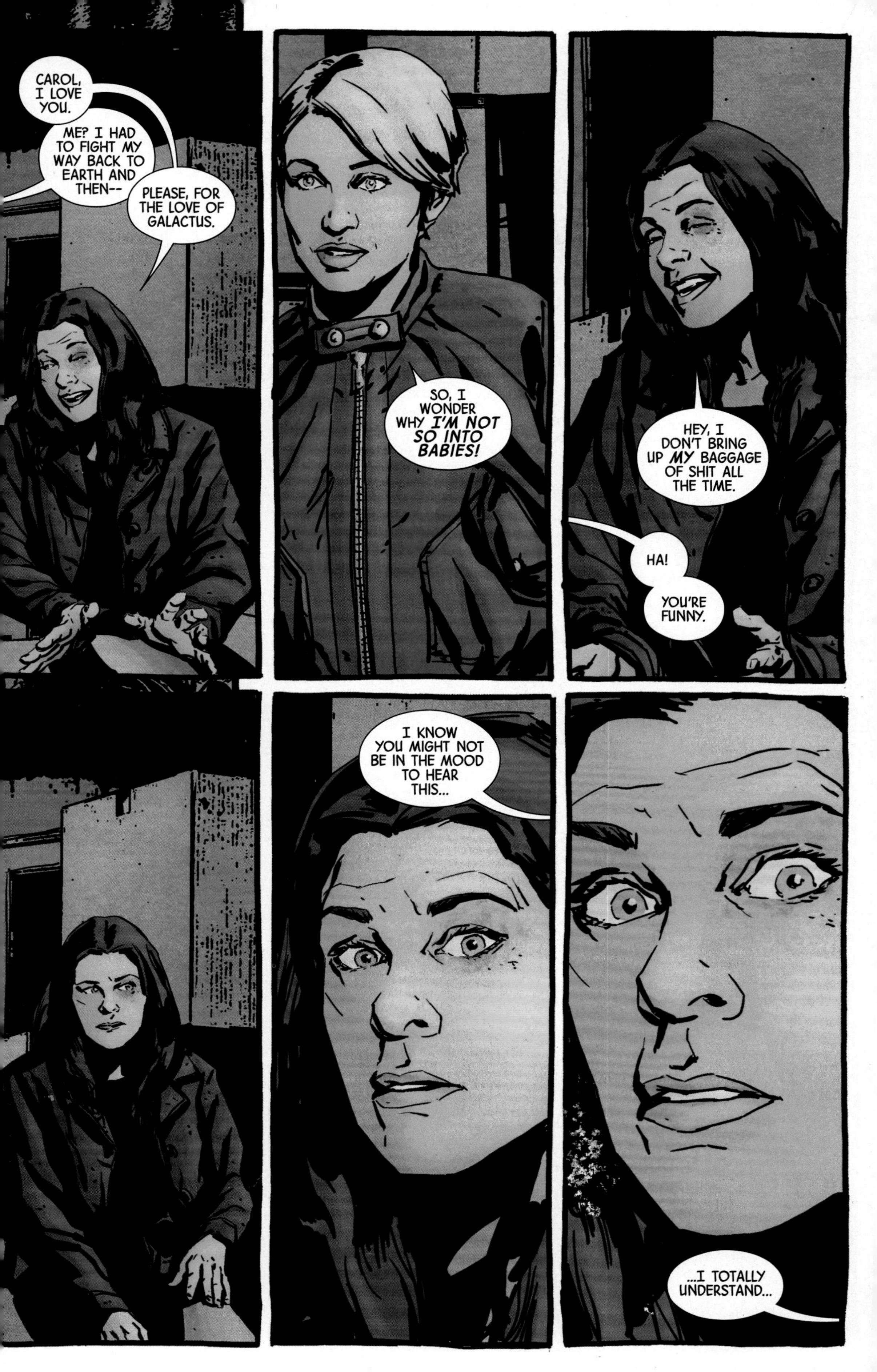
CAROL, I LOVE YOU.
ME? I HAD TO FIGHT MY WAY BACK TO EARTH AND THEN--
PLEASE, FOR THE LOVE OF GALACTUS.
SO, I WONDER WHY I'M NOT SO INTO BABIES!
HEY, I DON'T BRING UP MY BAGGAGE OF SHIT ALL THE TIME.
HA!
YOU'RE FUNNY.
I KNOW YOU MIGHT NOT BE IN THE MOOD TO HEAR THIS...
...I TOTALLY UNDERSTAND...

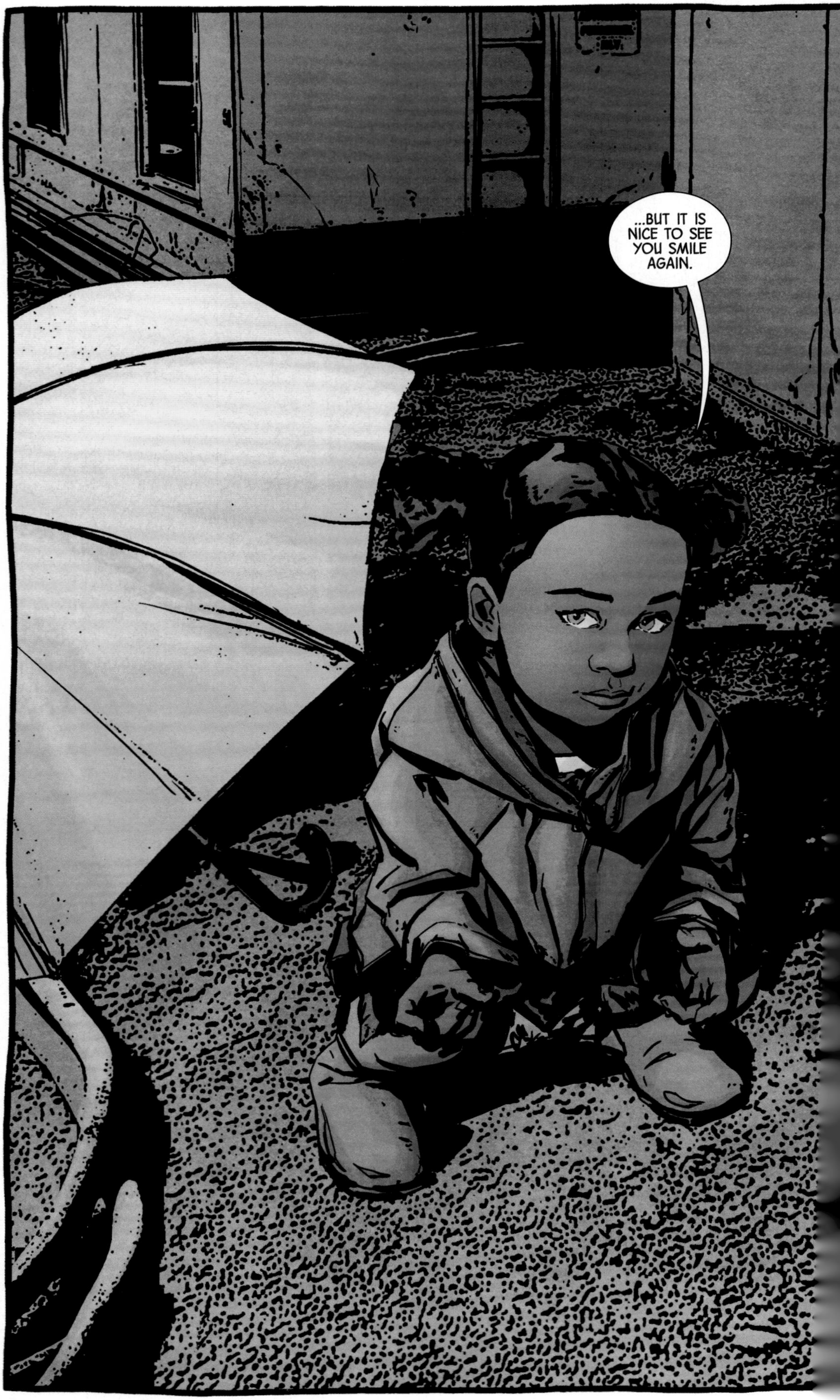
...BUT IT IS NICE TO SEE YOU SMILE AGAIN.

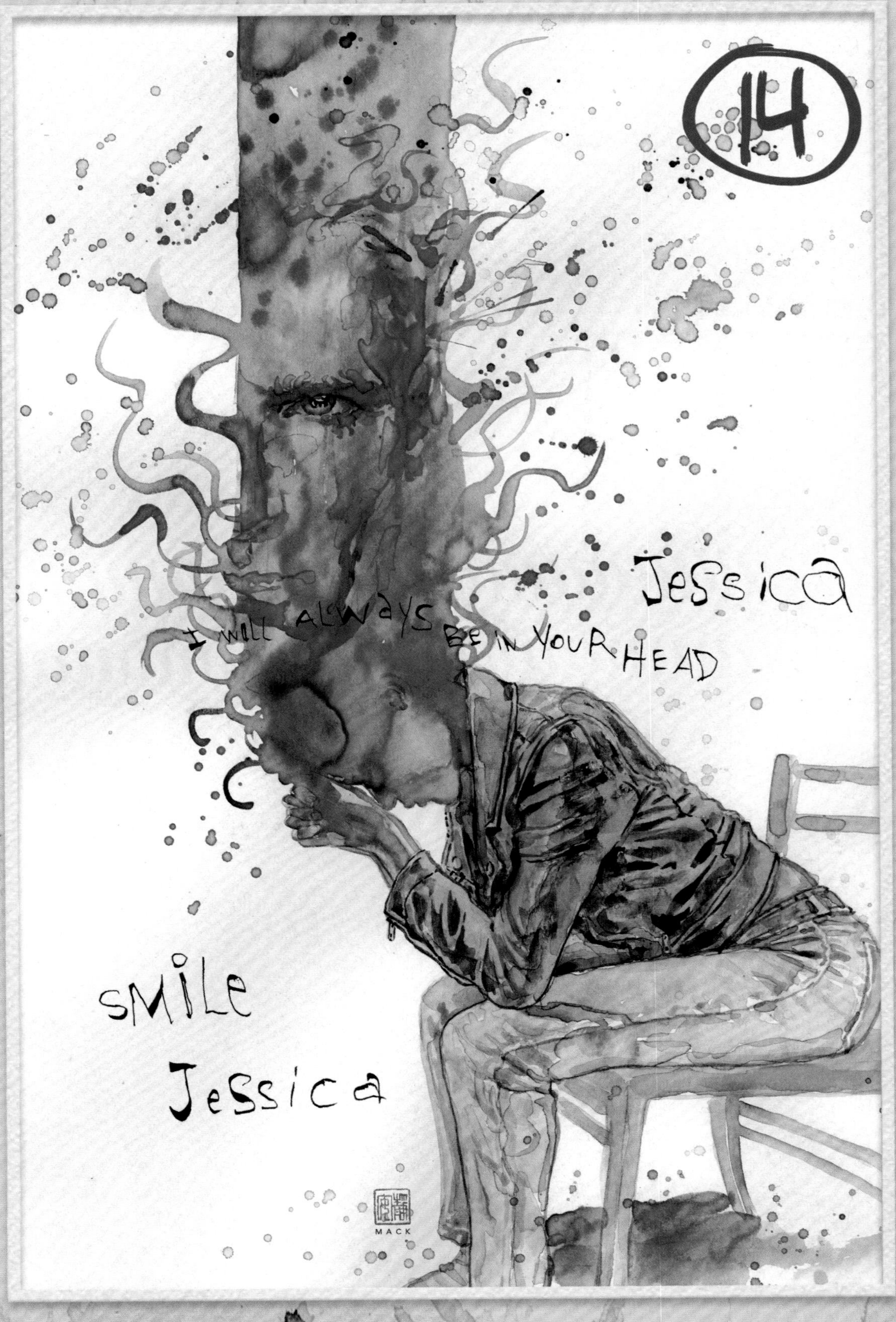
14
Jessica
I WILL ALWAYS BE IN YOUR HEAD
SMILE
Jessica
MACK

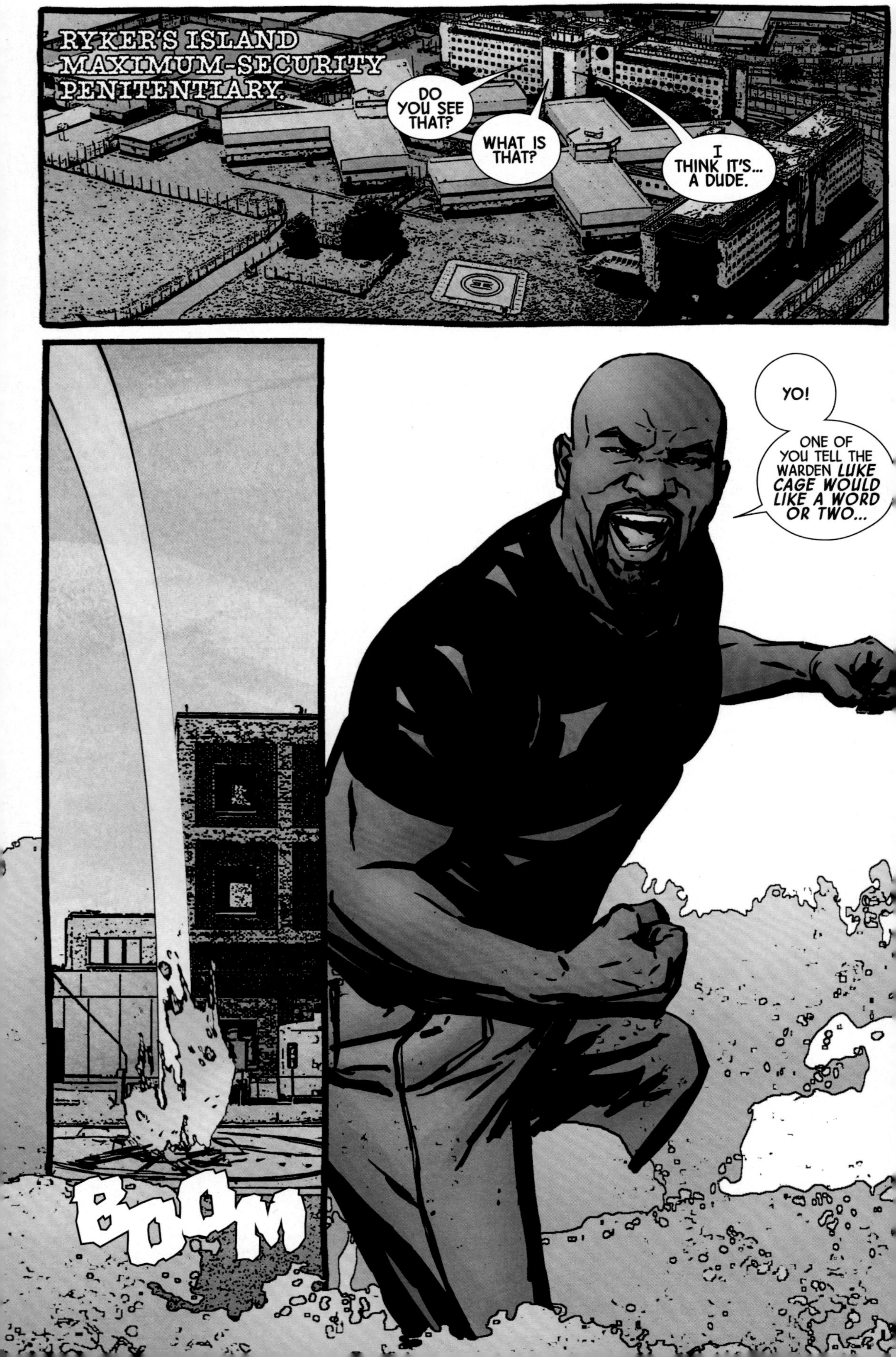
RYKER'S ISLAND MAXIMUM-SECURITY PENITENTIARY.
DO YOU SEE THAT?
WHAT IS THAT?
I THINK IT'S... A DUDE.
BOOM
YO!
ONE OF YOU TELL THE WARDEN LUKE CAGE WOULD LIKE A WORD OR TWO...

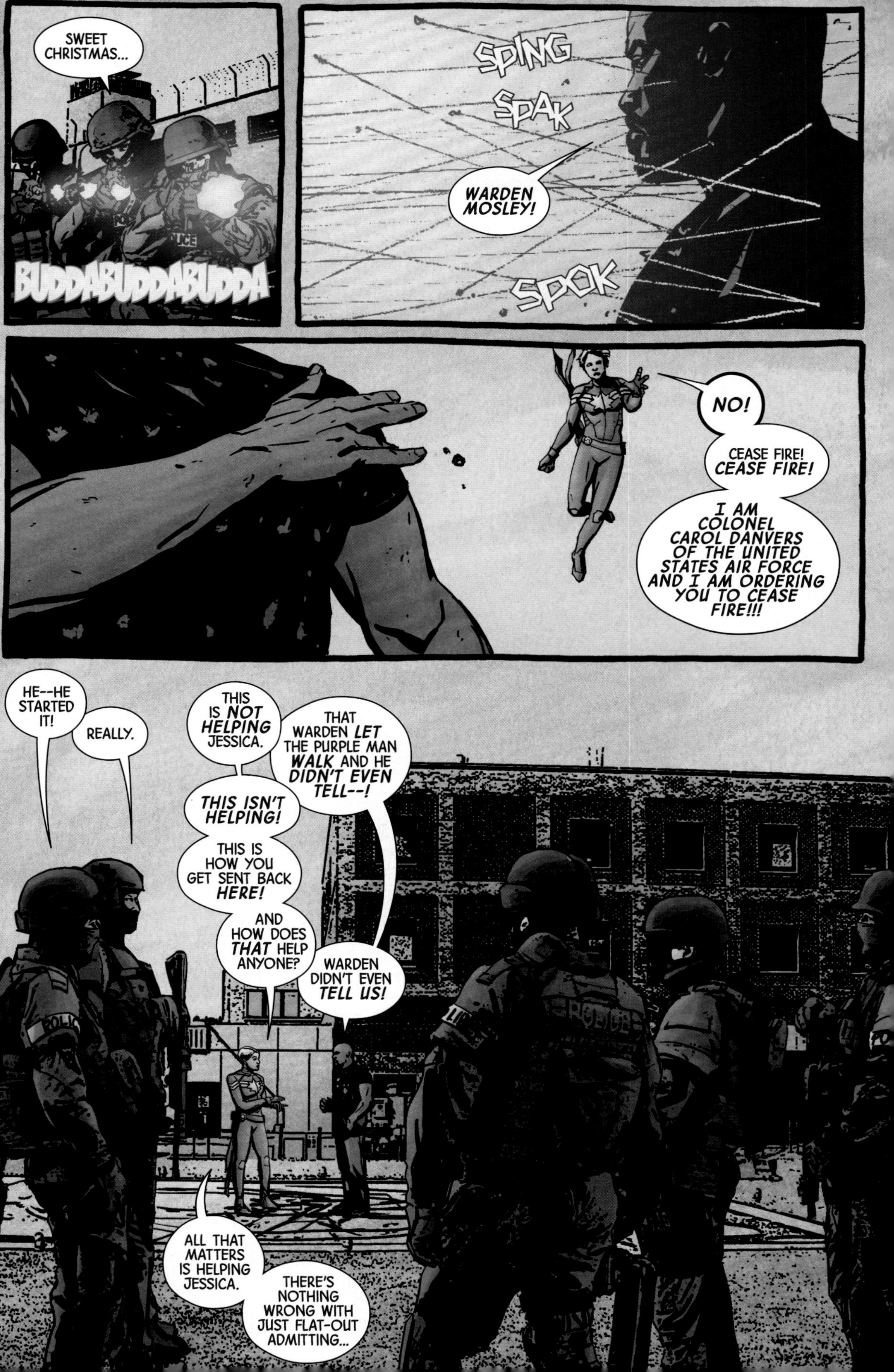
SWEET CHRISTMAS...
BUDDABUDDABUDDA
SPING
SPAK
WARDEN MOSLEY!
SPOK
NO!
CEASE FIRE! CEASE FIRE!
I AM COLONEL CAROL DANVERS OF THE UNITED STATES AIR FORCE AND I AM ORDERING YOU TO CEASE FIRE!!!
HE--HE STARTED IT!
REALLY.
THIS IS NOT HELPING JESSICA.
THAT WARDEN LET THE PURPLE MAN WALK AND HE DIDN'T EVEN TELL--!
THIS ISN'T HELPING!
THIS IS HOW YOU GET SENT BACK HERE!
AND HOW DOES THAT HELP ANYONE?
WARDEN DIDN'T EVEN TELL US!
ALL THAT MATTERS IS HELPING JESSICA.
THERE'S NOTHING WRONG WITH JUST FLAT-OUT ADMITTING...

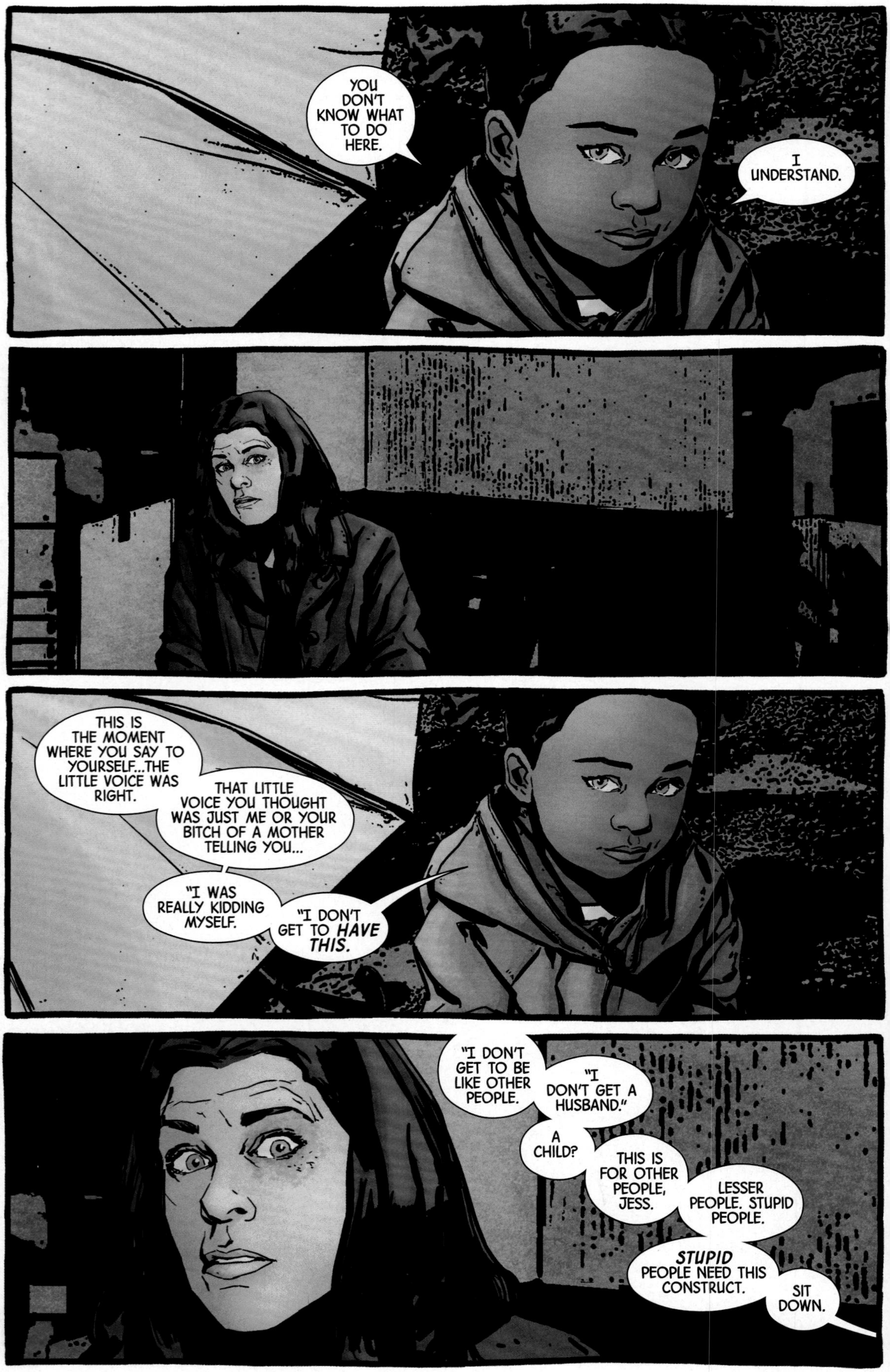

YOU DON'T KNOW WHAT TO DO HERE.
I UNDERSTAND.
THIS IS THE MOMENT WHERE YOU SAY TO YOURSELF...THE LITTLE VOICE WAS RIGHT.
THAT LITTLE VOICE YOU THOUGHT WAS JUST ME OR YOUR BITCH OF A MOTHER TELLING YOU...
"I WAS REALLY KIDDING MYSELF.
"I DON'T GET TO *HAVE THIS.*
"I DON'T GET TO BE LIKE OTHER PEOPLE.
"I DON'T GET A HUSBAND."
A CHILD?
THIS IS FOR OTHER PEOPLE, JESS.
LESSER PEOPLE. STUPID PEOPLE.
STUPID PEOPLE NEED THIS CONSTRUCT.
SIT DOWN.

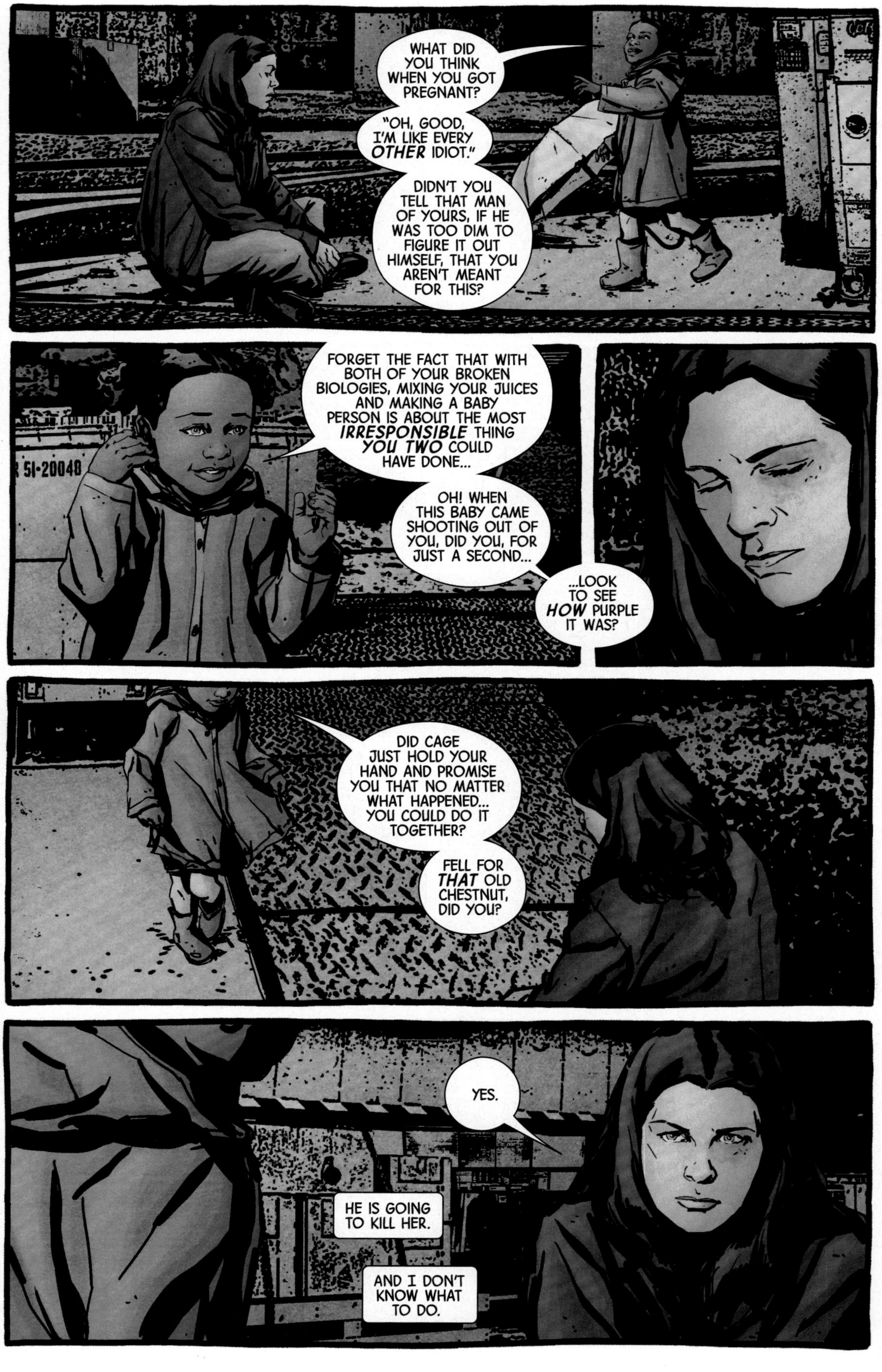
WHAT DID YOU THINK WHEN YOU GOT PREGNANT?
"OH, GOOD, I'M LIKE EVERY OTHER IDIOT."
DIDN'T YOU TELL THAT MAN OF YOURS, IF HE WAS TOO DIM TO FIGURE IT OUT HIMSELF, THAT YOU AREN'T MEANT FOR THIS?
R 51-20040
FORGET THE FACT THAT WITH BOTH OF YOUR BROKEN BIOLOGIES, MIXING YOUR JUICES AND MAKING A BABY PERSON IS ABOUT THE MOST IRRESPONSIBLE THING YOU TWO COULD HAVE DONE...
OH! WHEN THIS BABY CAME SHOOTING OUT OF YOU, DID YOU, FOR JUST A SECOND...
...LOOK TO SEE HOW PURPLE IT WAS?
DID CAGE JUST HOLD YOUR HAND AND PROMISE YOU THAT NO MATTER WHAT HAPPENED... YOU COULD DO IT TOGETHER?
FELL FOR THAT OLD CHESTNUT, DID YOU?
YES.
HE IS GOING TO KILL HER.
AND I DON'T KNOW WHAT TO DO.

IF I GRAB HER... HE'LL KILL HER.

IF I GRAB HER, HE COULD USE HER TO ATTACK AND KILL ME.

HE LIVES FOR MOMENTS LIKE THIS...

IMPOSSIBLE MORAL QUANDARIES.

THE SPORT OF IT.

WOULD I FIGHT MY OWN BABY TO SAVE MY LIFE?

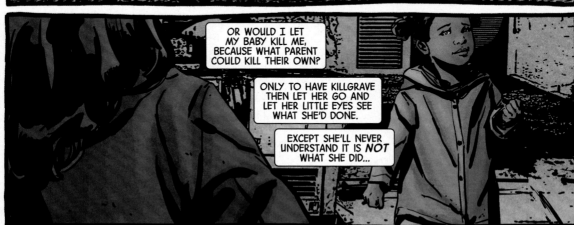

OR WOULD I LET MY BABY KILL ME, BECAUSE WHAT PARENT COULD KILL THEIR OWN?

ONLY TO HAVE KILLGRAVE THEN LET HER GO AND LET HER LITTLE EYES SEE WHAT SHE'D DONE.

EXCEPT SHE'LL NEVER UNDERSTAND IT IS *NOT* WHAT SHE DID...

...IT IS WHAT *HE* DID.

IF.

IF HE EVER LETS GO OF HER.

I DON'T KNOW WHAT TO DO.

KILLGRAVE...

...EVERY SECOND, EVERY BREATH YOU STEAL FROM MY DAUGHTER...

YOU'LL KILL ME.

YES.

I FULLY BELIEVE YOU.

YOU ALMOST KILLED ME A COUPLE OF TIMES.

IT'S INTERESTING, WHEN I AM FACED WITH REAL MORTAL DANGER, SOMETIMES MY POWERS KICK INTO THIS EXTRA--

KILLGRAVE!

DO NOT SPEAK TO ME THROUGH MY DAUGHTER.

WELL...

...I NEED TO SPEAK TO YOU.

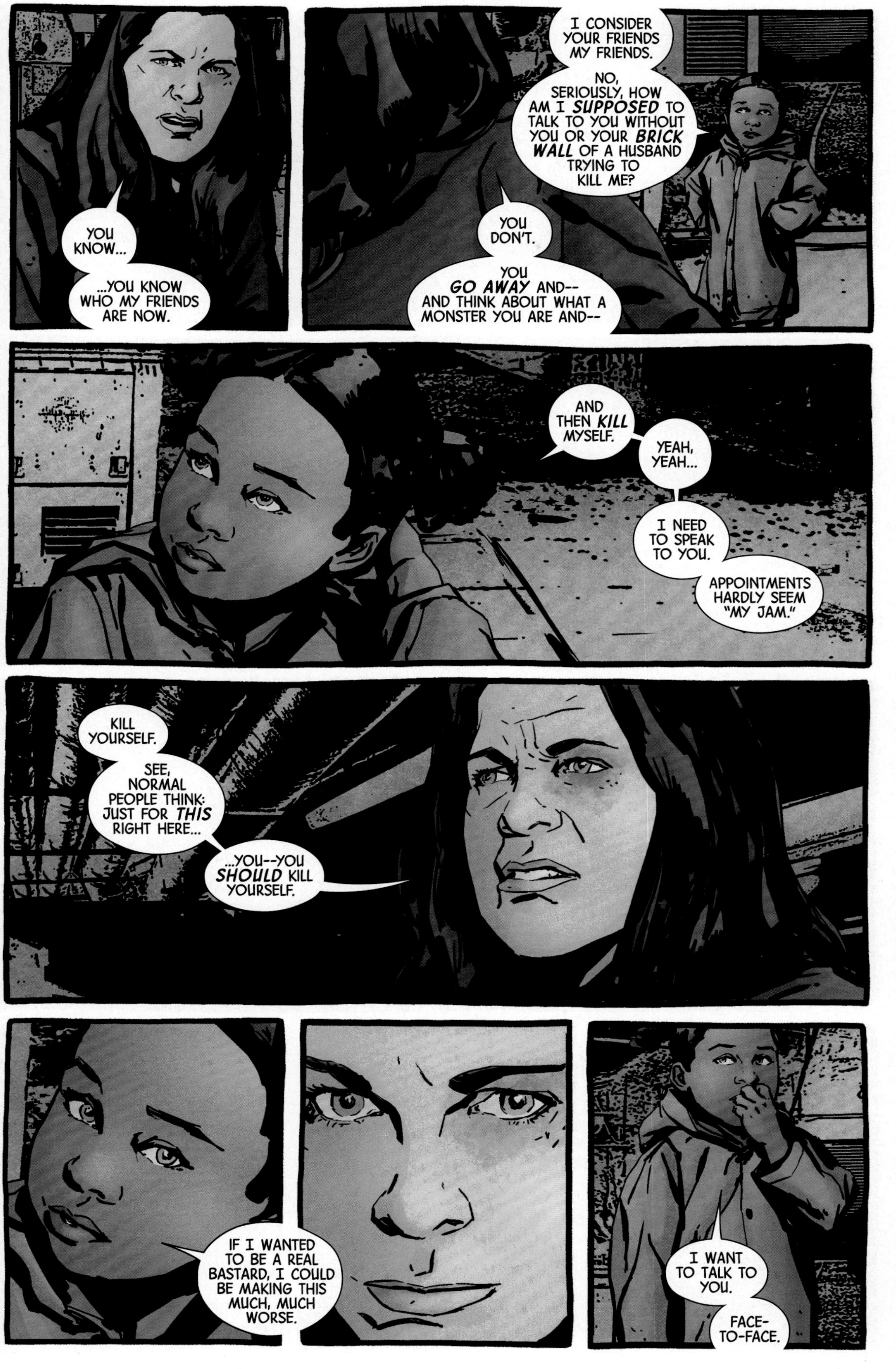

YOU KNOW...
...YOU KNOW WHO MY FRIENDS ARE NOW.
I CONSIDER YOUR FRIENDS MY FRIENDS.
NO, SERIOUSLY, HOW AM I SUPPOSED TO TALK TO YOU WITHOUT YOU OR YOUR BRICK WALL OF A HUSBAND TRYING TO KILL ME?
YOU DON'T.
YOU GO AWAY AND-- AND THINK ABOUT WHAT A MONSTER YOU ARE AND--
AND THEN KILL MYSELF.
YEAH, YEAH...
I NEED TO SPEAK TO YOU.
APPOINTMENTS HARDLY SEEM "MY JAM."
KILL YOURSELF.
SEE, NORMAL PEOPLE THINK: JUST FOR THIS RIGHT HERE...
...YOU--YOU SHOULD KILL YOURSELF.
IF I WANTED TO BE A REAL BASTARD, I COULD BE MAKING THIS MUCH, MUCH WORSE.
I WANT TO TALK TO YOU.
FACE-TO-FACE.

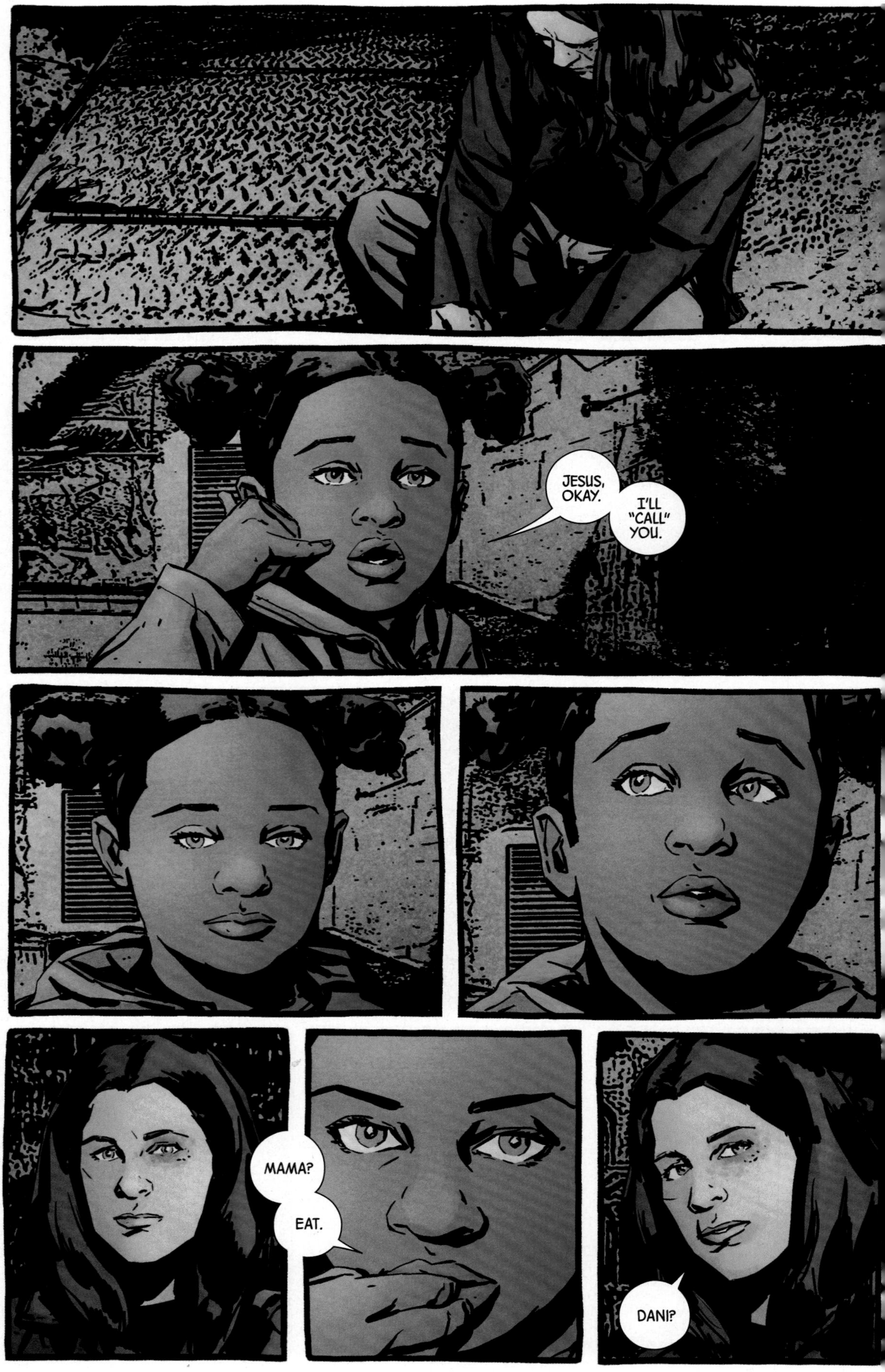
JESUS, OKAY.
I'LL "CALL" YOU.
MAMA?
EAT.
DANI?

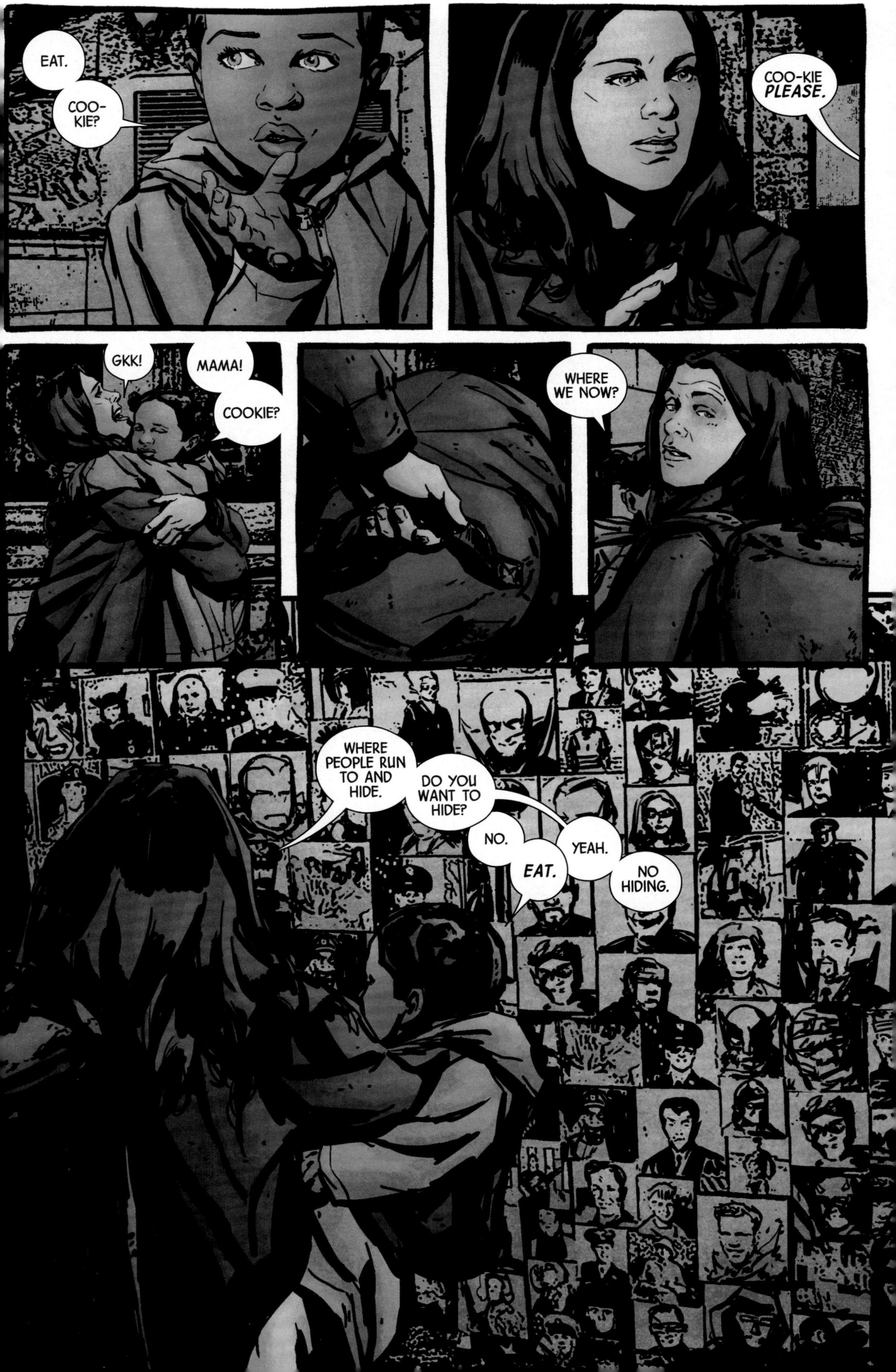
EAT.
COO-KIE?
COO-KIE PLEASE.
GKK!
MAMA!
COOKIE?
WHERE WE NOW?
WHERE PEOPLE RUN TO AND HIDE.
DO YOU WANT TO HIDE?
NO.
EAT.
YEAH.
NO HIDING.

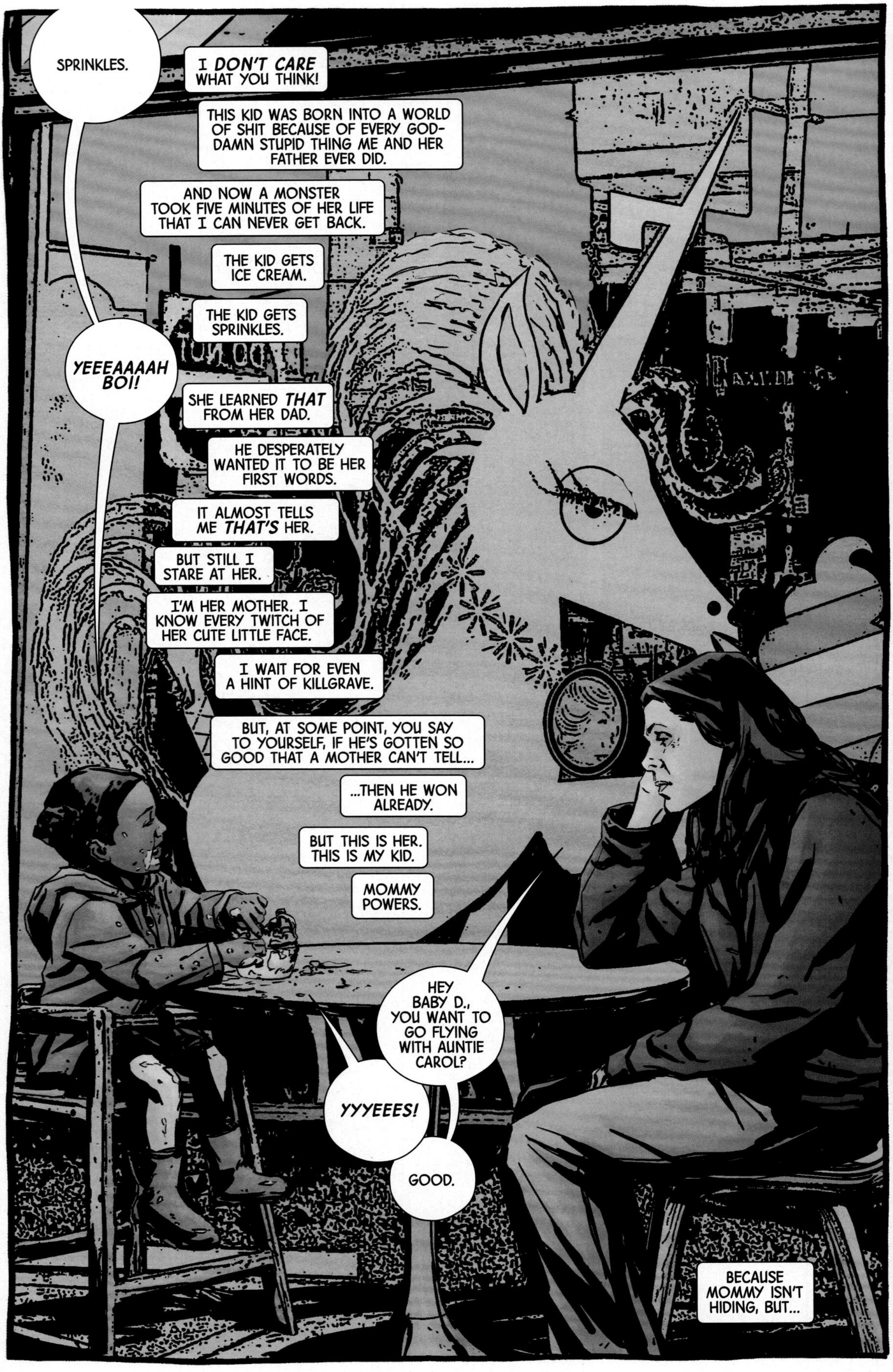
SPRINKLES.
I *DON'T CARE* WHAT YOU THINK!
THIS KID WAS BORN INTO A WORLD OF SHIT BECAUSE OF EVERY GOD-DAMN STUPID THING ME AND HER FATHER EVER DID.
AND NOW A MONSTER TOOK FIVE MINUTES OF HER LIFE THAT I CAN NEVER GET BACK.
THE KID GETS ICE CREAM.
THE KID GETS SPRINKLES.
YEEEAAAAH BOI!
SHE LEARNED *THAT* FROM HER DAD.
HE DESPERATELY WANTED IT TO BE HER FIRST WORDS.
IT ALMOST TELLS ME *THAT'S* HER.
BUT STILL I STARE AT HER.
I'M HER MOTHER. I KNOW EVERY TWITCH OF HER CUTE LITTLE FACE.
I WAIT FOR EVEN A HINT OF KILLGRAVE.
BUT, AT SOME POINT, YOU SAY TO YOURSELF, IF HE'S GOTTEN SO GOOD THAT A MOTHER CAN'T TELL...
...THEN HE WON ALREADY.
BUT THIS IS HER. THIS IS MY KID.
MOMMY POWERS.
HEY BABY D., YOU WANT TO GO FLYING WITH AUNTIE CAROL?
YYYEEES!
GOOD.
BECAUSE MOMMY ISN'T HIDING, BUT...

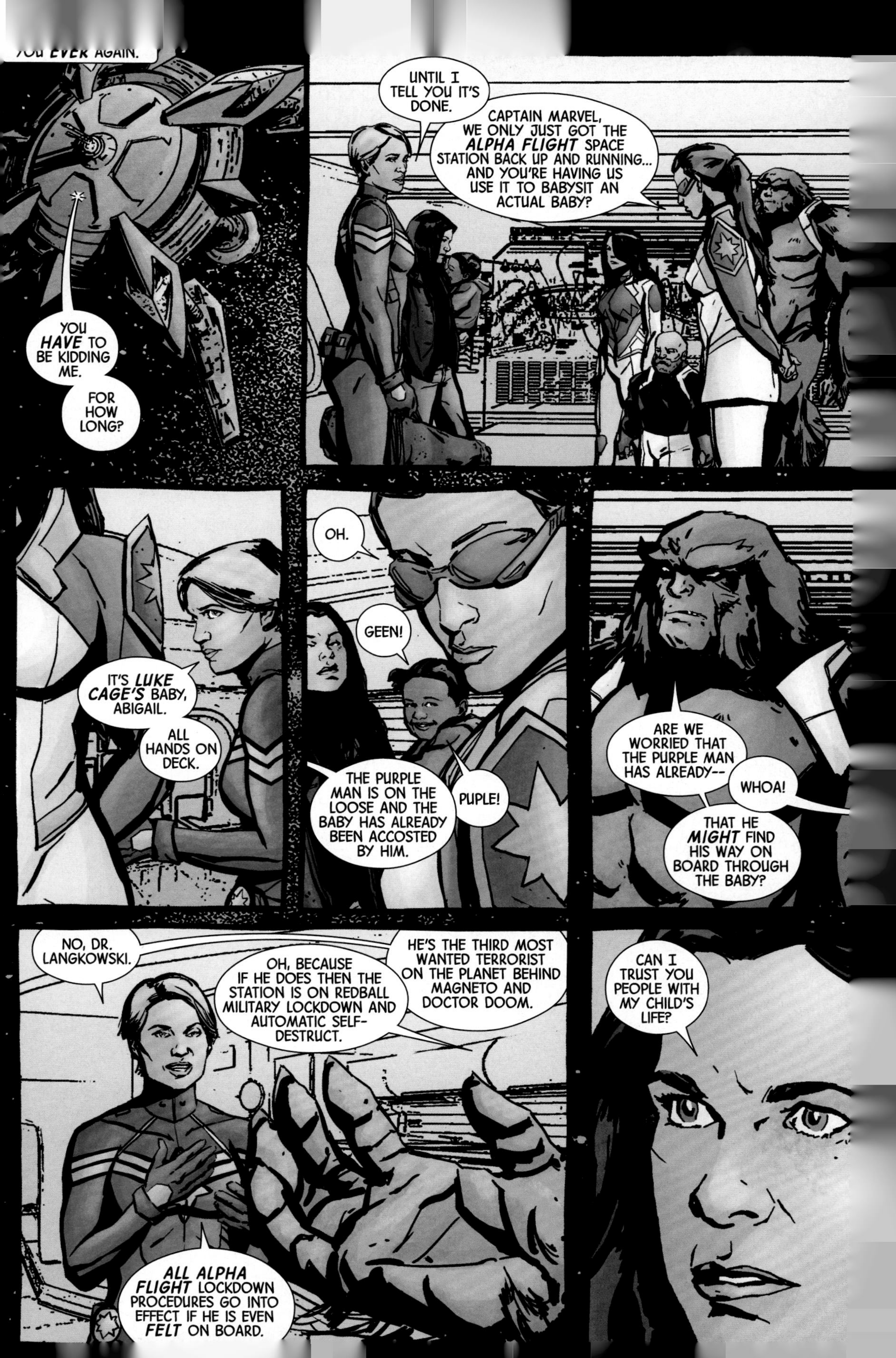
YOU EVER AGAIN.
YOU HAVE TO BE KIDDING ME.
FOR HOW LONG?
UNTIL I TELL YOU IT'S DONE.
CAPTAIN MARVEL, WE ONLY JUST GOT THE ALPHA FLIGHT SPACE STATION BACK UP AND RUNNING... AND YOU'RE HAVING US USE IT TO BABYSIT AN ACTUAL BABY?
IT'S LUKE CAGE'S BABY, ABIGAIL.
ALL HANDS ON DECK.
OH.
GEEN!
THE PURPLE MAN IS ON THE LOOSE AND THE BABY HAS ALREADY BEEN ACCOSTED BY HIM.
PUPLE!
ARE WE WORRIED THAT THE PURPLE MAN HAS ALREADY--
WHOA!
THAT HE MIGHT FIND HIS WAY ON BOARD THROUGH THE BABY?
NO, DR. LANGKOWSKI.
OH, BECAUSE IF HE DOES THEN THE STATION IS ON REDBALL MILITARY LOCKDOWN AND AUTOMATIC SELF-DESTRUCT.
HE'S THE THIRD MOST WANTED TERRORIST ON THE PLANET BEHIND MAGNETO AND DOCTOR DOOM.
ALL ALPHA FLIGHT LOCKDOWN PROCEDURES GO INTO EFFECT IF HE IS EVEN FELT ON BOARD.
CAN I TRUST YOU PEOPLE WITH MY CHILD'S LIFE?

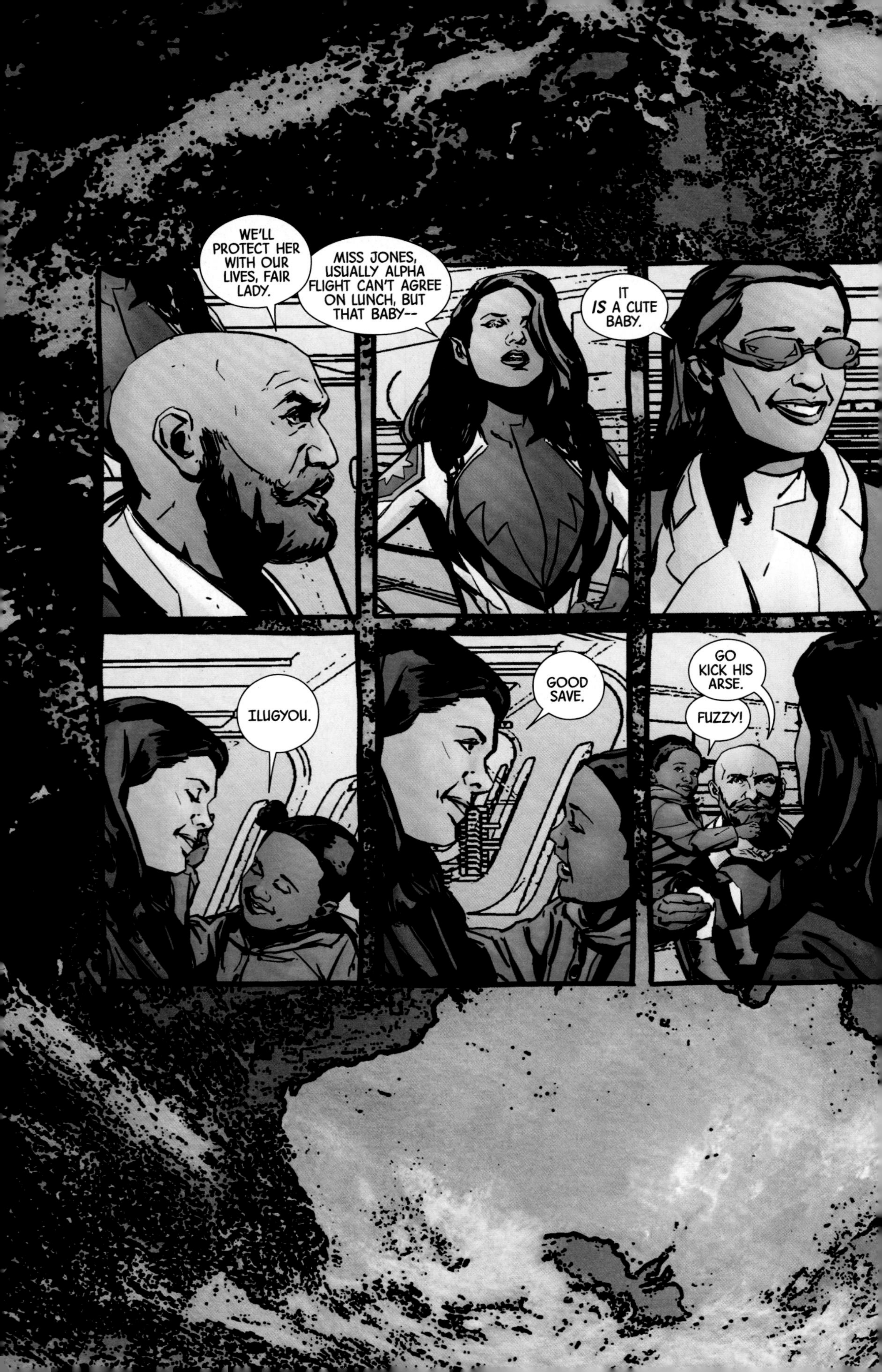
WE'LL PROTECT HER WITH OUR LIVES, FAIR LADY.
MISS JONES, USUALLY ALPHA FLIGHT CAN'T AGREE ON LUNCH, BUT THAT BABY--
IT IS A CUTE BABY.
ILUGYOU.
GOOD SAVE.
GO KICK HIS ARSE.
FUZZY!

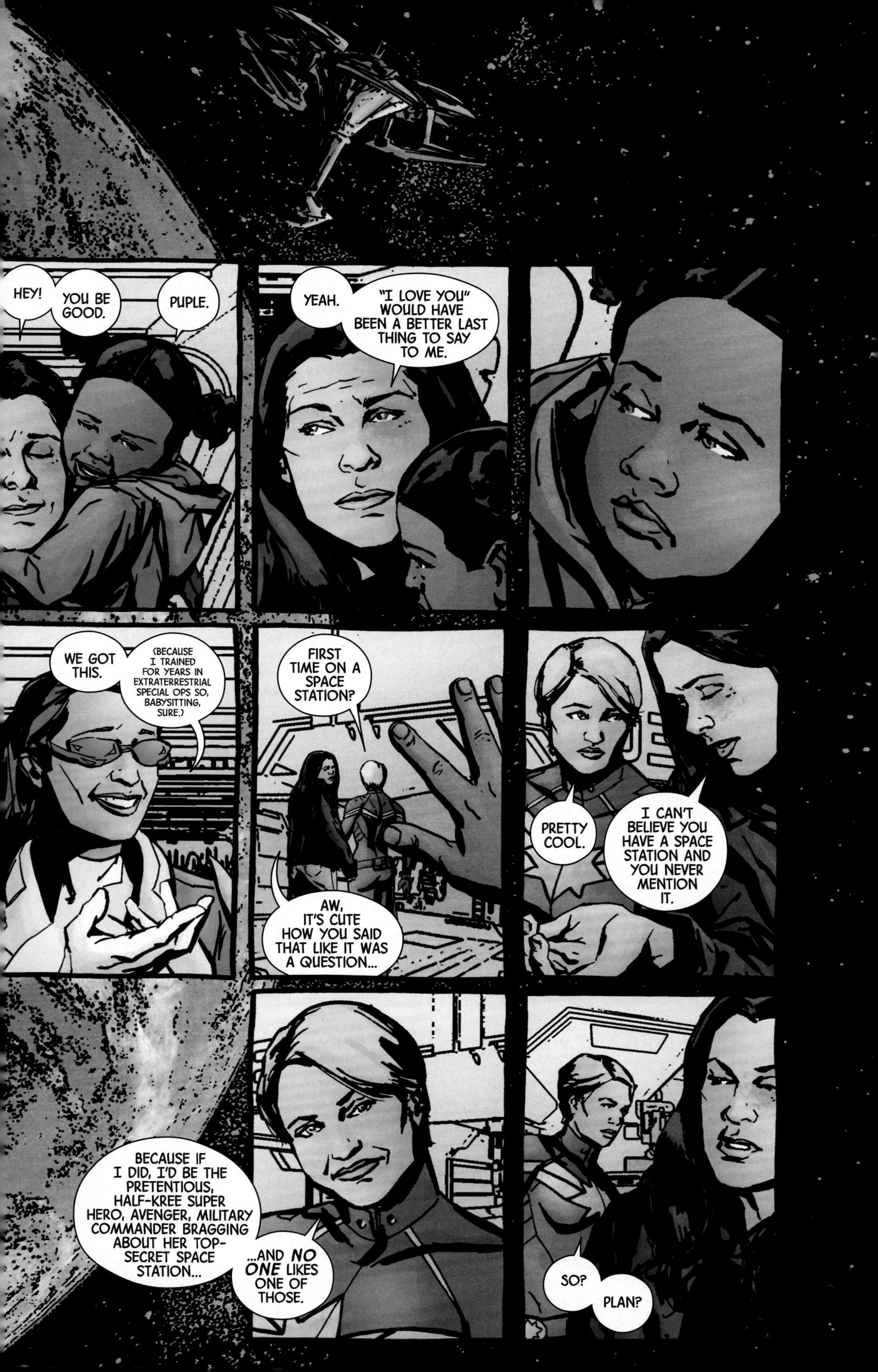
HEY!
YOU BE GOOD.
PUPLE.
YEAH.
"I LOVE YOU" WOULD HAVE BEEN A BETTER LAST THING TO SAY TO ME.
WE GOT THIS.
(BECAUSE I TRAINED FOR YEARS IN EXTRATERRESTRIAL SPECIAL OPS SO, BABYSITTING, SURE.)
FIRST TIME ON A SPACE STATION?
AW, IT'S CUTE HOW YOU SAID THAT LIKE IT WAS A QUESTION...
PRETTY COOL.
I CAN'T BELIEVE YOU HAVE A SPACE STATION AND YOU NEVER MENTION IT.
BECAUSE IF I DID, I'D BE THE PRETENTIOUS, HALF-KREE SUPER HERO, AVENGER, MILITARY COMMANDER BRAGGING ABOUT HER TOP-SECRET SPACE STATION...
...AND *NO ONE* LIKES ONE OF THOSE.
SO?
PLAN?

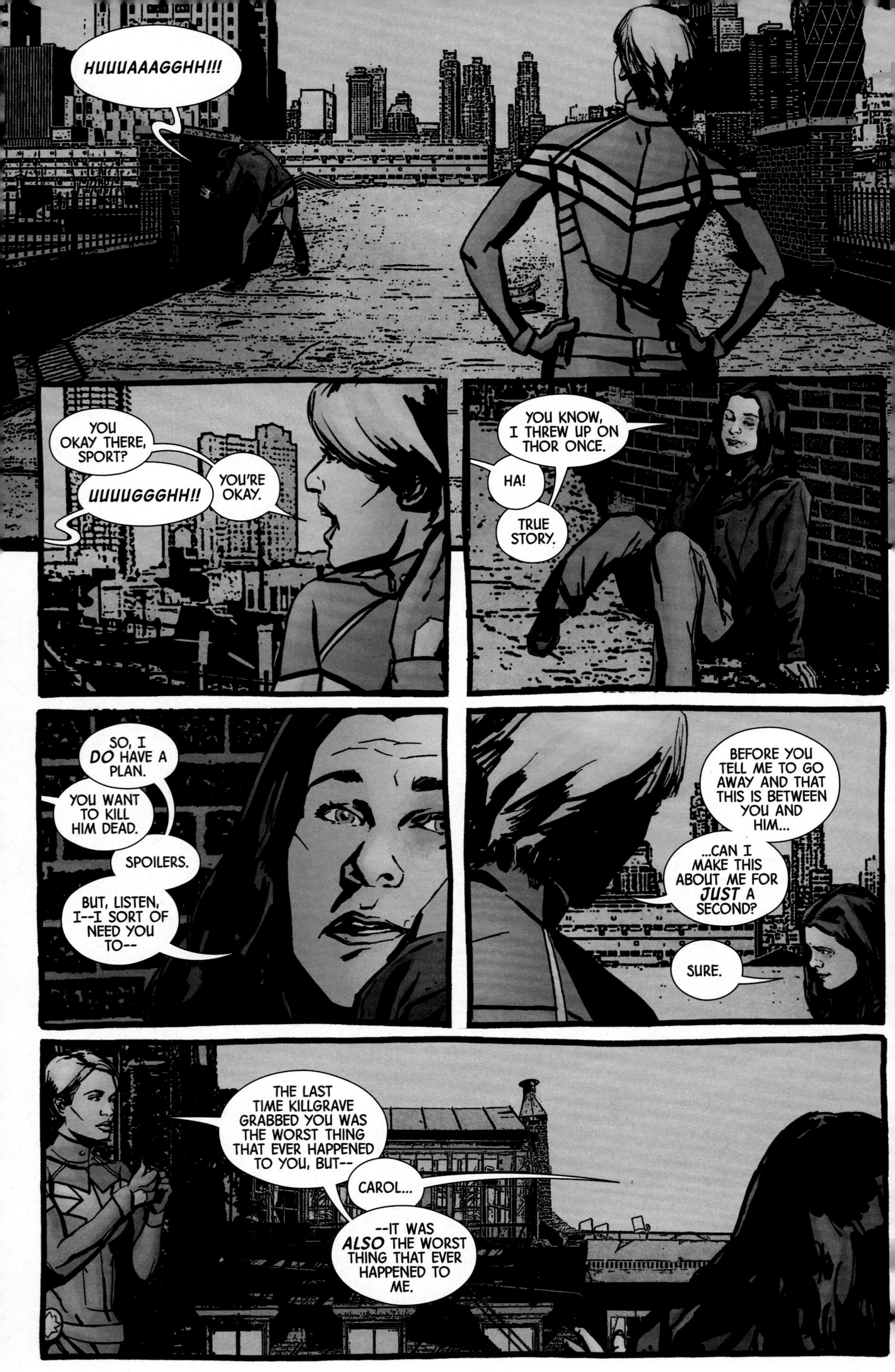
HUUUAAAGGHH!!!
YOU OKAY THERE, SPORT?
UUUUGGGHH!!
YOU'RE OKAY.
YOU KNOW, I THREW UP ON THOR ONCE.
HA!
TRUE STORY.
SO, I DO HAVE A PLAN.
YOU WANT TO KILL HIM DEAD.
SPOILERS.
BUT, LISTEN, I--I SORT OF NEED YOU TO--
BEFORE YOU TELL ME TO GO AWAY AND THAT THIS IS BETWEEN YOU AND HIM...
...CAN I MAKE THIS ABOUT ME FOR JUST A SECOND?
SURE.
THE LAST TIME KILLGRAVE GRABBED YOU WAS THE WORST THING THAT EVER HAPPENED TO YOU, BUT--
CAROL...
--IT WAS ALSO THE WORST THING THAT EVER HAPPENED TO ME.

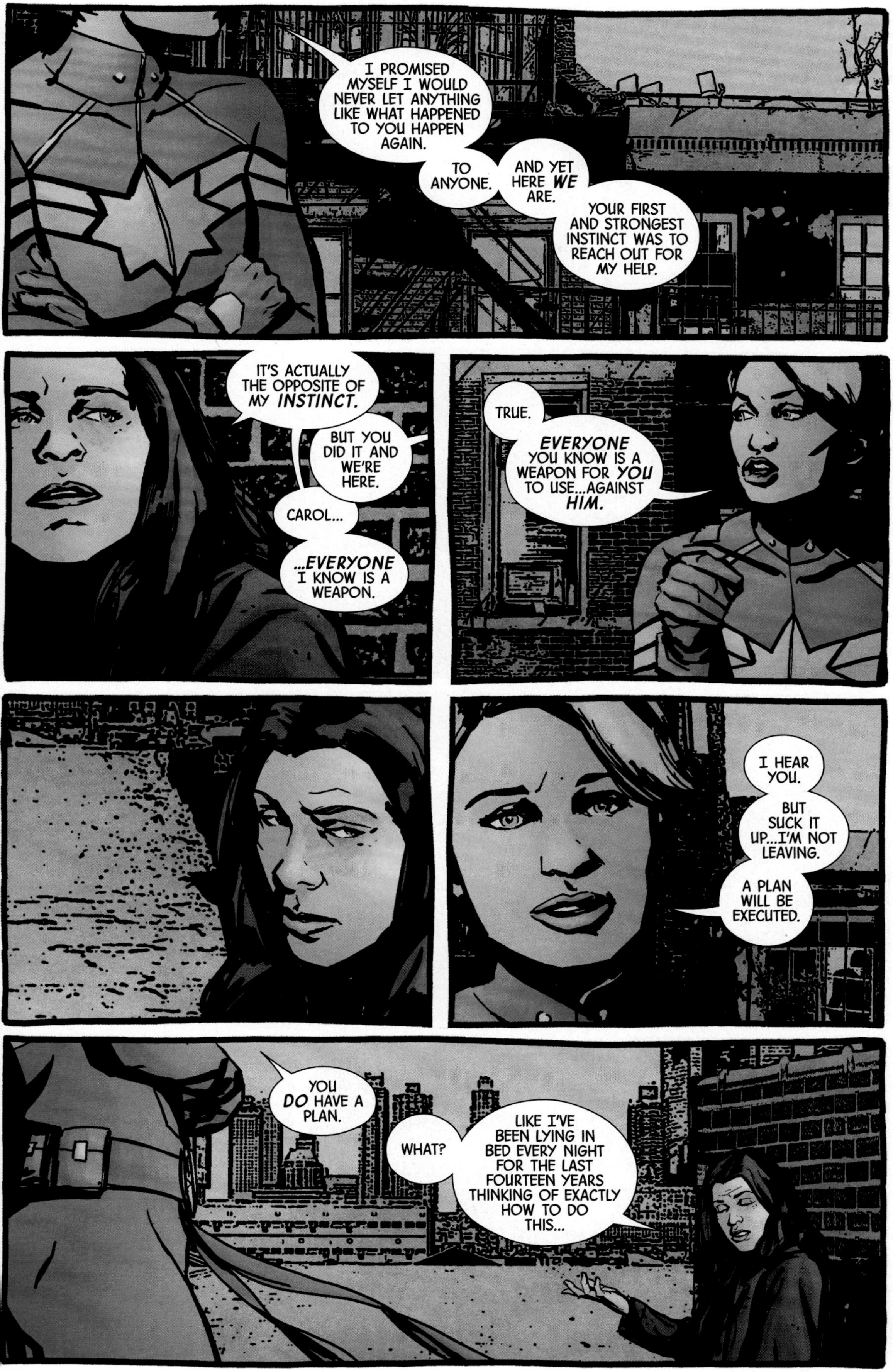
I PROMISED MYSELF I WOULD NEVER LET ANYTHING LIKE WHAT HAPPENED TO YOU HAPPEN AGAIN.
TO ANYONE.
AND YET HERE *WE* ARE.
YOUR FIRST AND STRONGEST INSTINCT WAS TO REACH OUT FOR MY HELP.
IT'S ACTUALLY THE OPPOSITE OF MY *INSTINCT.*
BUT YOU DID IT AND WE'RE HERE.
CAROL...
...*EVERYONE* I KNOW IS A WEAPON.
TRUE.
EVERYONE YOU KNOW IS A WEAPON FOR *YOU* TO USE...AGAINST *HIM.*
I HEAR YOU.
BUT SUCK IT UP...I'M NOT LEAVING.
A PLAN WILL BE EXECUTED.
YOU *DO* HAVE A PLAN.
WHAT?
LIKE I'VE BEEN LYING IN BED EVERY NIGHT FOR THE LAST FOURTEEN YEARS THINKING OF EXACTLY HOW TO DO THIS...

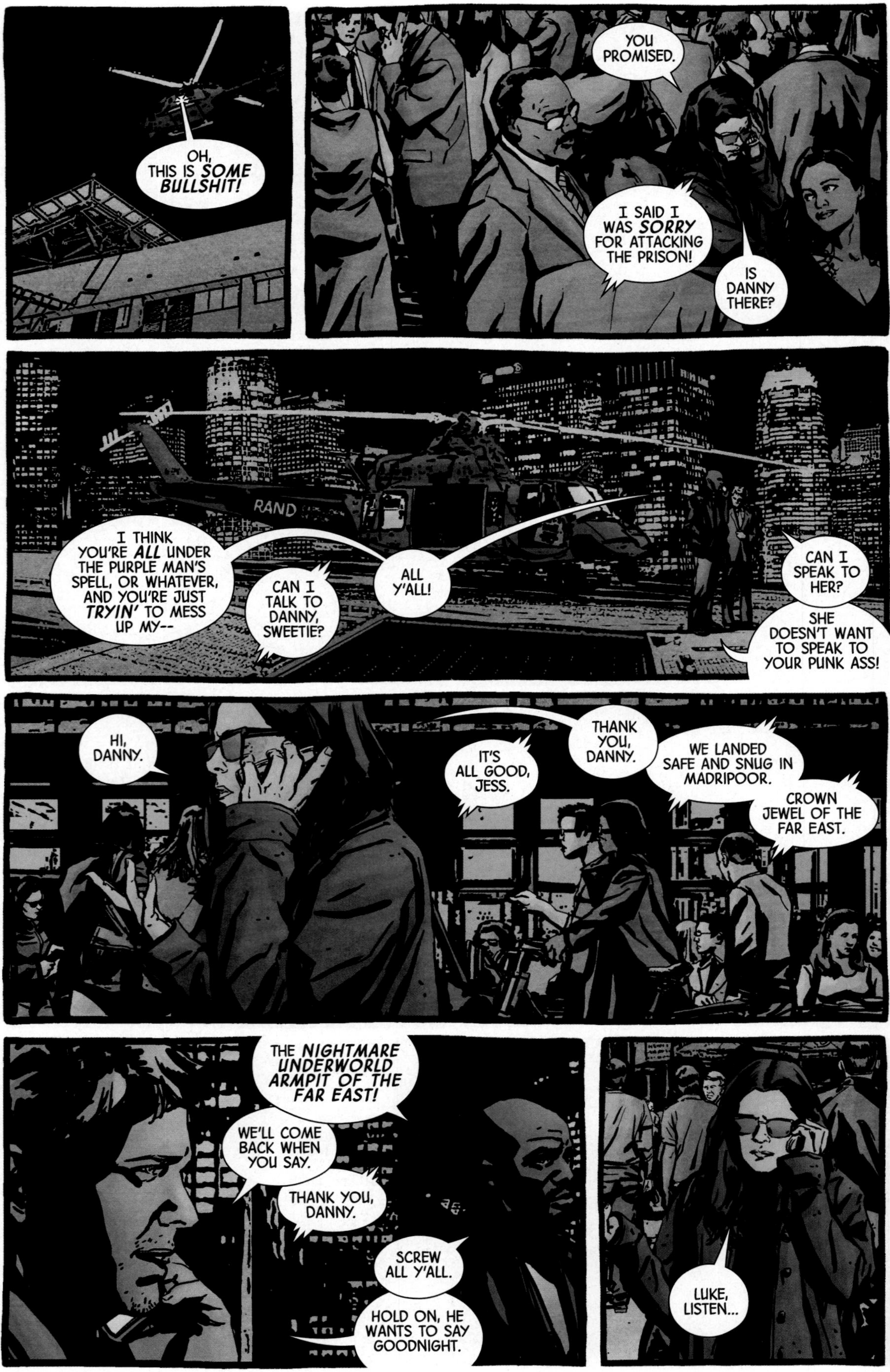
OH, THIS IS SOME BULLSHIT!
YOU PROMISED.
I SAID I WAS SORRY FOR ATTACKING THE PRISON!
IS DANNY THERE?
RAND
I THINK YOU'RE ALL UNDER THE PURPLE MAN'S SPELL, OR WHATEVER, AND YOU'RE JUST TRYIN' TO MESS UP MY--
CAN I TALK TO DANNY, SWEETIE?
ALL Y'ALL!
CAN I SPEAK TO HER?
SHE DOESN'T WANT TO SPEAK TO YOUR PUNK ASS!
HI, DANNY.
IT'S ALL GOOD, JESS.
THANK YOU, DANNY.
WE LANDED SAFE AND SNUG IN MADRIPOOR.
CROWN JEWEL OF THE FAR EAST.
THE NIGHTMARE UNDERWORLD ARMPIT OF THE FAR EAST!
WE'LL COME BACK WHEN YOU SAY.
THANK YOU, DANNY.
SCREW ALL Y'ALL.
HOLD ON, HE WANTS TO SAY GOODNIGHT.
LUKE, LISTEN...

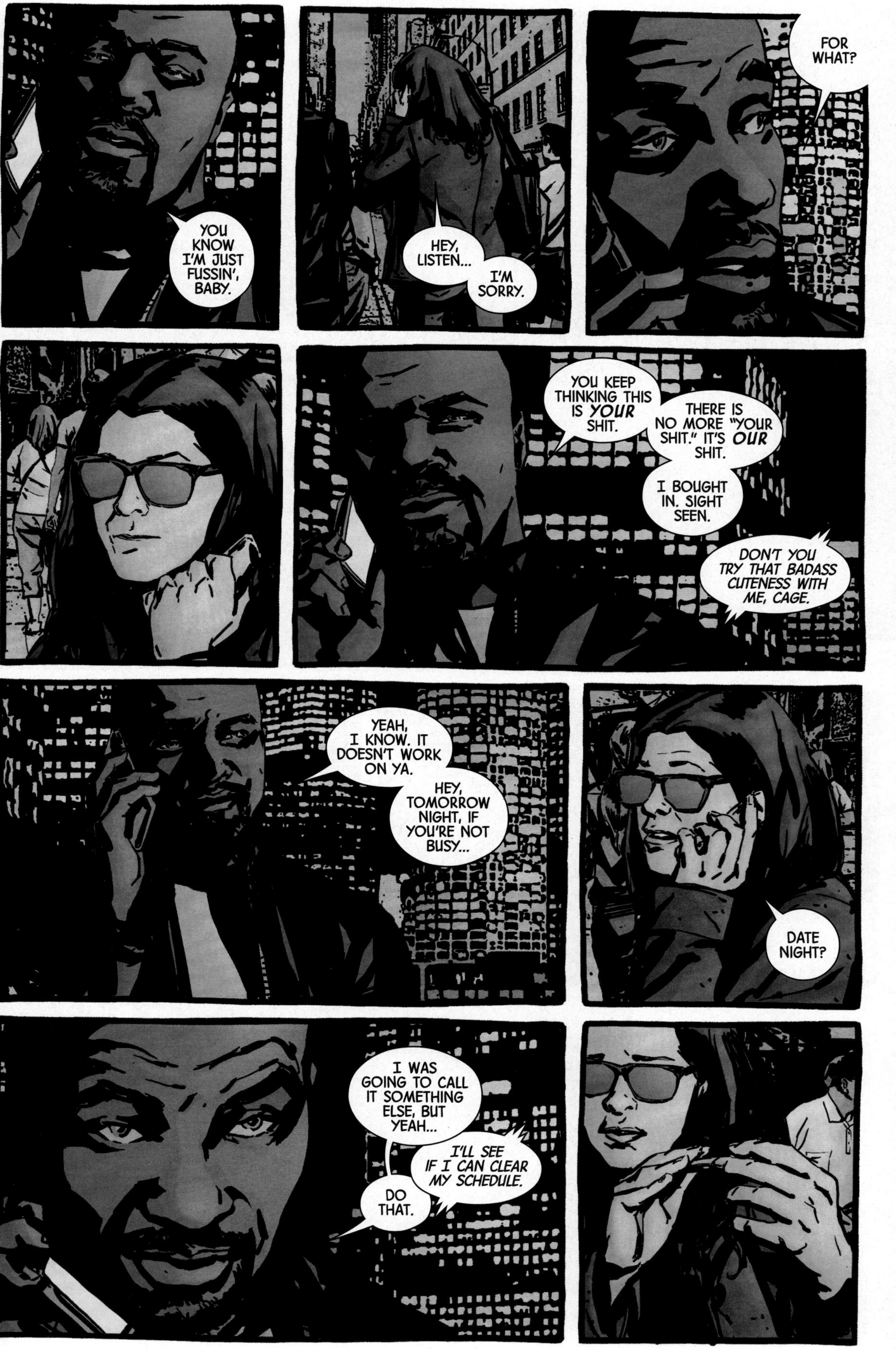
YOU KNOW I'M JUST FUSSIN', BABY.
HEY, LISTEN...
I'M SORRY.
FOR WHAT?
YOU KEEP THINKING THIS IS YOUR SHIT.
THERE IS NO MORE "YOUR SHIT." IT'S OUR SHIT.
I BOUGHT IN. SIGHT SEEN.
DON'T YOU TRY THAT BADASS CUTENESS WITH ME, CAGE.
YEAH, I KNOW. IT DOESN'T WORK ON YA.
HEY, TOMORROW NIGHT, IF YOU'RE NOT BUSY...
DATE NIGHT?
I WAS GOING TO CALL IT SOMETHING ELSE, BUT YEAH...
I'LL SEE IF I CAN CLEAR MY SCHEDULE.
DO THAT.

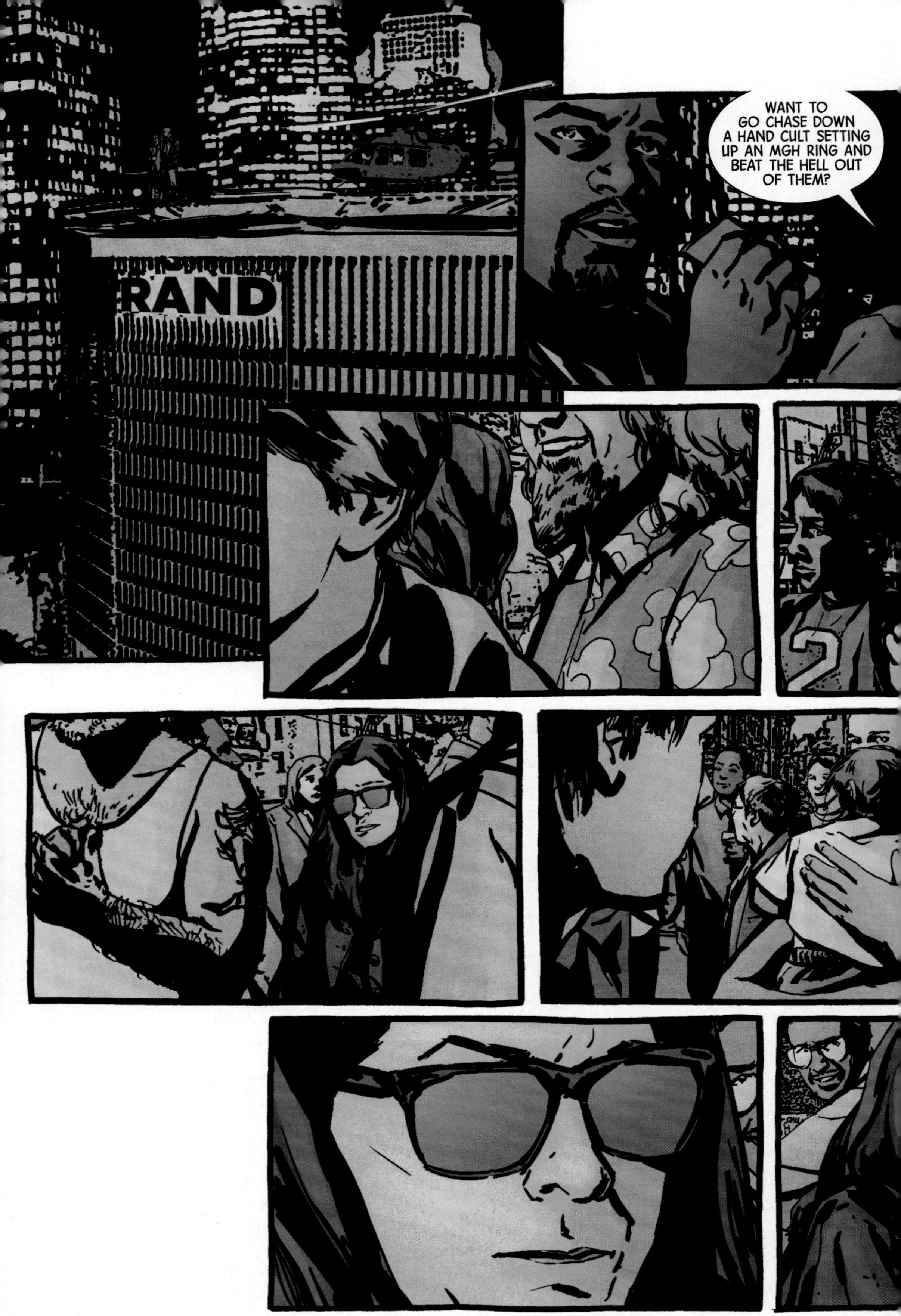
RAND
WANT TO GO CHASE DOWN A HAND CULT SETTING UP AN MGH RING AND BEAT THE HELL OUT OF THEM?

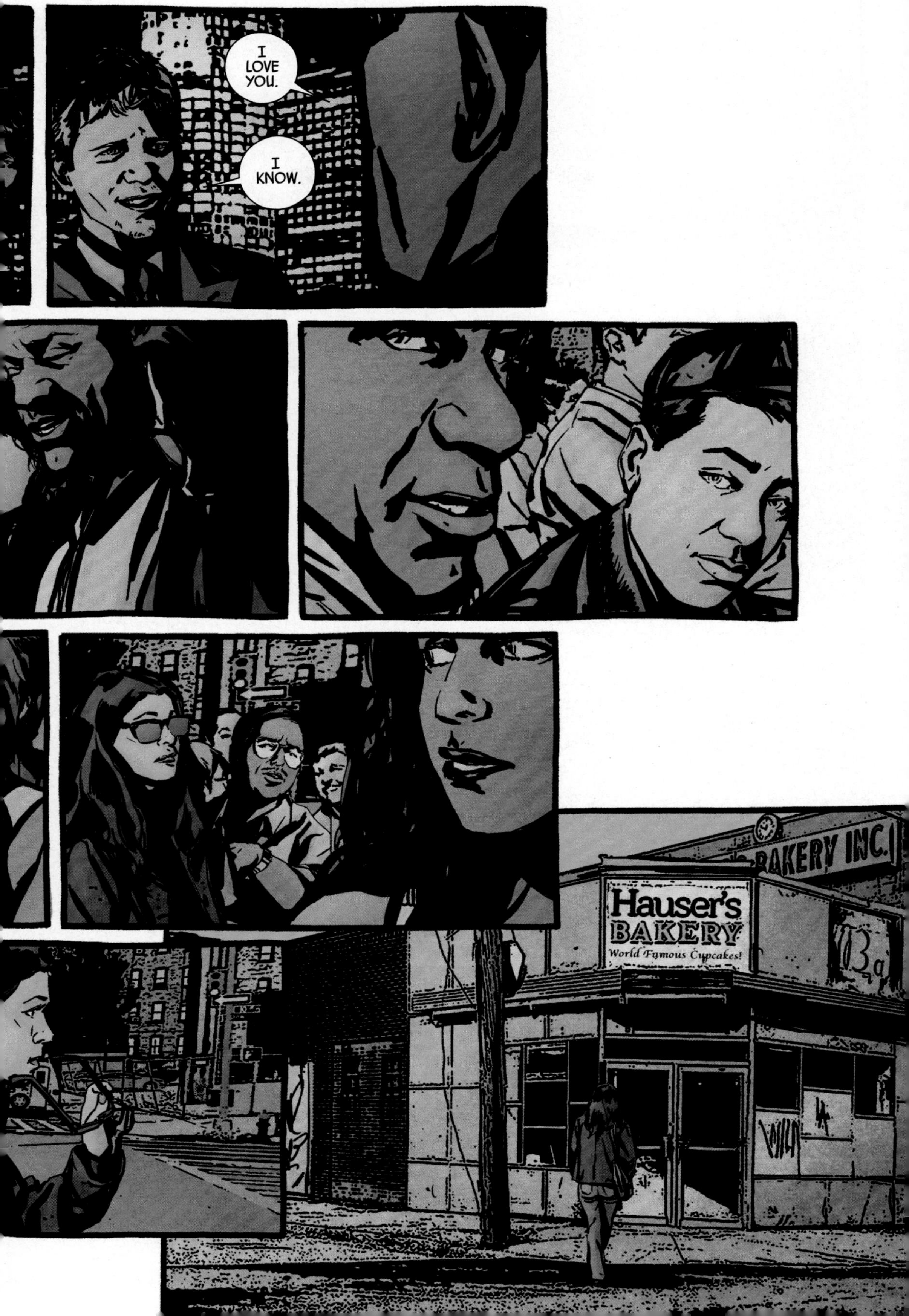
I LOVE YOU.
I KNOW.
BAKERY INC.
Hauser's BAKERY
World Famous Cupcakes!

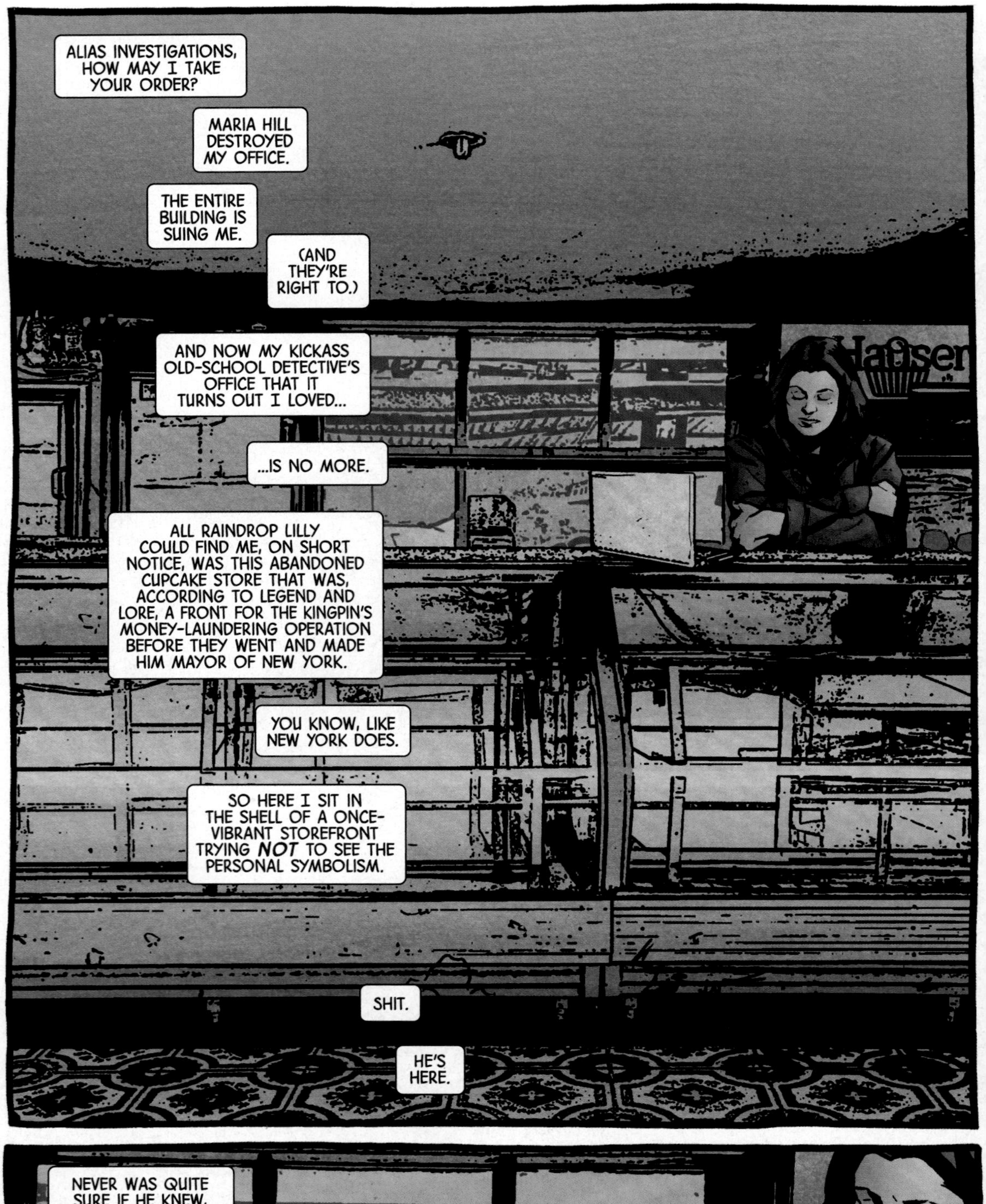
ALIAS INVESTIGATIONS, HOW MAY I TAKE YOUR ORDER?
MARIA HILL DESTROYED MY OFFICE.
THE ENTIRE BUILDING IS SUING ME.
(AND THEY'RE RIGHT TO.)
AND NOW MY KICKASS OLD-SCHOOL DETECTIVE'S OFFICE THAT IT TURNS OUT I LOVED...
...IS NO MORE.
ALL RAINDROP LILLY COULD FIND ME, ON SHORT NOTICE, WAS THIS ABANDONED CUPCAKE STORE THAT WAS, ACCORDING TO LEGEND AND LORE, A FRONT FOR THE KINGPIN'S MONEY-LAUNDERING OPERATION BEFORE THEY WENT AND MADE HIM MAYOR OF NEW YORK.
YOU KNOW, LIKE NEW YORK DOES.
SO HERE I SIT IN THE SHELL OF A ONCE-VIBRANT STOREFRONT TRYING *NOT* TO SEE THE PERSONAL SYMBOLISM.
SHIT.
HE'S HERE.

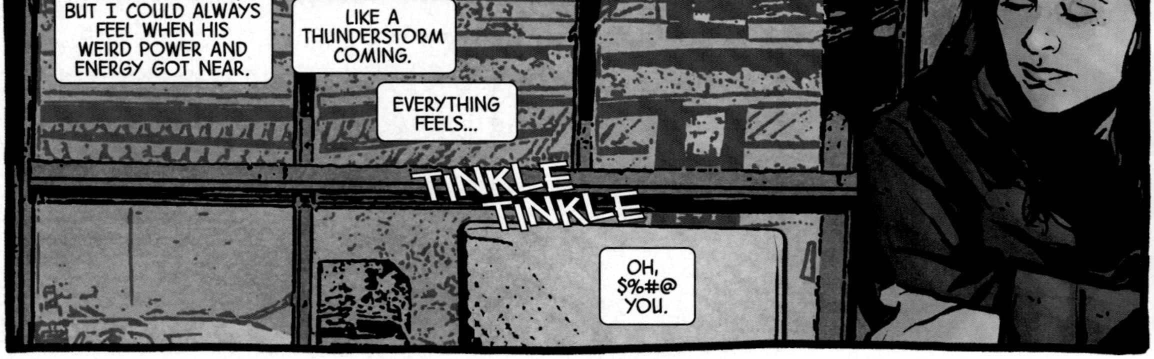
NEVER WAS QUITE SURE IF HE KNEW, BUT I COULD ALWAYS FEEL WHEN HIS WEIRD POWER AND ENERGY GOT NEAR.
LIKE A THUNDERSTORM COMING.
EVERYTHING FEELS...
TINKLE TINKLE
OH, $%#@ YOU.

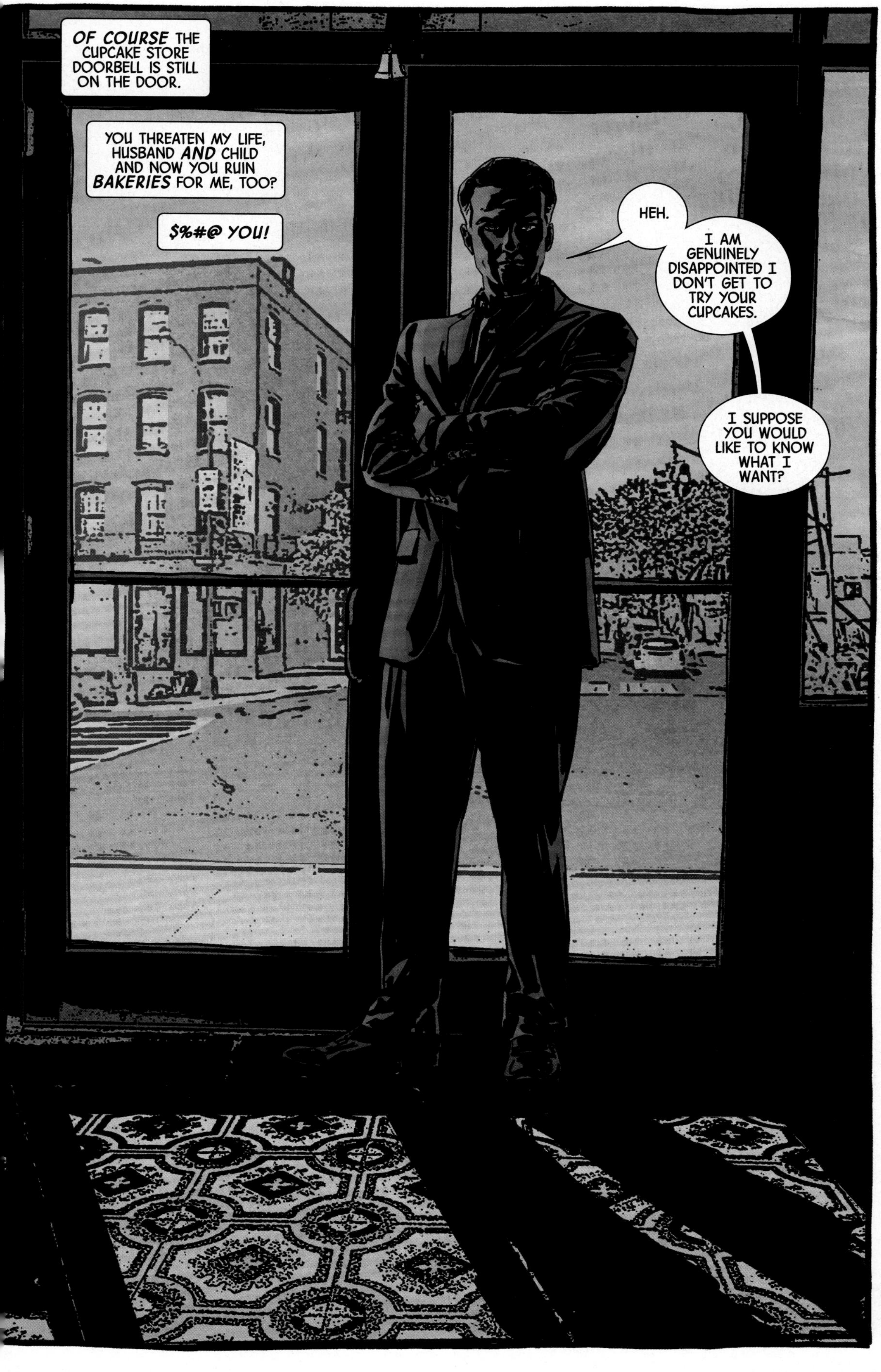
OF COURSE THE CUPCAKE STORE DOORBELL IS STILL ON THE DOOR.
YOU THREATEN MY LIFE, HUSBAND *AND* CHILD AND NOW YOU RUIN *BAKERIES* FOR ME, TOO?
$%#@ YOU!
HEH.
I AM GENUINELY DISAPPOINTED I DON'T GET TO TRY YOUR CUPCAKES.
I SUPPOSE YOU WOULD LIKE TO KNOW WHAT I WANT?

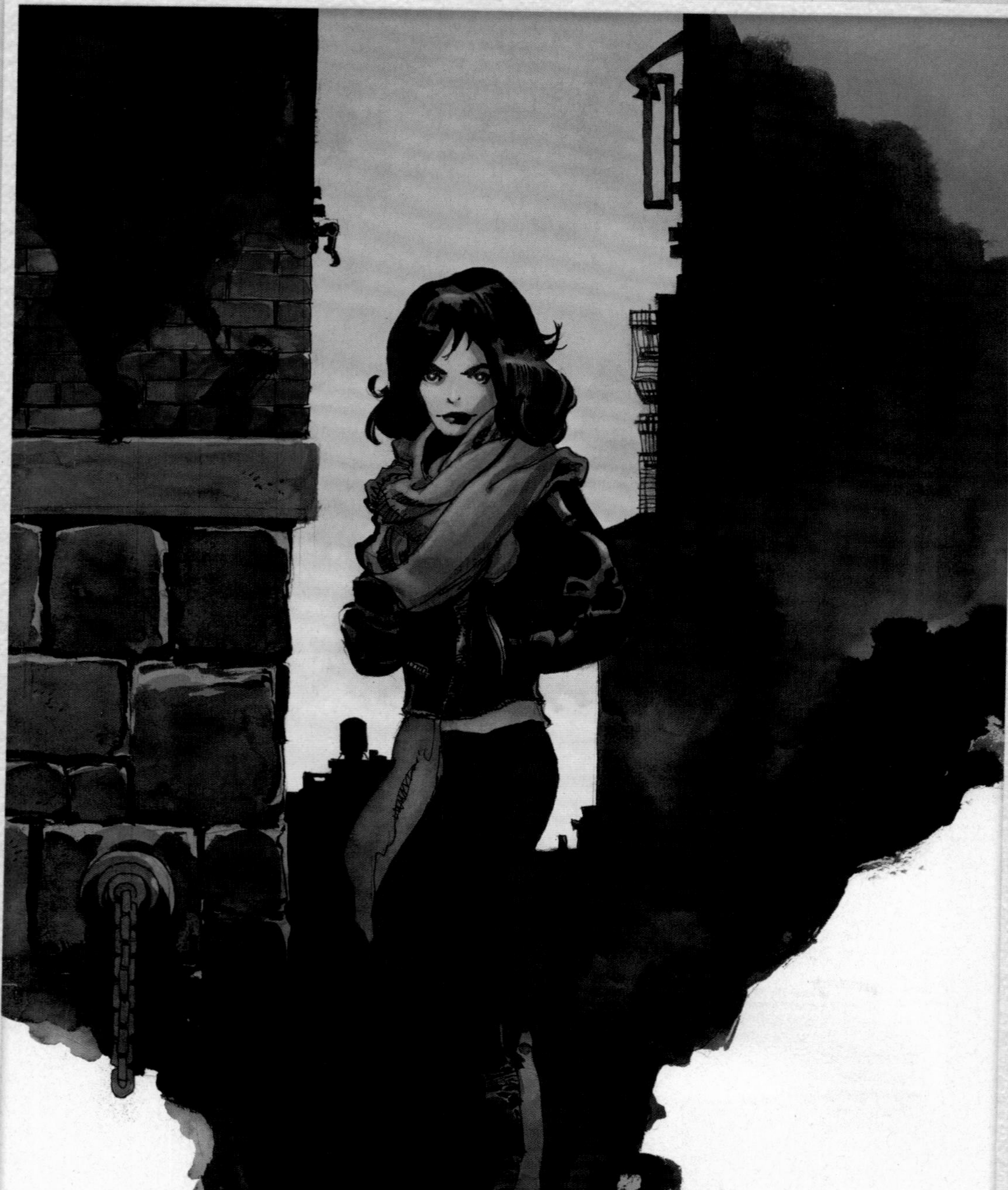
T SALE
2017

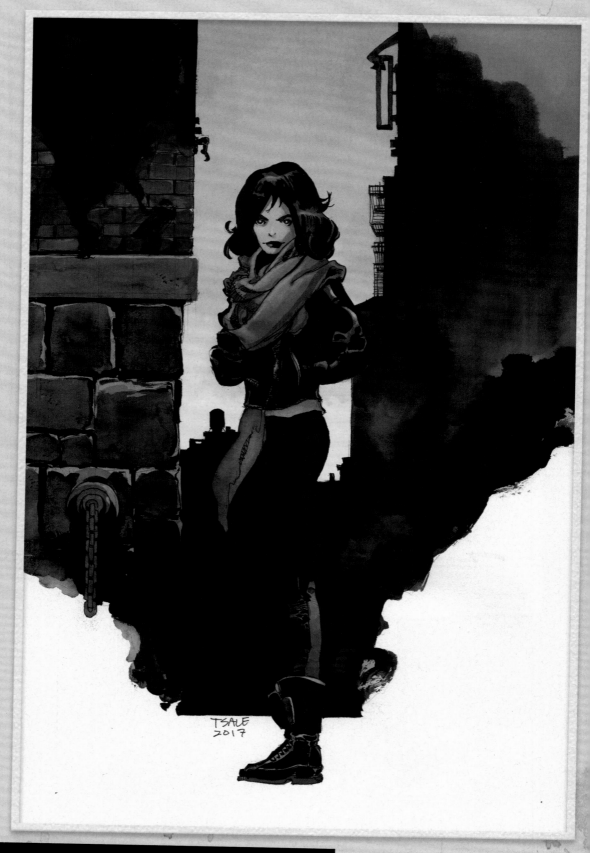

#13 variant by **Tim Sale** & **Dave Stewart**

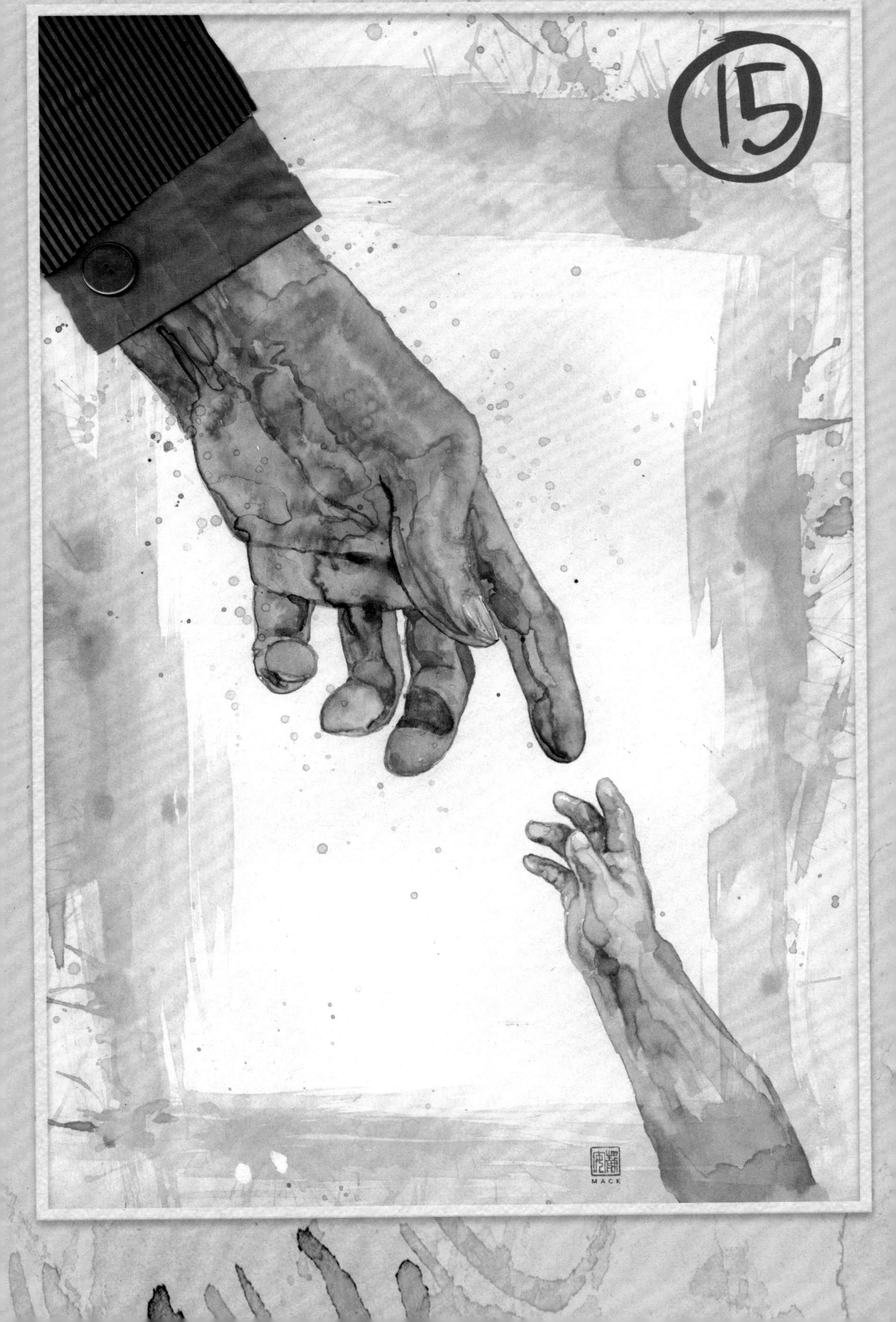
15
MACK

I SAID: I SUPPOSE YOU WOULD LIKE TO KNOW WHAT I WANT.

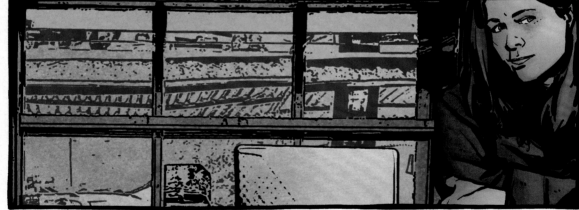

WELL...

...FIRST OF ALL, I *MISS* YOU, JESSICA.

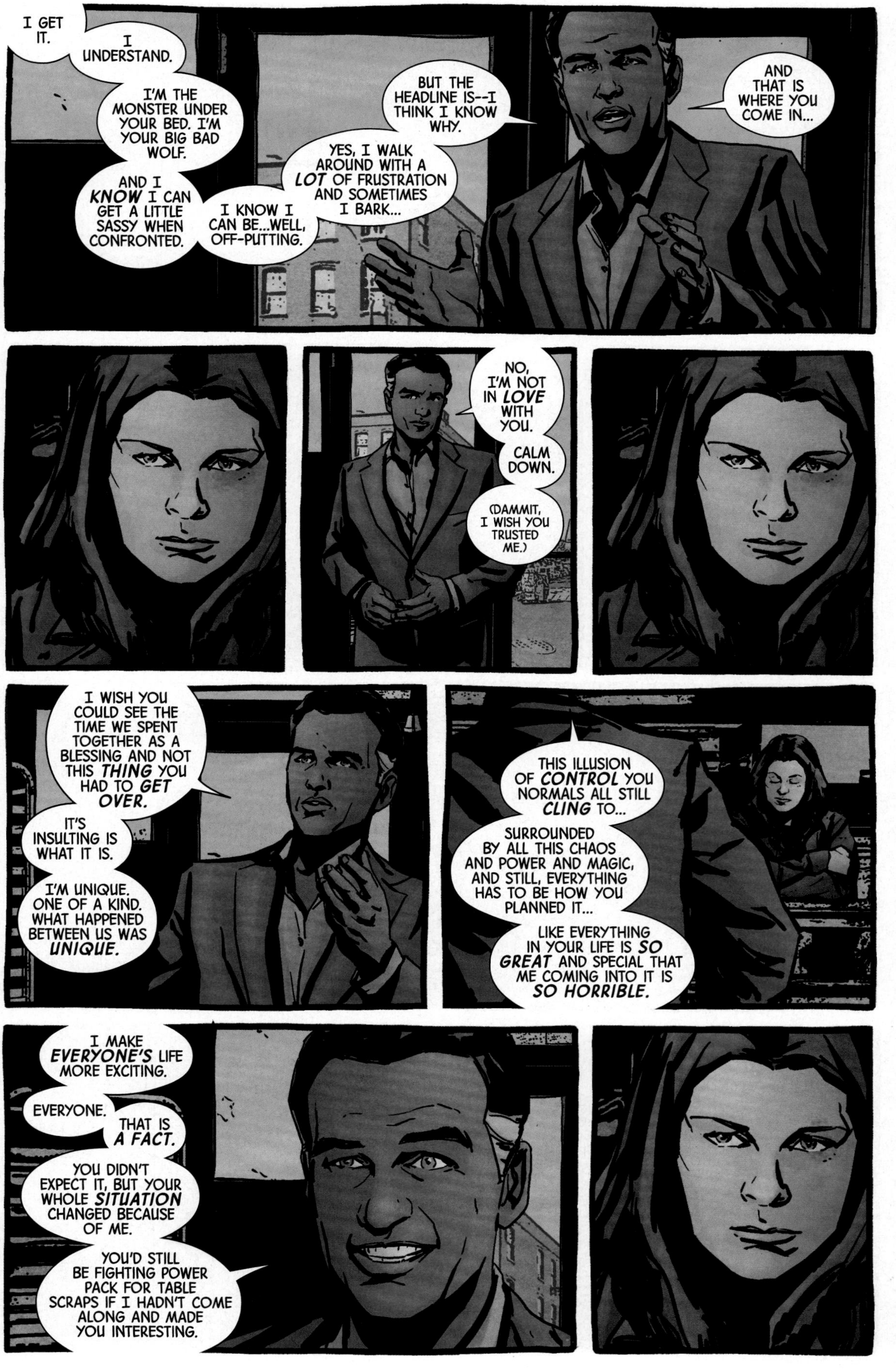
I GET IT.
I UNDERSTAND.
I'M THE MONSTER UNDER YOUR BED. I'M YOUR BIG BAD WOLF.
AND I KNOW I CAN GET A LITTLE SASSY WHEN CONFRONTED.
I KNOW I CAN BE...WELL, OFF-PUTTING.
YES, I WALK AROUND WITH A LOT OF FRUSTRATION AND SOMETIMES I BARK...
BUT THE HEADLINE IS--I THINK I KNOW WHY.
AND THAT IS WHERE YOU COME IN...
NO, I'M NOT IN LOVE WITH YOU.
CALM DOWN.
(DAMMIT, I WISH YOU TRUSTED ME.)
I WISH YOU COULD SEE THE TIME WE SPENT TOGETHER AS A BLESSING AND NOT THIS THING YOU HAD TO GET OVER.
IT'S INSULTING IS WHAT IT IS.
I'M UNIQUE. ONE OF A KIND. WHAT HAPPENED BETWEEN US WAS UNIQUE.
THIS ILLUSION OF CONTROL YOU NORMALS ALL STILL CLING TO...
SURROUNDED BY ALL THIS CHAOS AND POWER AND MAGIC, AND STILL, EVERYTHING HAS TO BE HOW YOU PLANNED IT...
LIKE EVERYTHING IN YOUR LIFE IS SO GREAT AND SPECIAL THAT ME COMING INTO IT IS SO HORRIBLE.
I MAKE EVERYONE'S LIFE MORE EXCITING.
EVERYONE.
THAT IS A FACT.
YOU DIDN'T EXPECT IT, BUT YOUR WHOLE SITUATION CHANGED BECAUSE OF ME.
YOU'D STILL BE FIGHTING POWER PACK FOR TABLE SCRAPS IF I HADN'T COME ALONG AND MADE YOU INTERESTING.

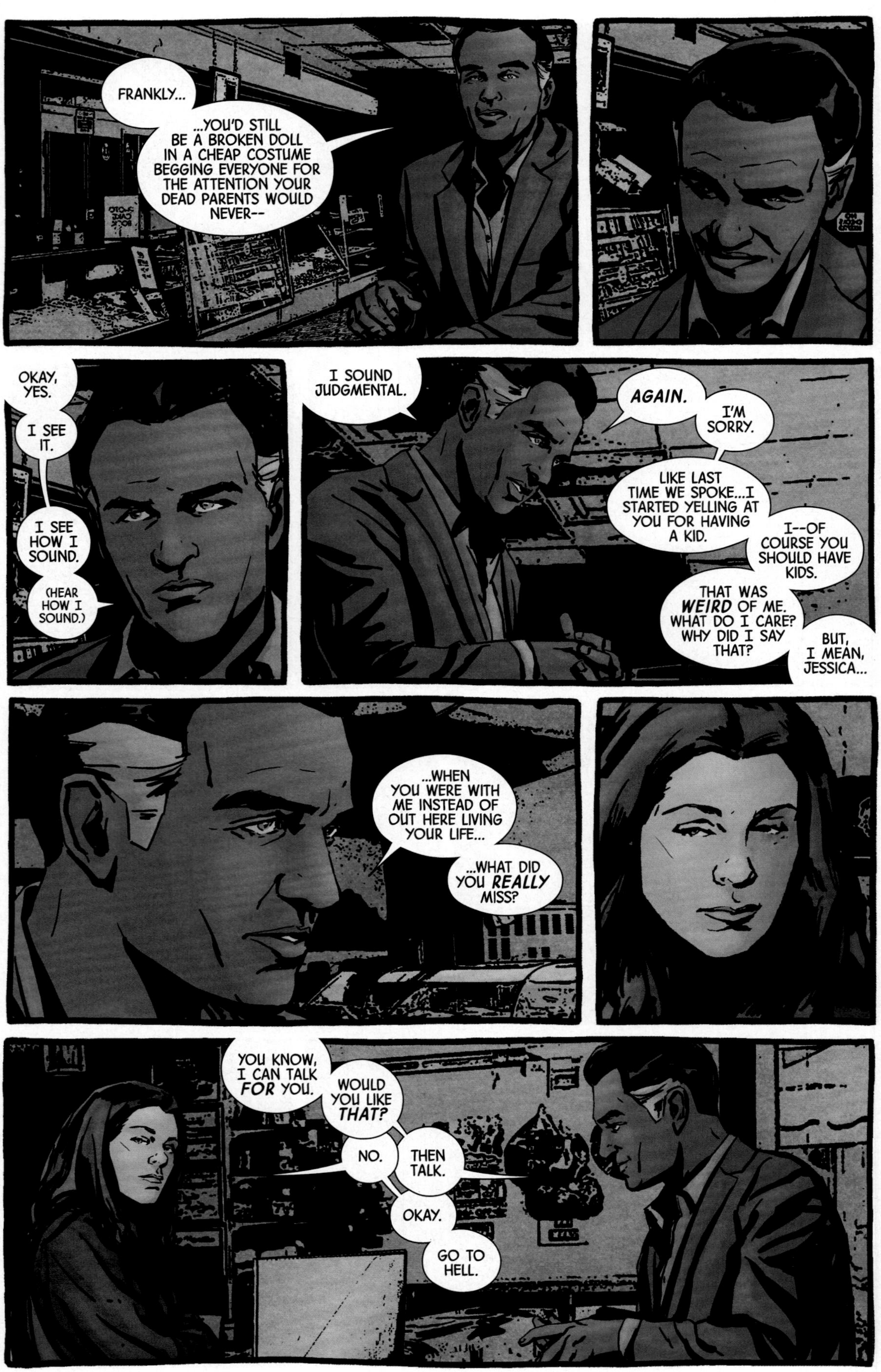
FRANKLY...
...YOU'D STILL BE A BROKEN DOLL IN A CHEAP COSTUME BEGGING EVERYONE FOR THE ATTENTION YOUR DEAD PARENTS WOULD NEVER--
OKAY, YES.
I SEE IT.
I SEE HOW I SOUND.
(HEAR HOW I SOUND.)
I SOUND JUDGMENTAL.
AGAIN.
I'M SORRY.
LIKE LAST TIME WE SPOKE...I STARTED YELLING AT YOU FOR HAVING A KID.
I--OF COURSE YOU SHOULD HAVE KIDS.
THAT WAS WEIRD OF ME. WHAT DO I CARE? WHY DID I SAY THAT?
BUT, I MEAN, JESSICA...
...WHEN YOU WERE WITH ME INSTEAD OF OUT HERE LIVING YOUR LIFE...
...WHAT DID YOU REALLY MISS?
YOU KNOW, I CAN TALK FOR YOU.
WOULD YOU LIKE THAT?
NO.
THEN TALK.
OKAY.
GO TO HELL.

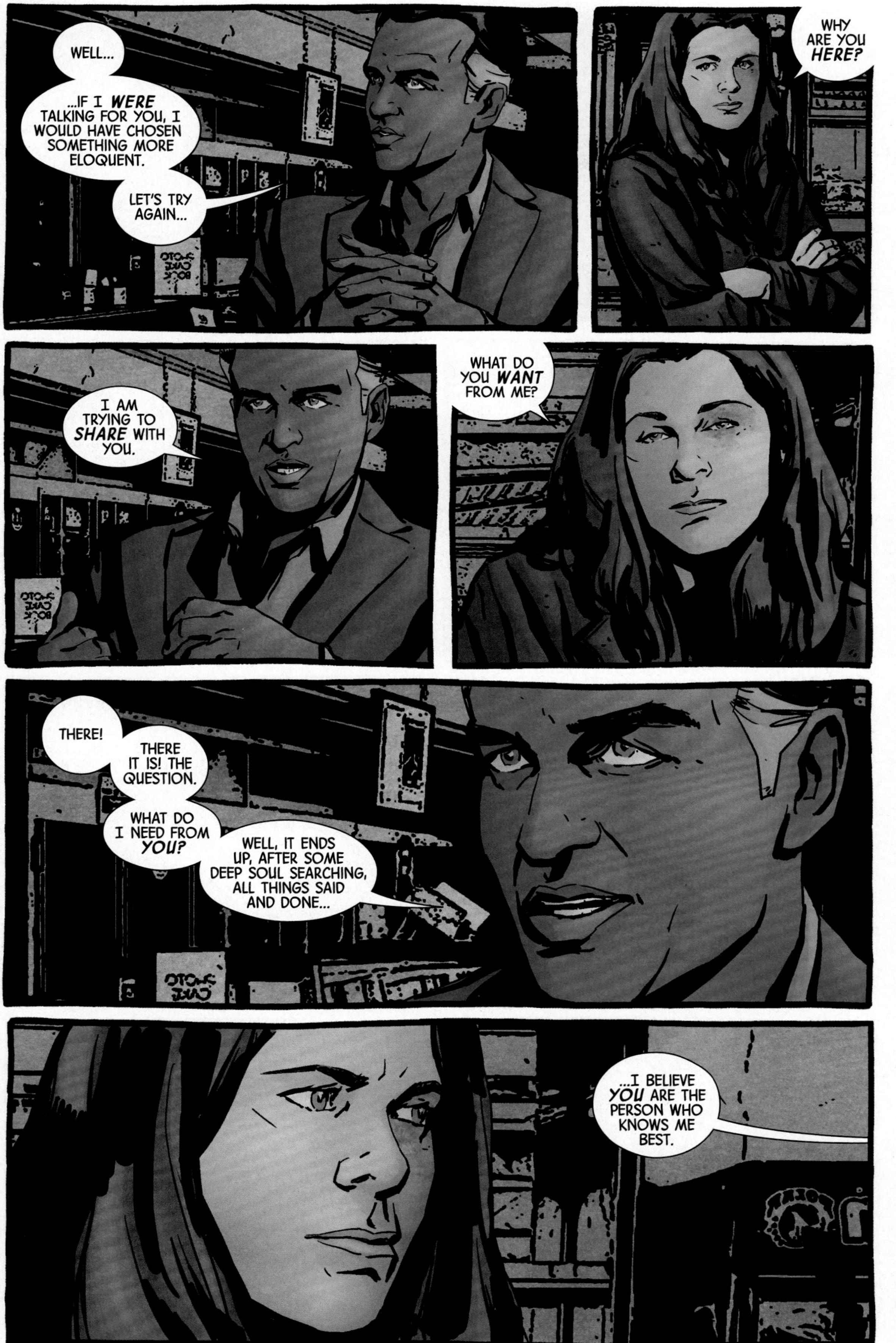
WELL...
...IF I WERE TALKING FOR YOU, I WOULD HAVE CHOSEN SOMETHING MORE ELOQUENT.
LET'S TRY AGAIN...
WHY ARE YOU HERE?
I AM TRYING TO SHARE WITH YOU.
WHAT DO YOU WANT FROM ME?
THERE!
THERE IT IS! THE QUESTION.
WHAT DO I NEED FROM YOU?
WELL, IT ENDS UP, AFTER SOME DEEP SOUL SEARCHING, ALL THINGS SAID AND DONE...
...I BELIEVE YOU ARE THE PERSON WHO KNOWS ME BEST.

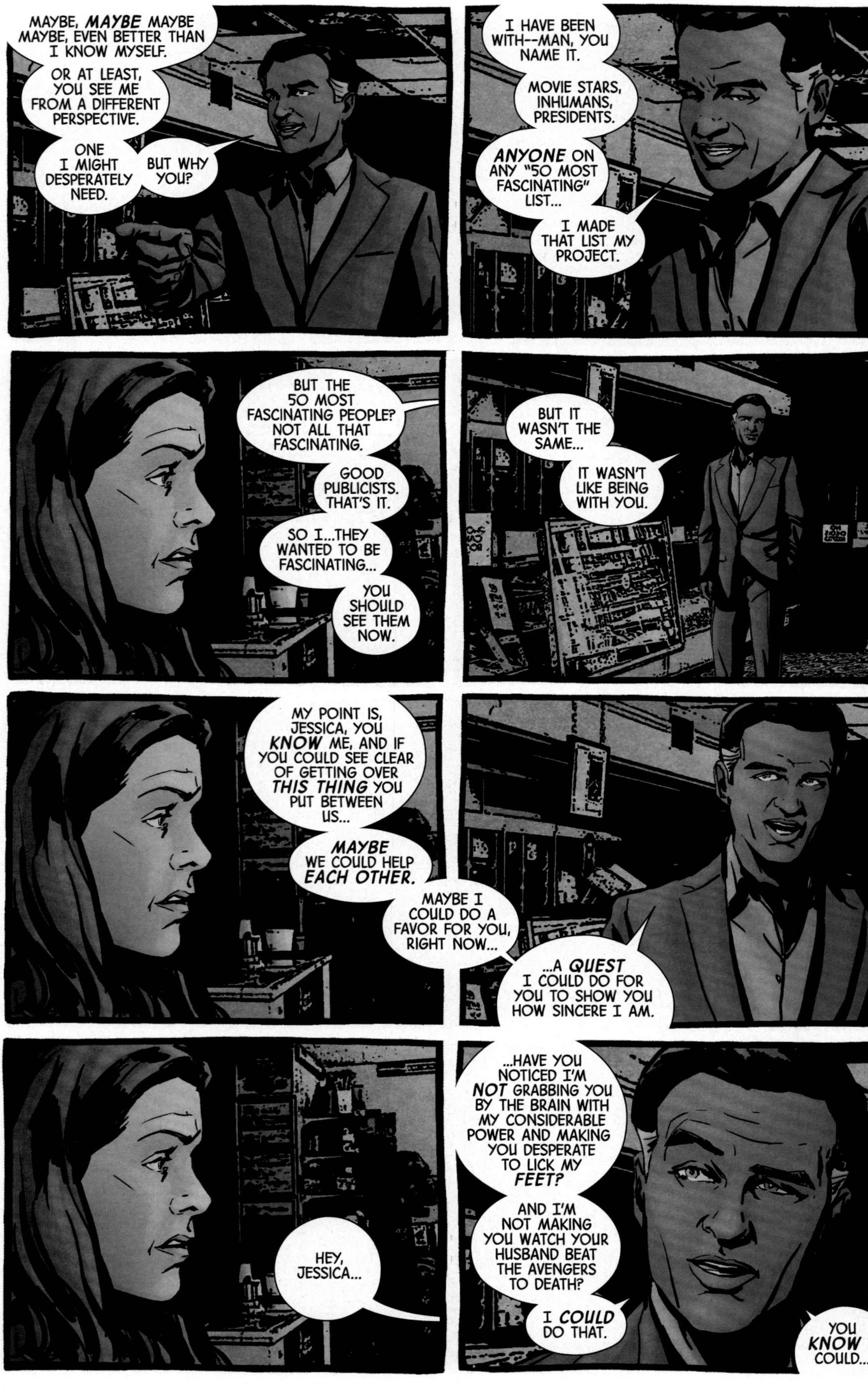
MAYBE, MAYBE MAYBE MAYBE, EVEN BETTER THAN I KNOW MYSELF.
OR AT LEAST, YOU SEE ME FROM A DIFFERENT PERSPECTIVE.
ONE I MIGHT DESPERATELY NEED.
BUT WHY YOU?
I HAVE BEEN WITH--MAN, YOU NAME IT.
MOVIE STARS, INHUMANS, PRESIDENTS.
ANYONE ON ANY "50 MOST FASCINATING" LIST...
I MADE THAT LIST MY PROJECT.
BUT THE 50 MOST FASCINATING PEOPLE? NOT ALL THAT FASCINATING.
GOOD PUBLICISTS. THAT'S IT.
SO I...THEY WANTED TO BE FASCINATING...
YOU SHOULD SEE THEM NOW.
BUT IT WASN'T THE SAME...
IT WASN'T LIKE BEING WITH YOU.
MY POINT IS, JESSICA, YOU KNOW ME, AND IF YOU COULD SEE CLEAR OF GETTING OVER THIS THING YOU PUT BETWEEN US...
MAYBE WE COULD HELP EACH OTHER.
MAYBE I COULD DO A FAVOR FOR YOU, RIGHT NOW...
...A QUEST I COULD DO FOR YOU TO SHOW YOU HOW SINCERE I AM.
HEY, JESSICA...
...HAVE YOU NOTICED I'M NOT GRABBING YOU BY THE BRAIN WITH MY CONSIDERABLE POWER AND MAKING YOU DESPERATE TO LICK MY FEET?
AND I'M NOT MAKING YOU WATCH YOUR HUSBAND BEAT THE AVENGERS TO DEATH?
I COULD DO THAT.
YOU KNOW I COULD...

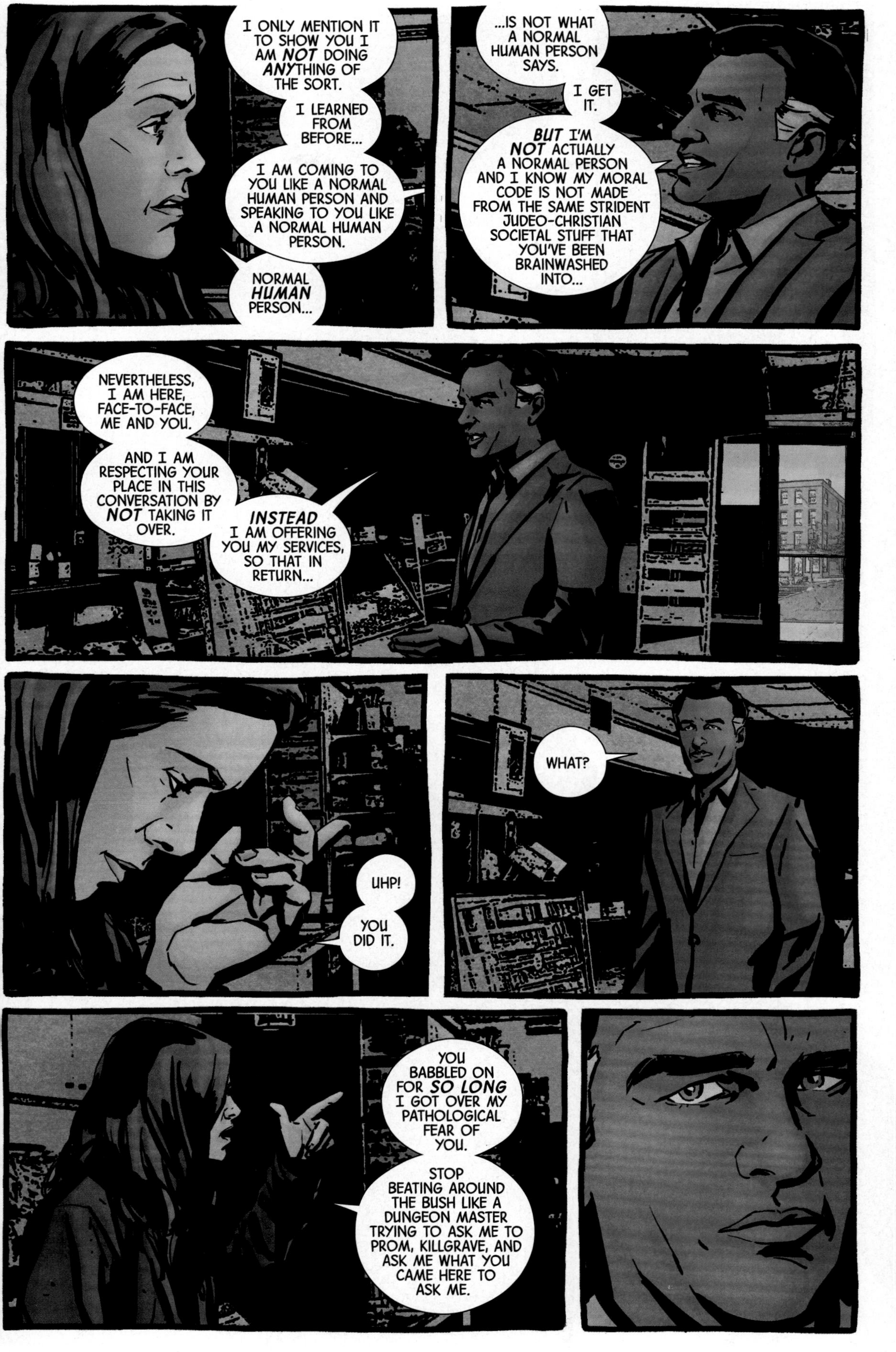
I ONLY MENTION IT TO SHOW YOU I AM NOT DOING ANYTHING OF THE SORT.
I LEARNED FROM BEFORE...
I AM COMING TO YOU LIKE A NORMAL HUMAN PERSON AND SPEAKING TO YOU LIKE A NORMAL HUMAN PERSON.
NORMAL HUMAN PERSON...
...IS NOT WHAT A NORMAL HUMAN PERSON SAYS.
I GET IT.
BUT I'M NOT ACTUALLY A NORMAL PERSON AND I KNOW MY MORAL CODE IS NOT MADE FROM THE SAME STRIDENT JUDEO-CHRISTIAN SOCIETAL STUFF THAT YOU'VE BEEN BRAINWASHED INTO...
NEVERTHELESS, I AM HERE, FACE-TO-FACE, ME AND YOU.
AND I AM RESPECTING YOUR PLACE IN THIS CONVERSATION BY NOT TAKING IT OVER.
INSTEAD I AM OFFERING YOU MY SERVICES, SO THAT IN RETURN...
UHP!
YOU DID IT.
WHAT?
YOU BABBLED ON FOR SO LONG I GOT OVER MY PATHOLOGICAL FEAR OF YOU.
STOP BEATING AROUND THE BUSH LIKE A DUNGEON MASTER TRYING TO ASK ME TO PROM, KILLGRAVE, AND ASK ME WHAT YOU CAME HERE TO ASK ME.

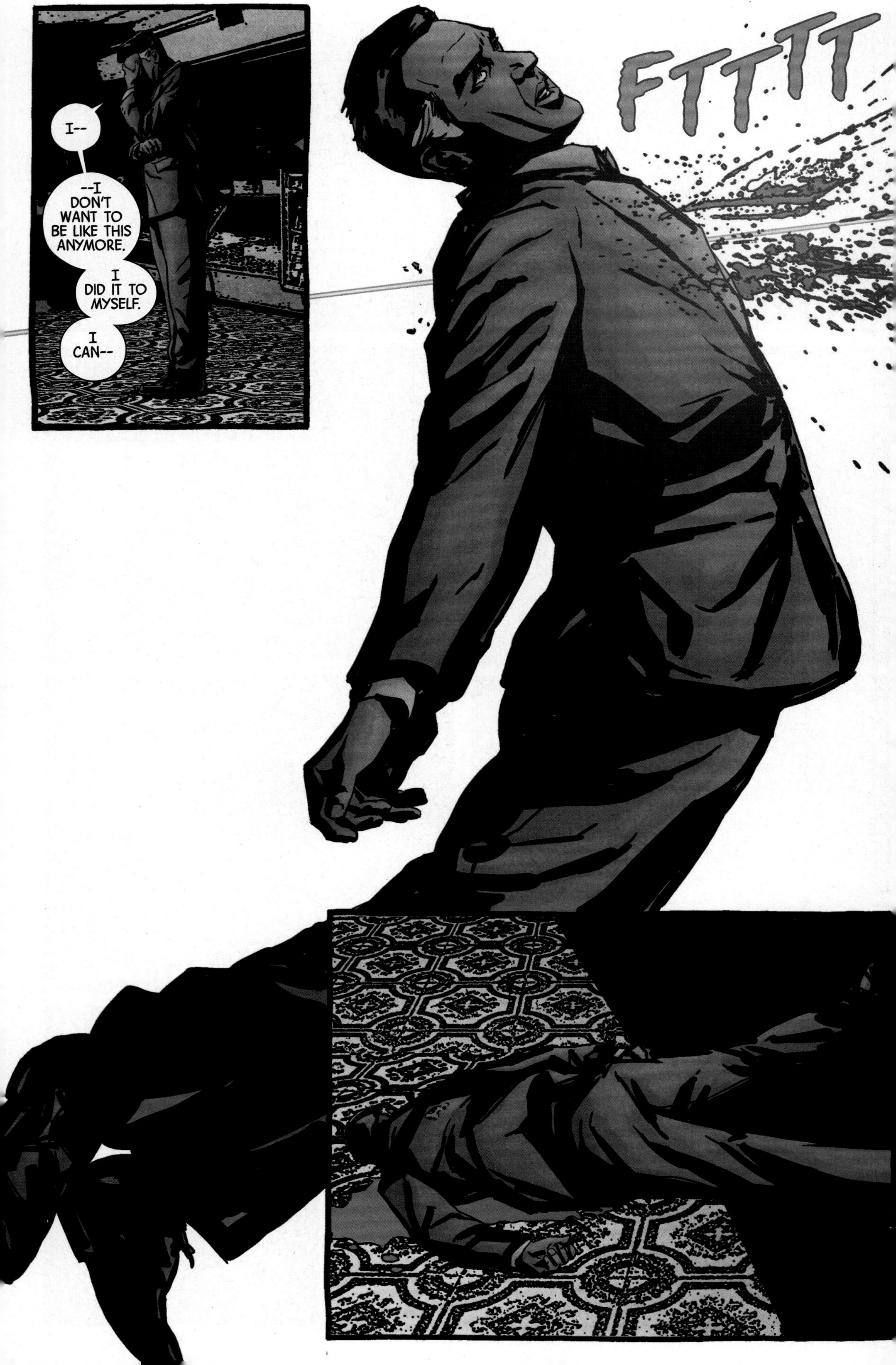
I--
--I DON'T WANT TO BE LIKE THIS ANYMORE.
I DID IT TO MYSELF.
I CAN--
FTTTT

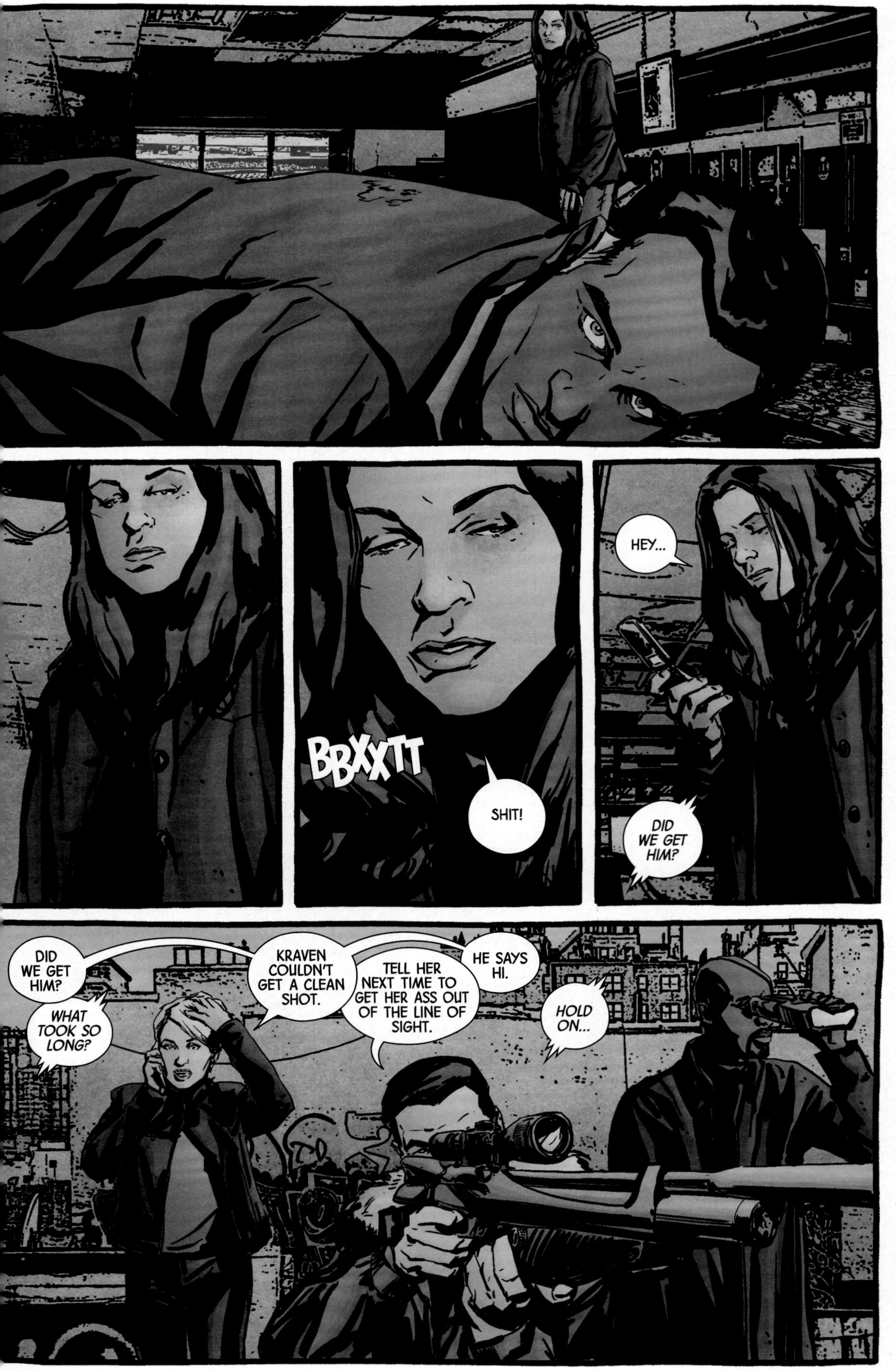
BBXXTT
SHIT!
HEY...
DID WE GET HIM?
DID WE GET HIM?
WHAT TOOK SO LONG?
KRAVEN COULDN'T GET A CLEAN SHOT.
TELL HER NEXT TIME TO GET HER ASS OUT OF THE LINE OF SIGHT.
HE SAYS HI.
HOLD ON...

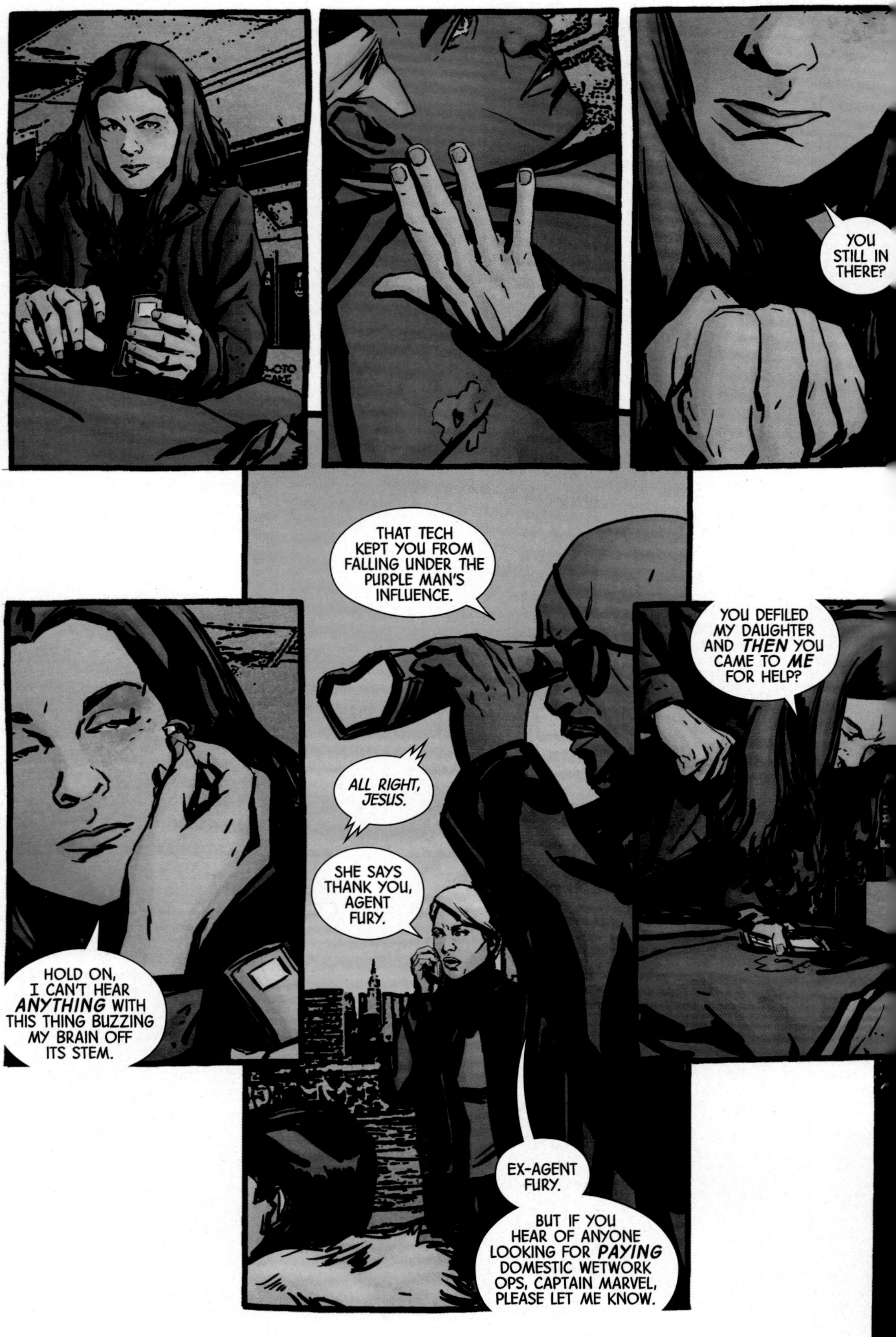
YOU STILL IN THERE?
THAT TECH KEPT YOU FROM FALLING UNDER THE PURPLE MAN'S INFLUENCE.
YOU DEFILED MY DAUGHTER AND *THEN* YOU CAME TO *ME* FOR HELP?
HOLD ON, I CAN'T HEAR *ANYTHING* WITH THIS THING BUZZING MY BRAIN OFF ITS STEM.
ALL RIGHT, JESUS.
SHE SAYS THANK YOU, AGENT FURY.
EX-AGENT FURY.
BUT IF YOU HEAR OF ANYONE LOOKING FOR *PAYING* DOMESTIC WETWORK OPS, CAPTAIN MARVEL, PLEASE LET ME KNOW.

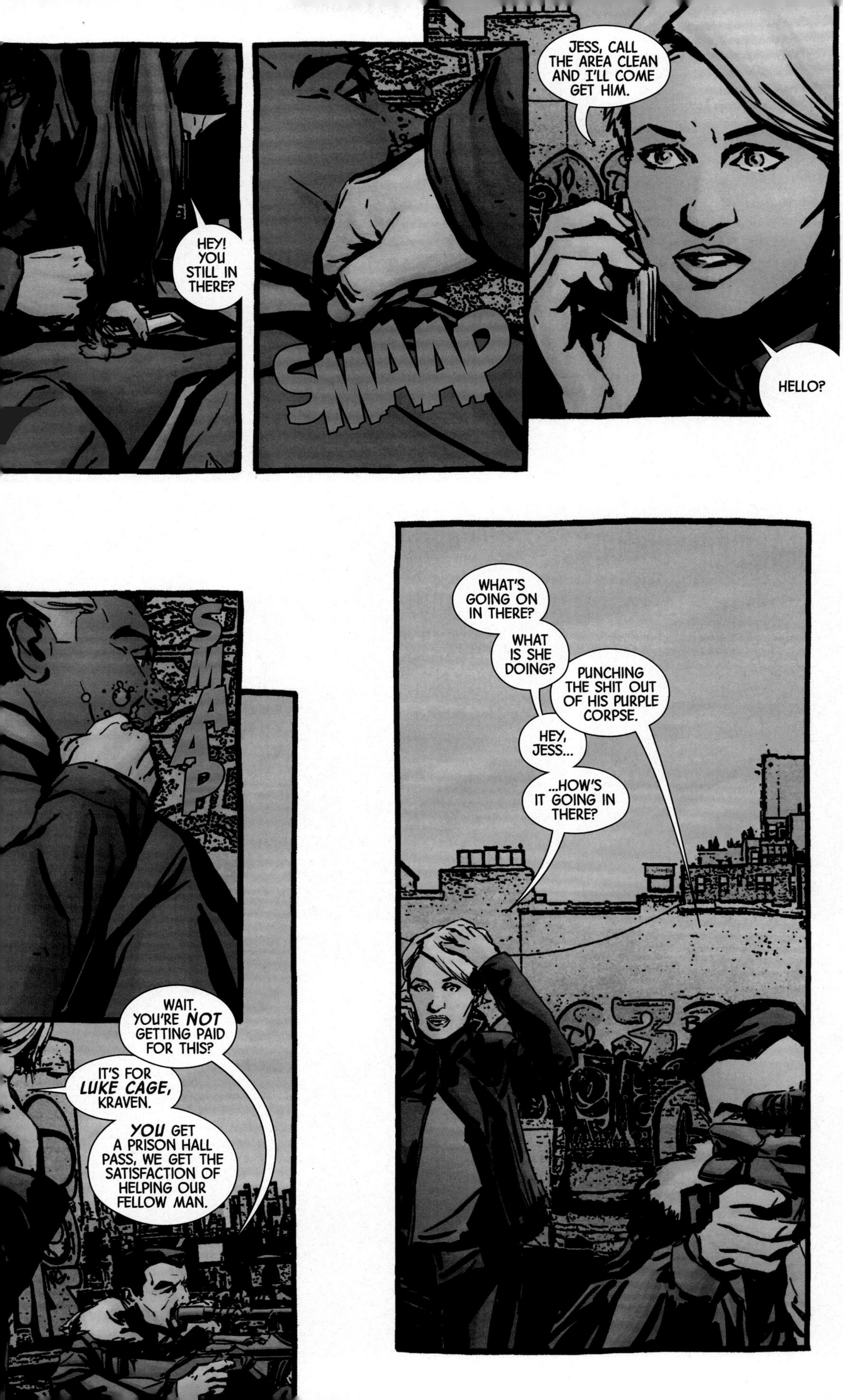
HEY! YOU STILL IN THERE?
SMAAP
JESS, CALL THE AREA CLEAN AND I'LL COME GET HIM.
HELLO?
SMAAP
WAIT. YOU'RE NOT GETTING PAID FOR THIS?
IT'S FOR LUKE CAGE, KRAVEN.
YOU GET A PRISON HALL PASS, WE GET THE SATISFACTION OF HELPING OUR FELLOW MAN.
WHAT'S GOING ON IN THERE?
WHAT IS SHE DOING?
PUNCHING THE SHIT OUT OF HIS PURPLE CORPSE.
HEY, JESS...
...HOW'S IT GOING IN THERE?

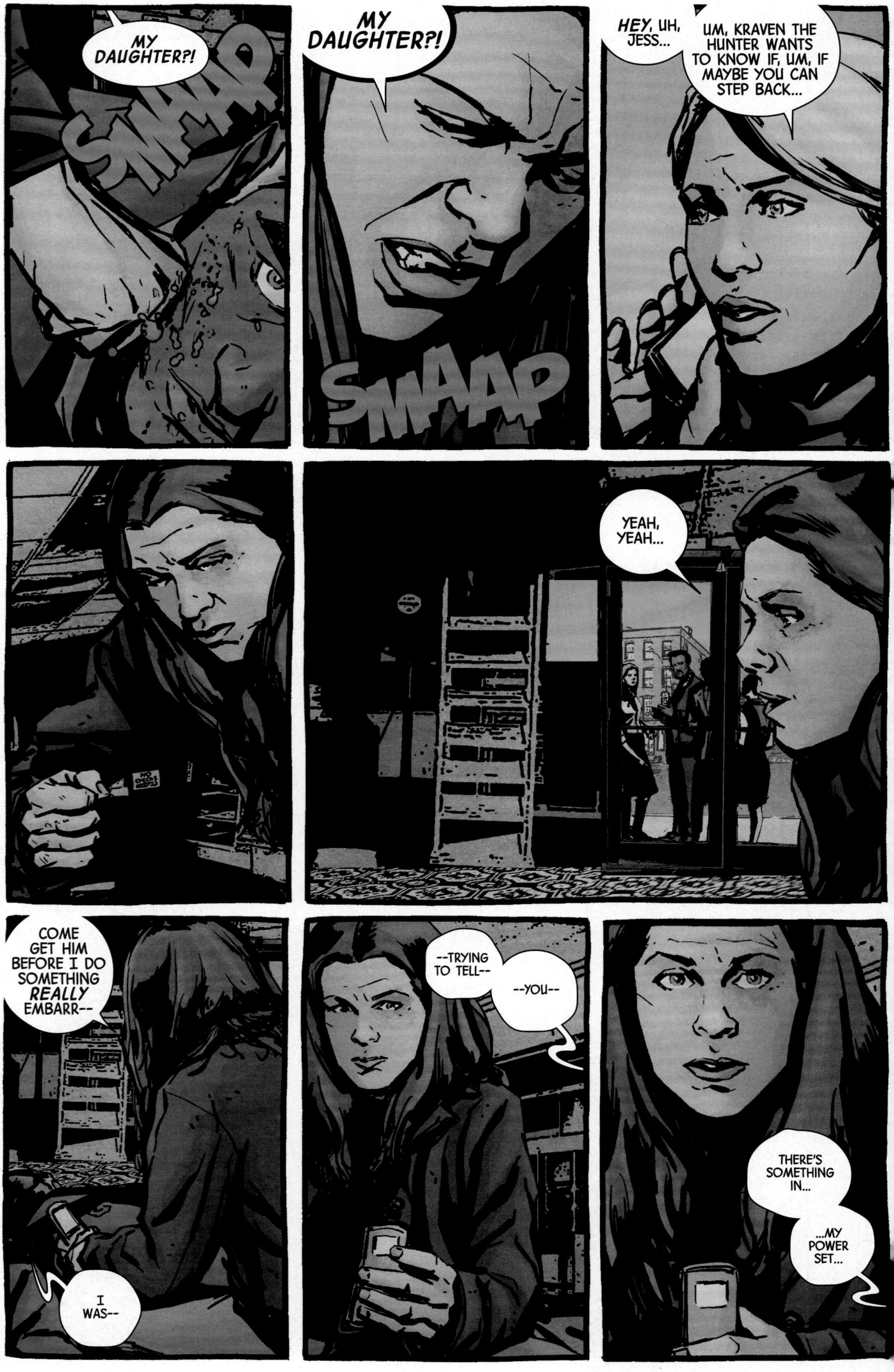
MY DAUGHTER?!
SMAAAP
MY DAUGHTER?!
SMAAAP
HEY, UH, JESS...
UM, KRAVEN THE HUNTER WANTS TO KNOW IF, UM, IF MAYBE YOU CAN STEP BACK...
YEAH, YEAH...
COME GET HIM BEFORE I DO SOMETHING REALLY EMBARR--
I WAS--
--TRYING TO TELL--
--YOU--
THERE'S SOMETHING IN...
...MY POWER SET...

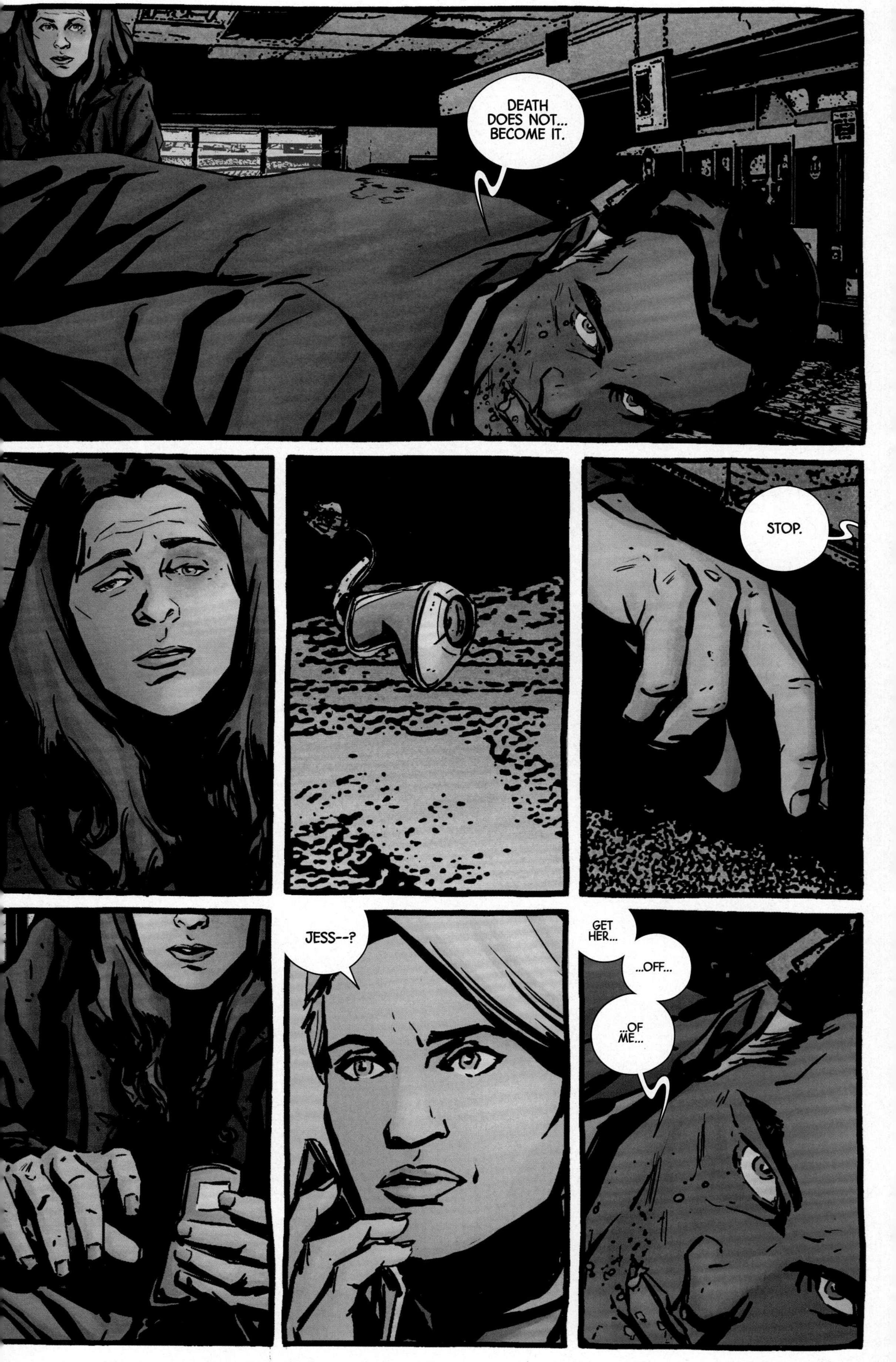
DEATH DOES NOT... BECOME IT.
STOP.
JESS--?
GET HER...
...OFF...
...OF ME...

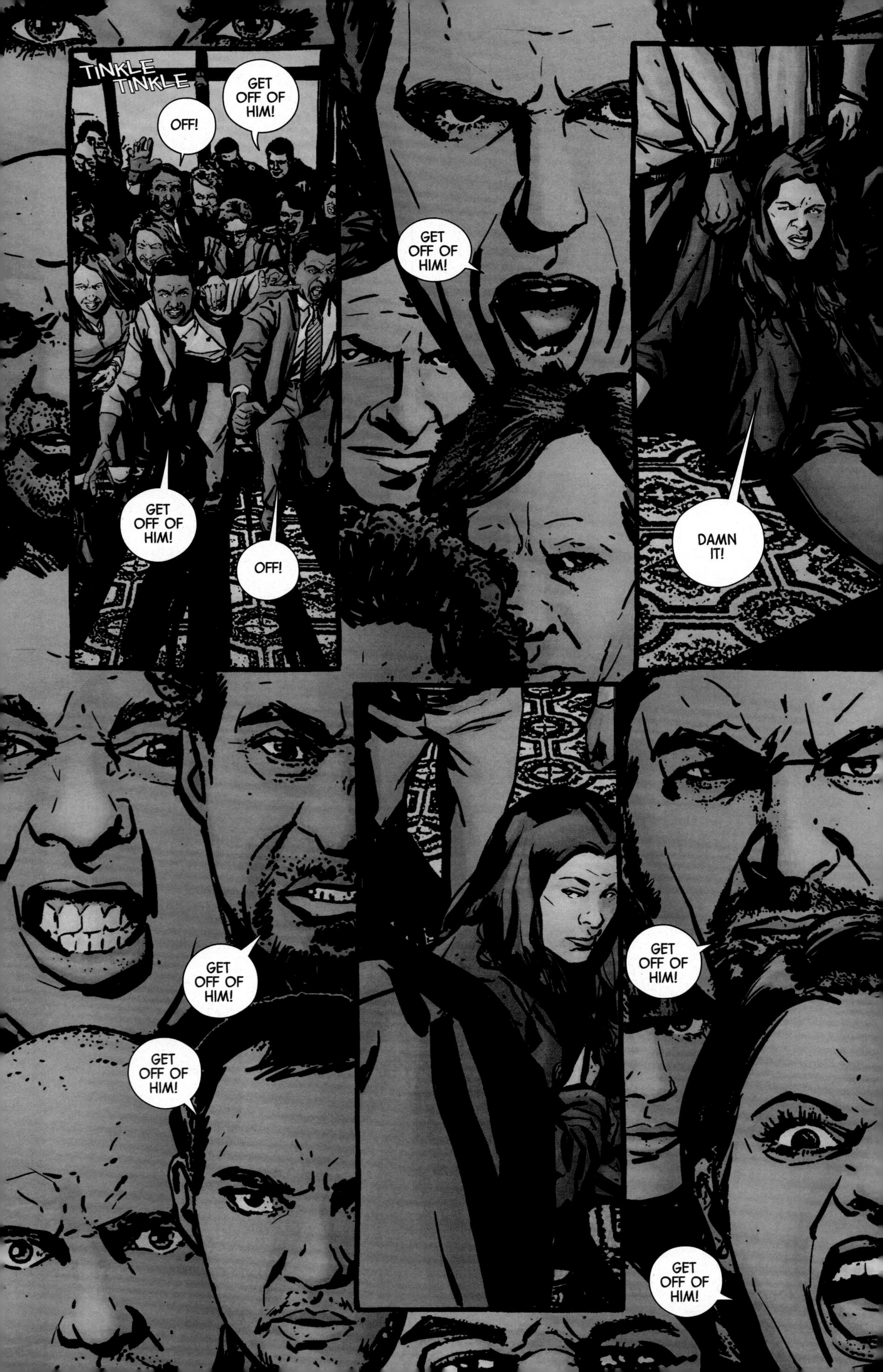
TINKLE TINKLE
OFF!
GET OFF OF HIM!
GET OFF OF HIM!
OFF!
GET OFF OF HIM!
DAMN IT!
GET OFF OF HIM!
GET OFF OF HIM!
GET OFF OF HIM!
GET OFF OF HIM!

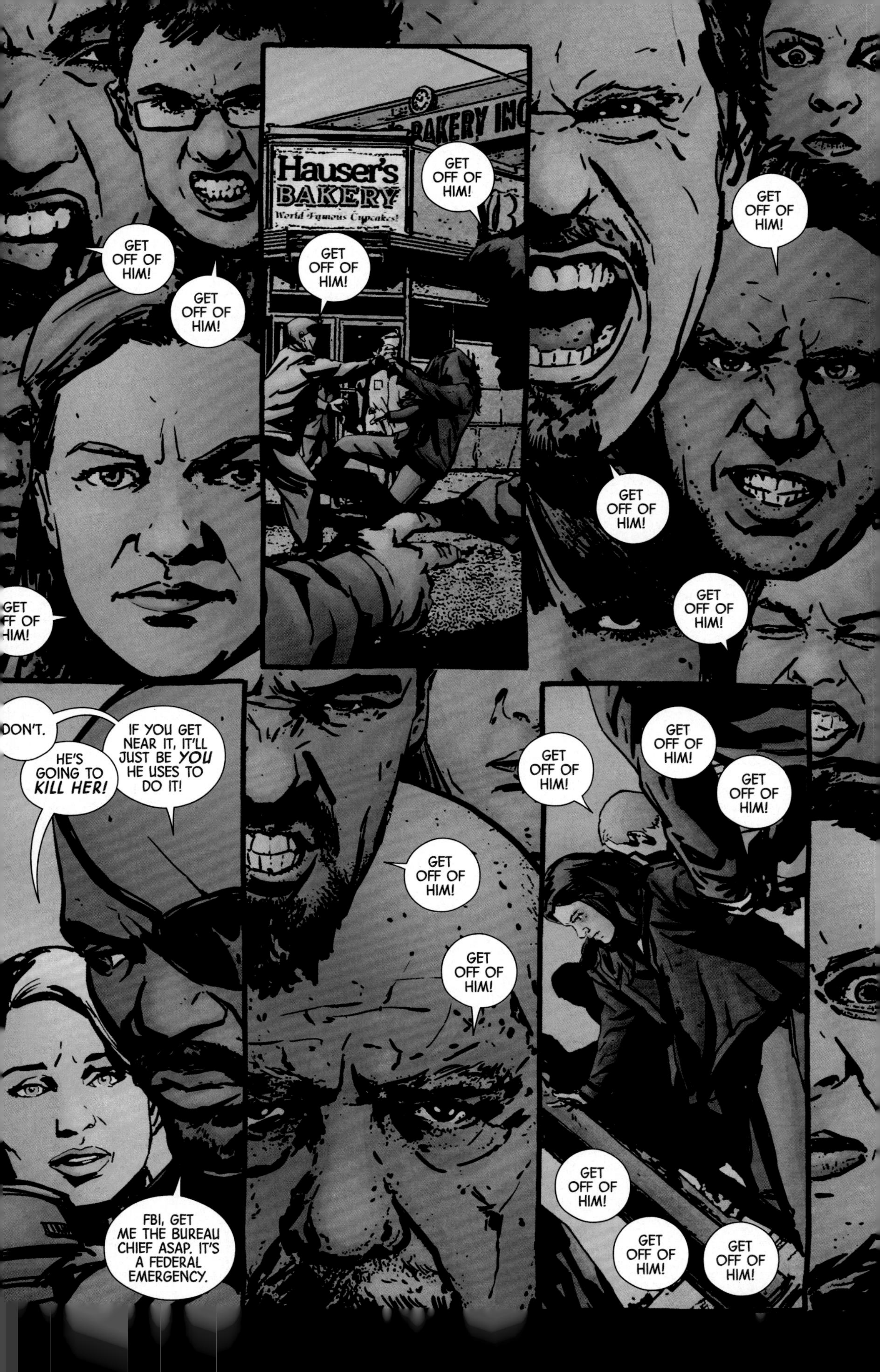

Hauser's BAKERY
World Famous Cupcakes!
BAKERY INC
GET OFF OF HIM!
GET OFF OF HIM!
GET OFF OF HIM!
GET OFF OF HIM!
GET OFF OF HIM!
GET OFF OF HIM!
GET OFF OF HIM!
GET OFF OF HIM!
DON'T.
HE'S GOING TO *KILL HER!*
IF YOU GET NEAR IT, IT'LL JUST BE *YOU* HE USES TO DO IT!
GET OFF OF HIM!
GET OFF OF HIM!
GET OFF OF HIM!
GET OFF OF HIM!
GET OFF OF HIM!
FBI, GET ME THE BUREAU CHIEF ASAP. IT'S A FEDERAL EMERGENCY.
GET OFF OF HIM!
GET OFF OF HIM!
GET OFF OF HIM!

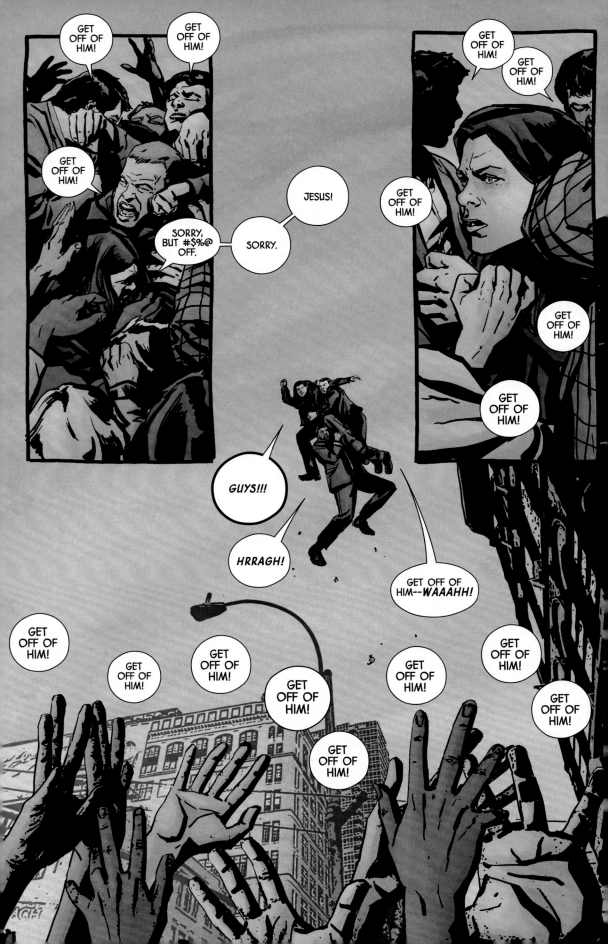

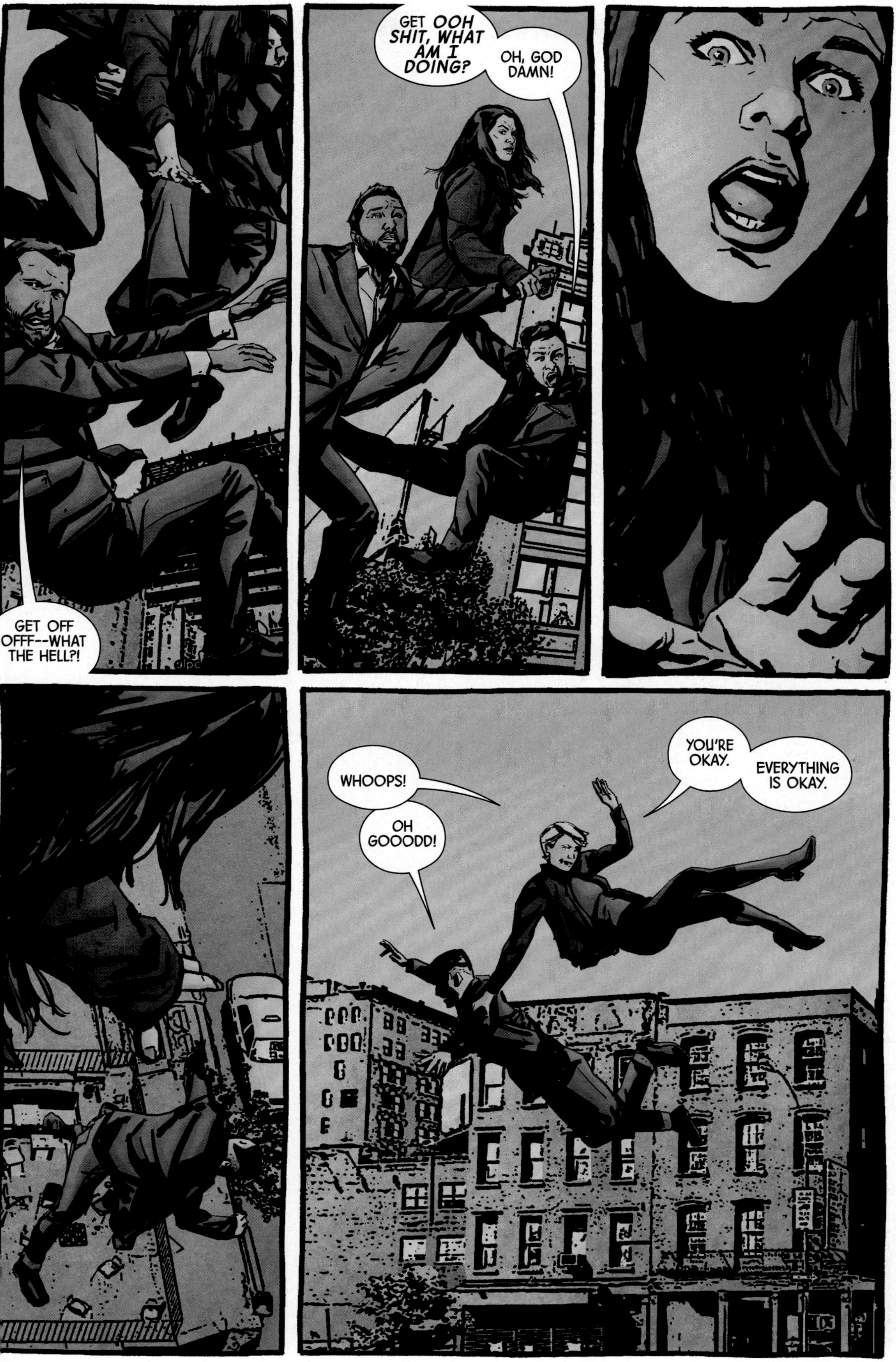
GET OFF OFFF--WHAT THE HELL?!
GET OOH SHIT, WHAT AM I DOING?
OH, GOD DAMN!
WHOOPS!
OH GOOODD!
YOU'RE OKAY.
EVERYTHING IS OKAY.

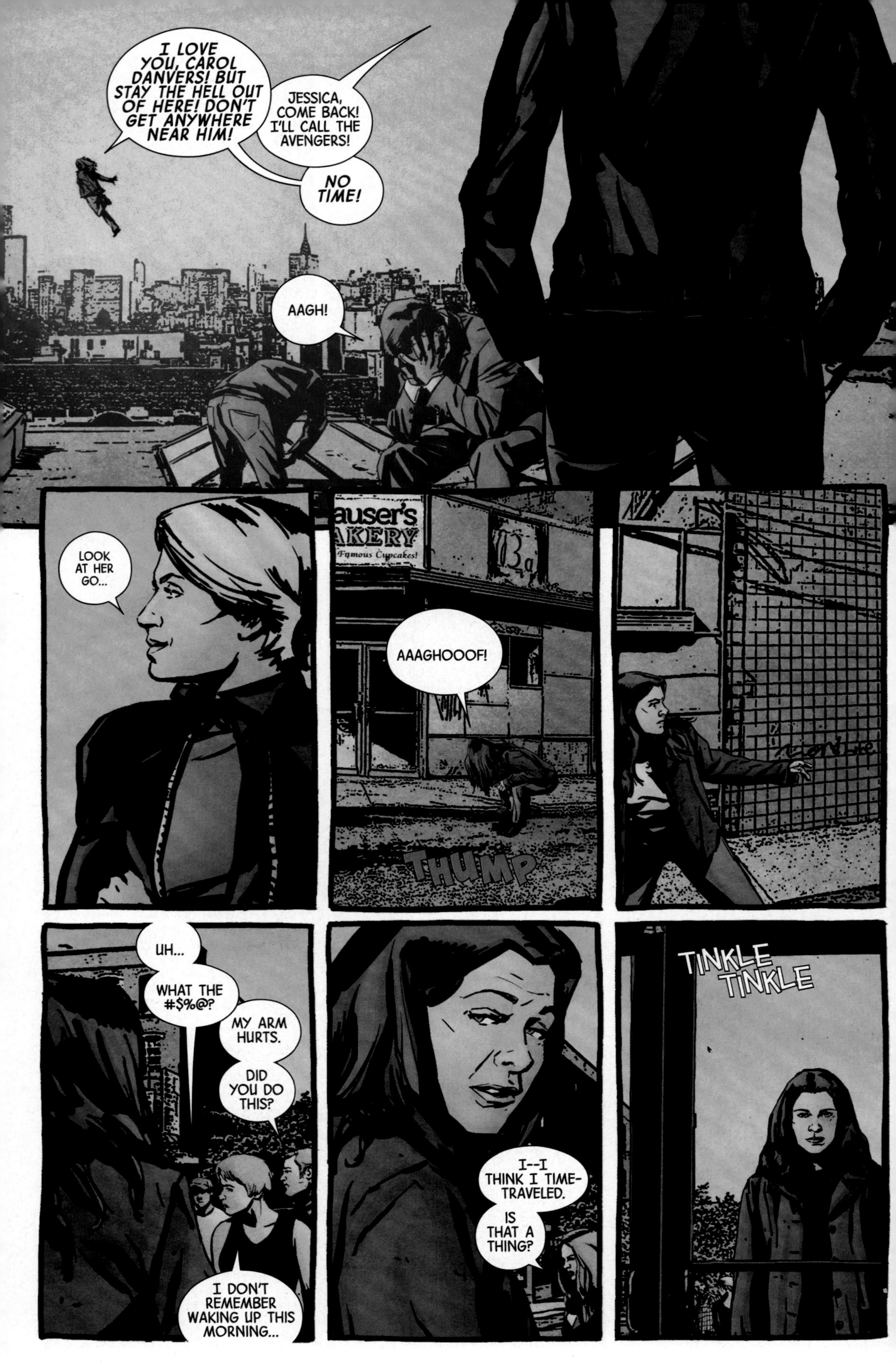
I LOVE YOU, CAROL DANVERS! BUT STAY THE HELL OUT OF HERE! DON'T GET ANYWHERE NEAR HIM!
JESSICA, COME BACK! I'LL CALL THE AVENGERS!
NO TIME!
AAGH!
LOOK AT HER GO...
AAAGHOOOF!
THUMP
UH...
WHAT THE #$%@?
MY ARM HURTS.
DID YOU DO THIS?
I DON'T REMEMBER WAKING UP THIS MORNING...
I--I THINK I TIME-TRAVELED.
IS THAT A THING?
TINKLE TINKLE

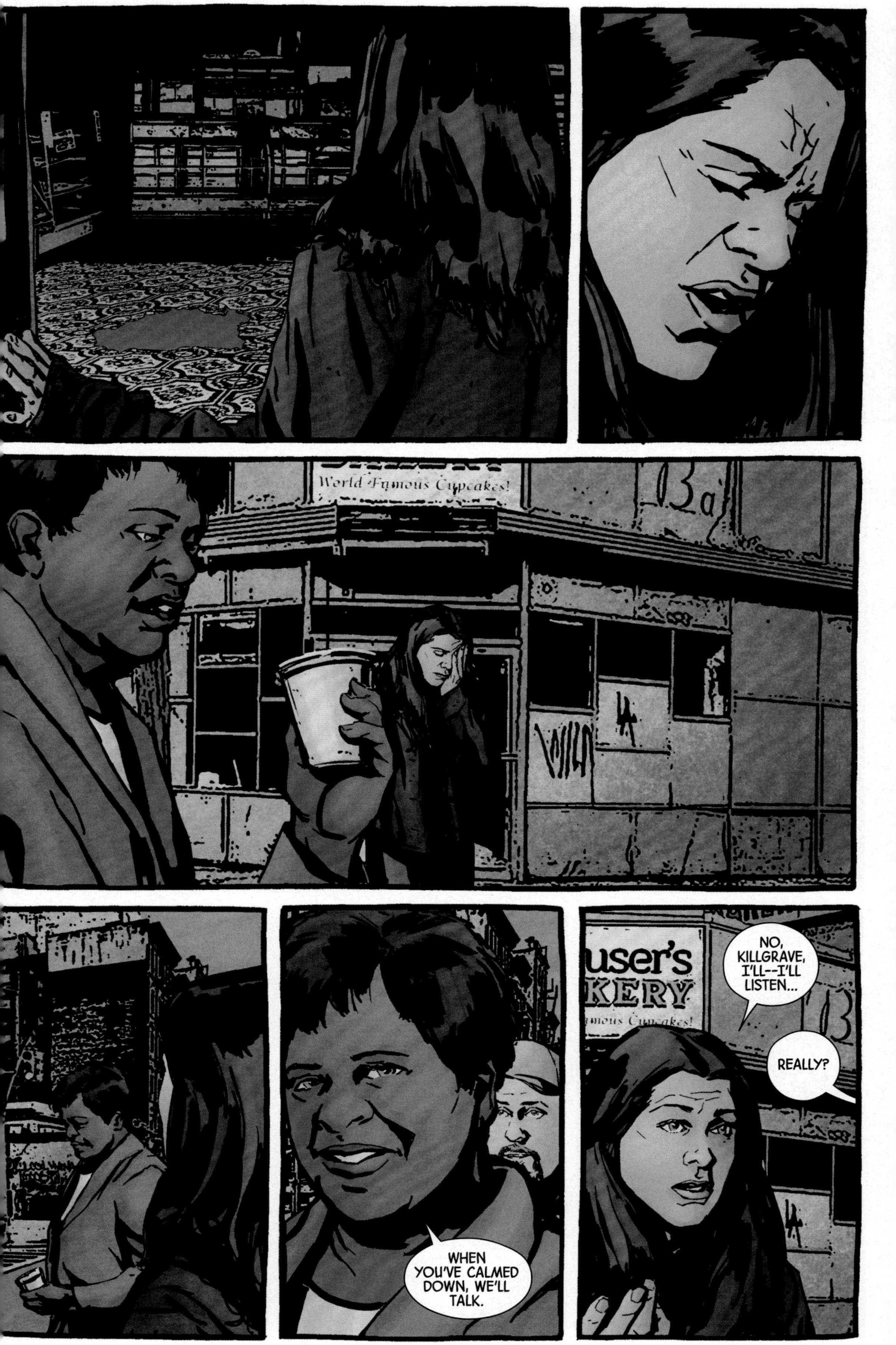
World Famous Cupcakes!
WHEN YOU'VE CALMED DOWN, WE'LL TALK.
NO, KILLGRAVE, I'LL--I'LL LISTEN...
REALLY?

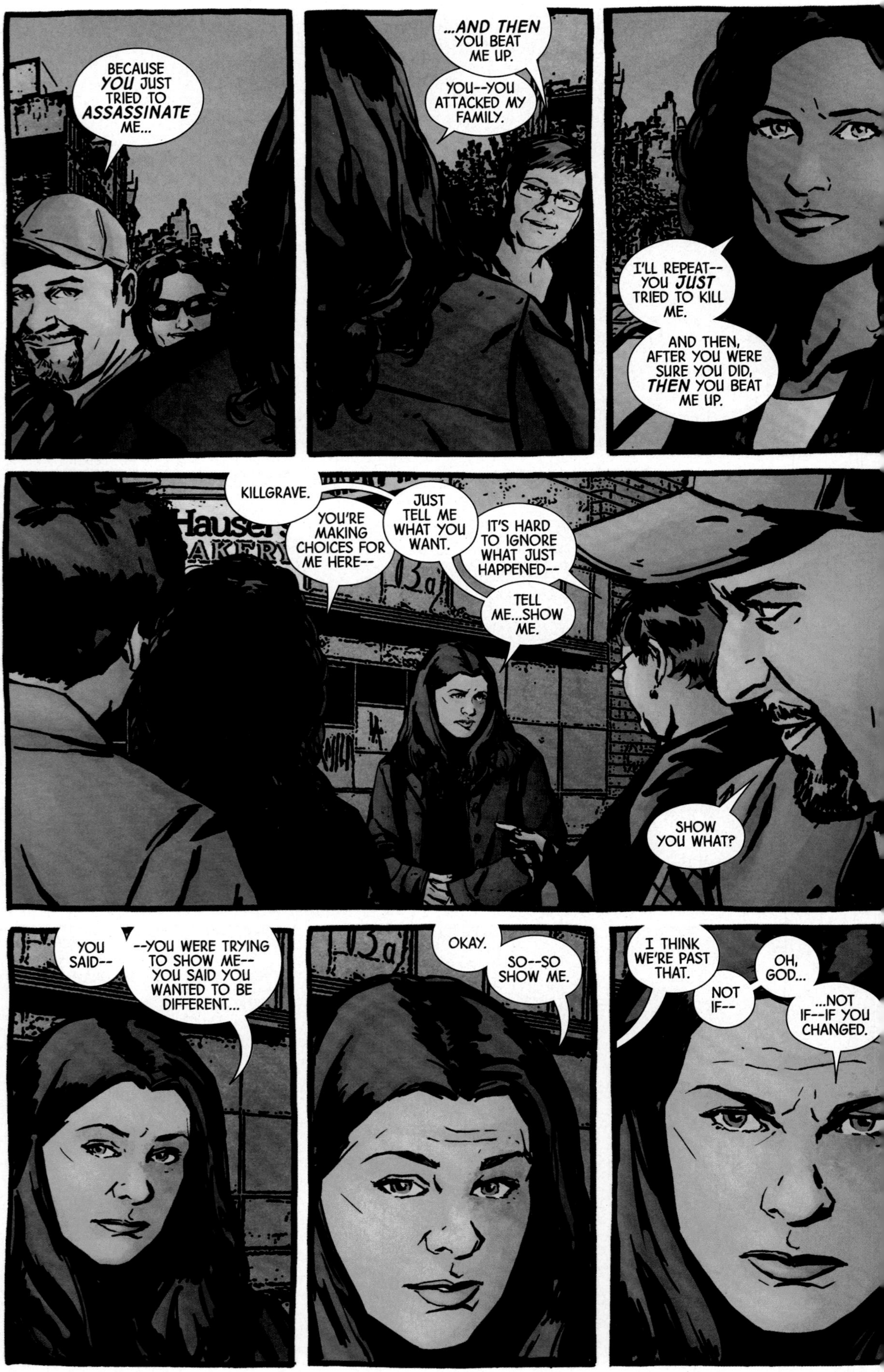
BECAUSE *YOU* JUST TRIED TO *ASSASSINATE* ME...
...AND THEN YOU BEAT ME UP.
YOU--YOU ATTACKED MY FAMILY.
I'LL REPEAT-- YOU *JUST* TRIED TO KILL ME.
AND THEN, AFTER YOU WERE SURE YOU DID, *THEN* YOU BEAT ME UP.
KILLGRAVE.
YOU'RE MAKING CHOICES FOR ME HERE--
JUST TELL ME WHAT YOU WANT.
IT'S HARD TO IGNORE WHAT JUST HAPPENED--
TELL ME...SHOW ME.
SHOW YOU WHAT?
YOU SAID--
--YOU WERE TRYING TO SHOW ME-- YOU SAID YOU WANTED TO BE DIFFERENT...
OKAY.
SO--SO SHOW ME.
I THINK WE'RE PAST THAT.
NOT IF--
OH, GOD...
...NOT IF--IF YOU CHANGED.

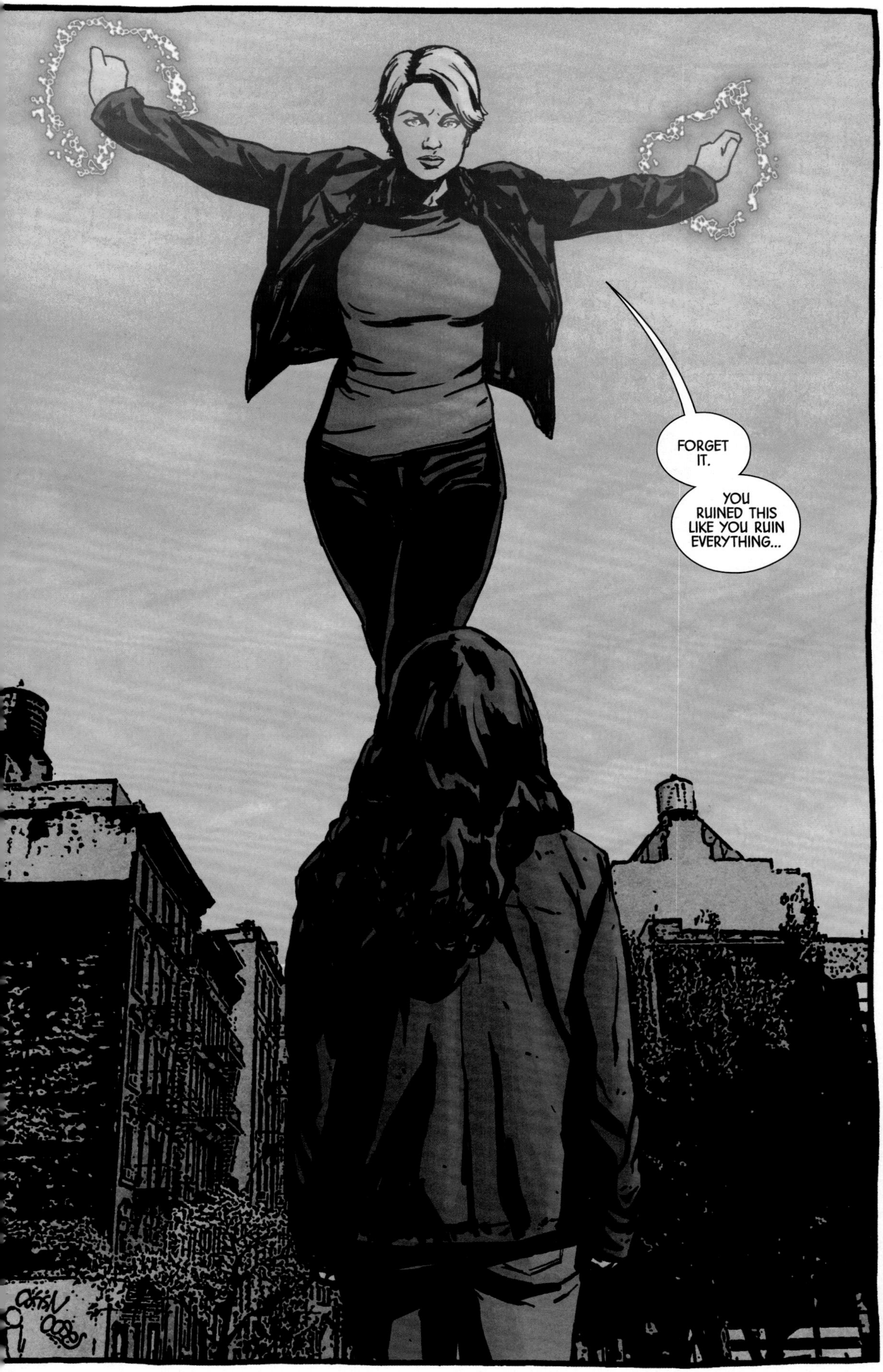
FORGET IT.
YOU RUINED THIS LIKE YOU RUIN EVERYTHING...

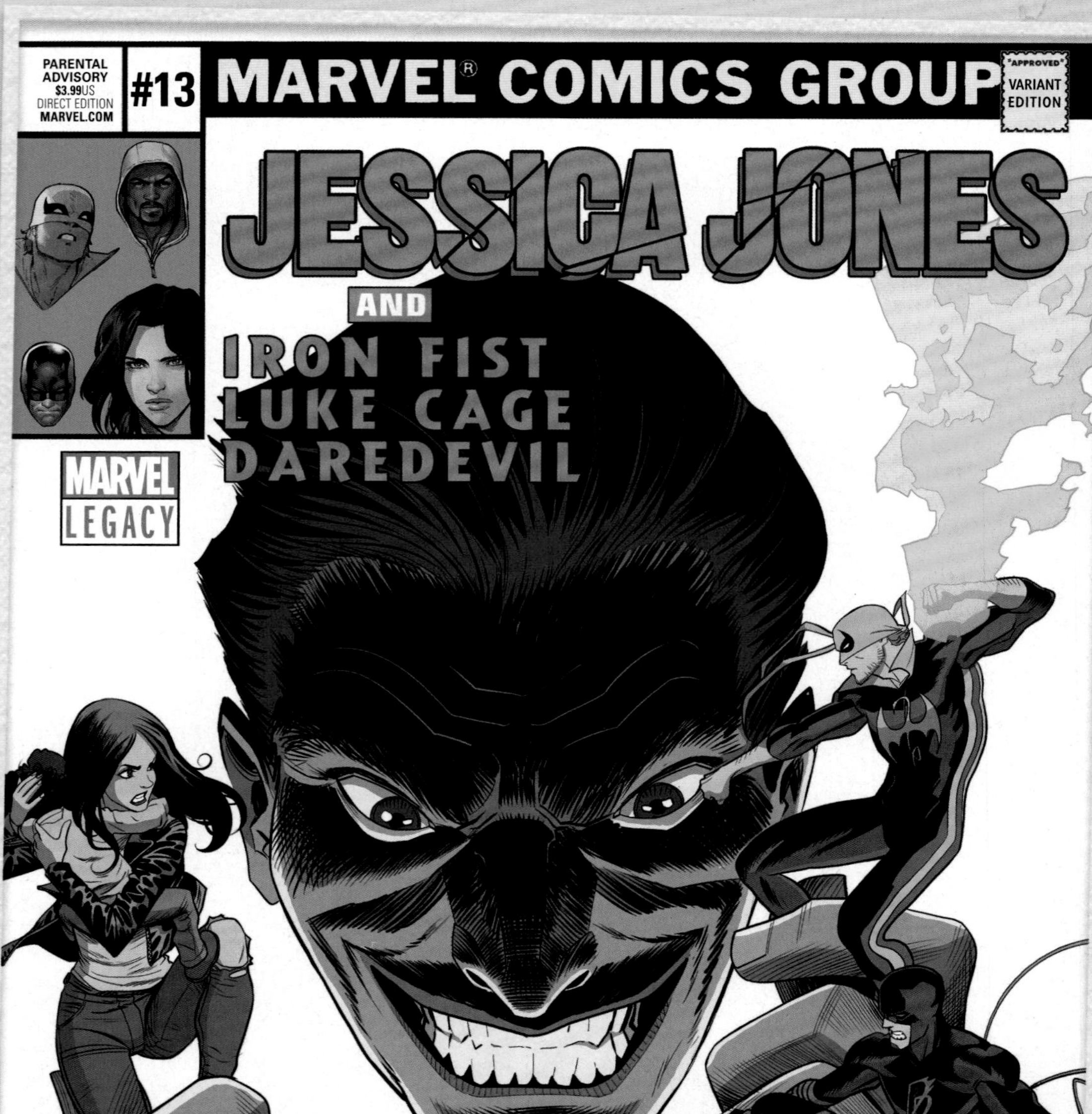
PARENTAL ADVISORY
$3.99US
DIRECT EDITION
MARVEL.COM
#13
MARVEL® COMICS GROUP
"APPROVED"
VARIANT EDITION
JESSICA JONES
AND
IRON FIST
LUKE CAGE
DAREDEVIL
MARVEL
LEGACY
PAWNS OF THE PURPLE MAN!

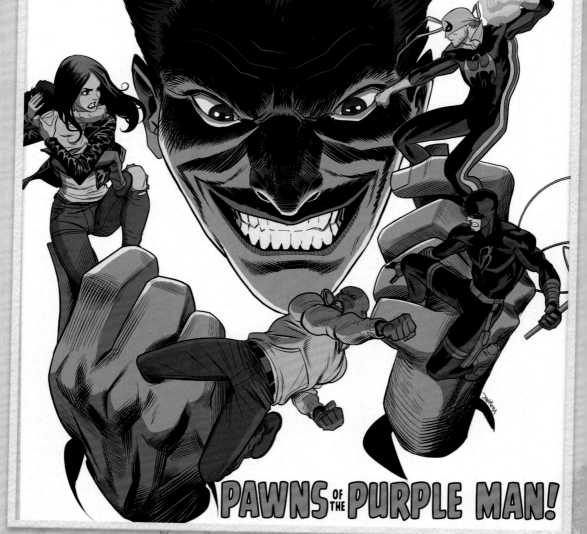

#13 Homage variant by **Dan Mora** & **Megan Wilson**

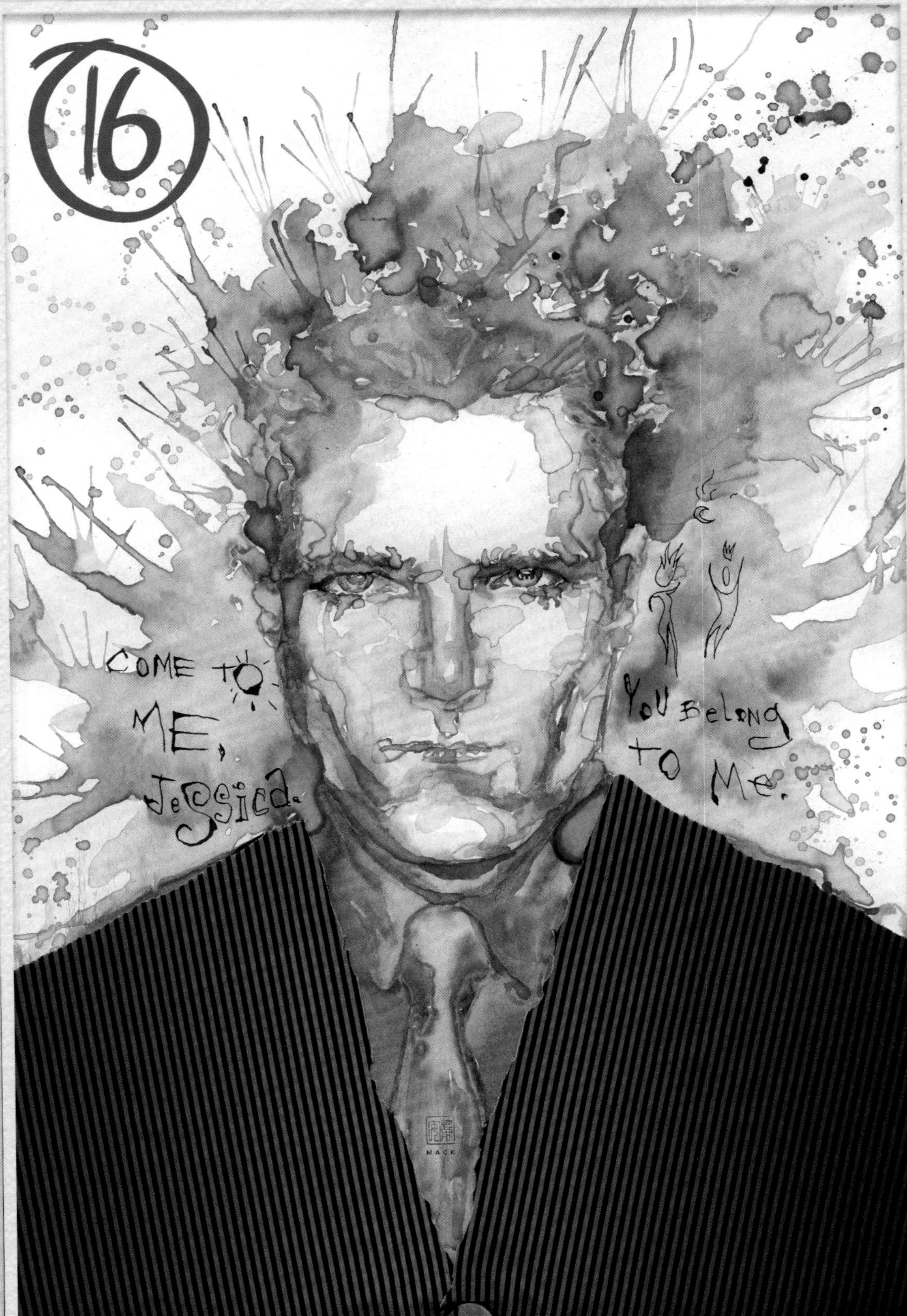
16
COME TO ME, Jessica.
YOU BELONG TO ME.
MACK

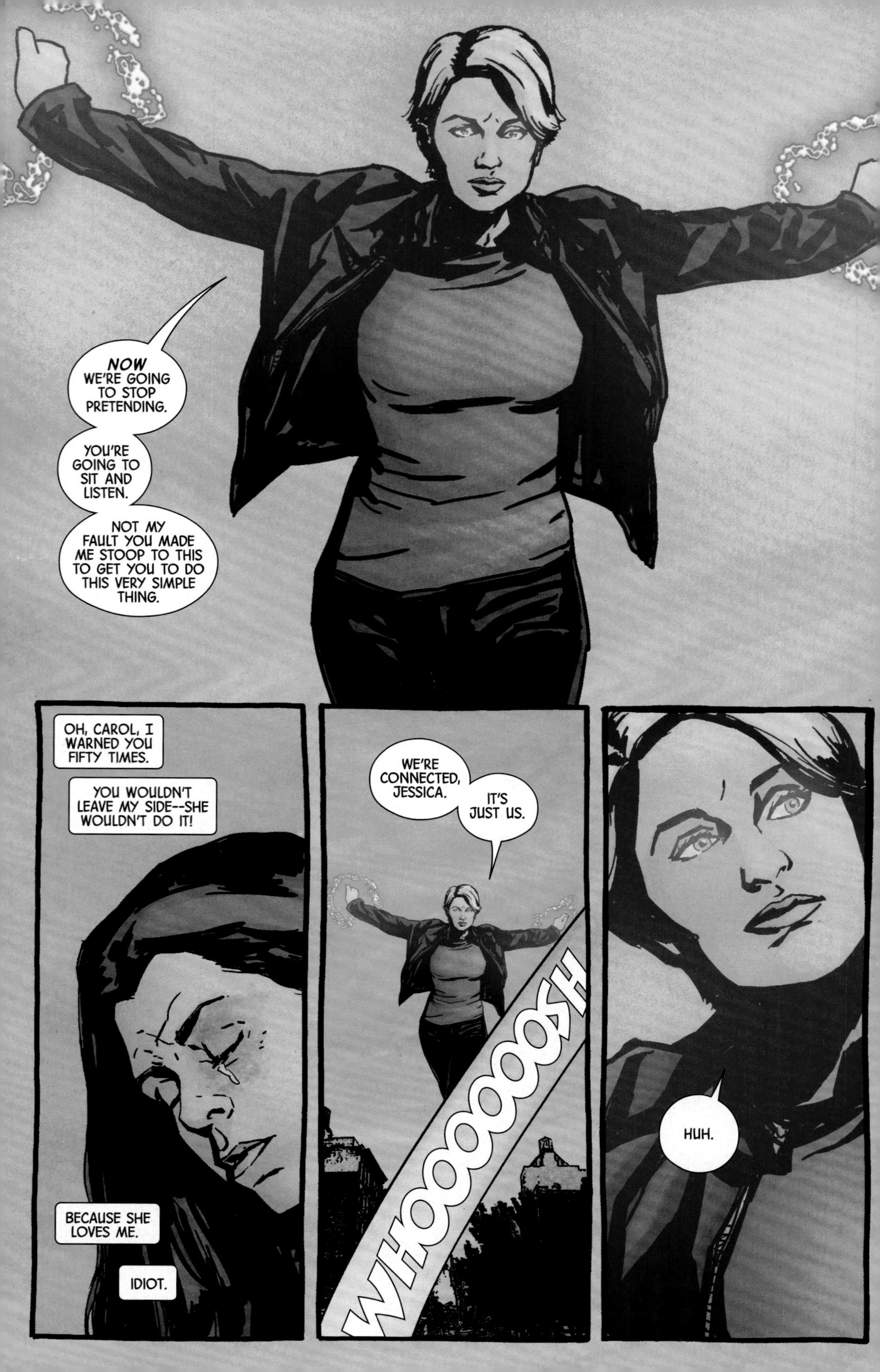

NOW WE'RE GOING TO STOP PRETENDING.
YOU'RE GOING TO SIT AND LISTEN.
NOT MY FAULT YOU MADE ME STOOP TO THIS TO GET YOU TO DO THIS VERY SIMPLE THING.
OH, CAROL, I WARNED YOU FIFTY TIMES.
YOU WOULDN'T LEAVE MY SIDE--SHE WOULDN'T DO IT!
BECAUSE SHE LOVES ME.
IDIOT.
WE'RE CONNECTED, JESSICA.
IT'S JUST US.
WHOOOOOOOSH
HUH.

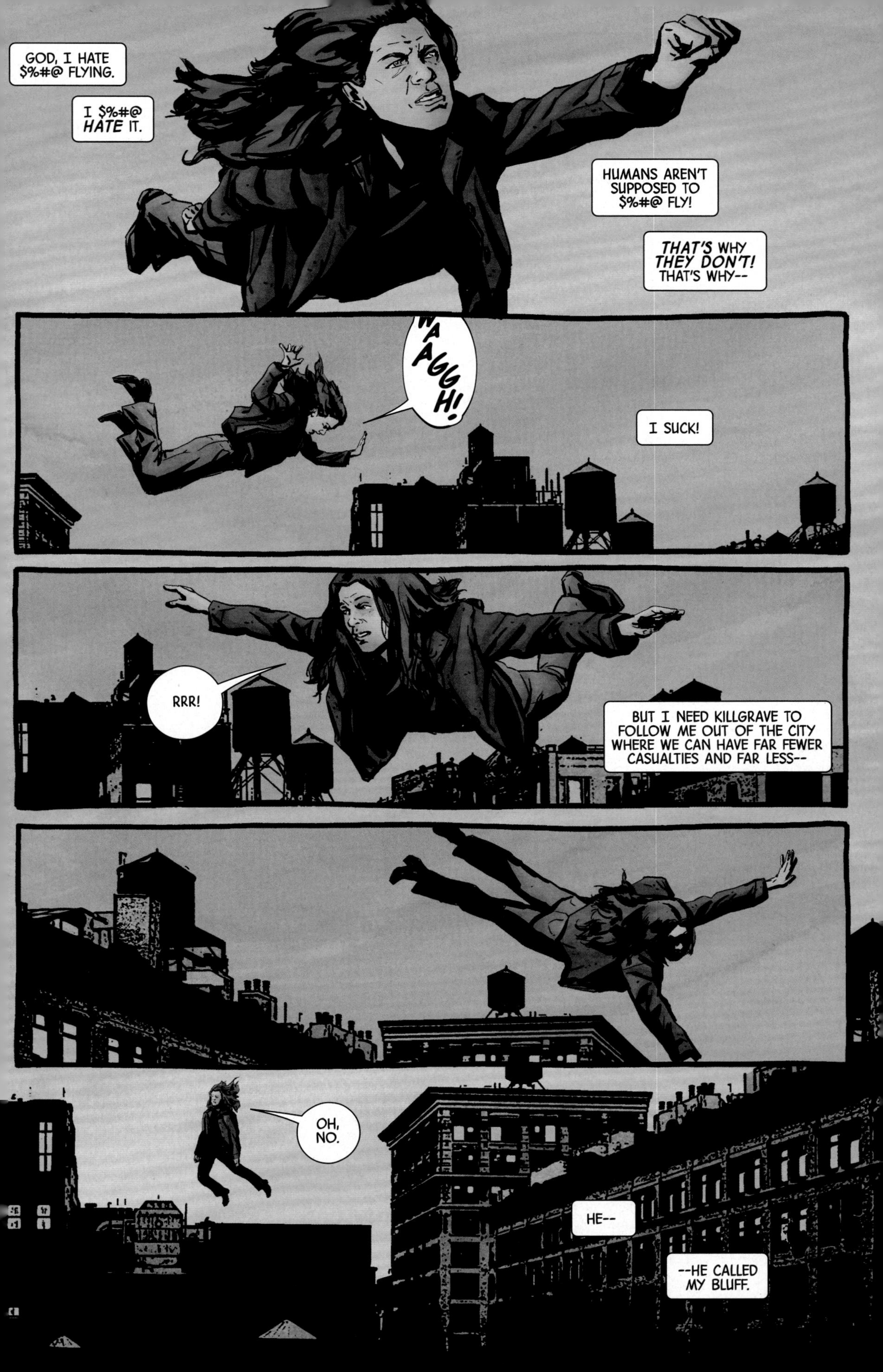
GOD, I HATE $%#@ FLYING.
I $%#@ *HATE* IT.
HUMANS AREN'T SUPPOSED TO $%#@ FLY!
THAT'S WHY *THEY DON'T!* THAT'S WHY--
WAAGGH!
I SUCK!
RRR!
BUT I NEED KILLGRAVE TO FOLLOW ME OUT OF THE CITY WHERE WE CAN HAVE FAR FEWER CASUALTIES AND FAR LESS--
OH, NO.
HE--
--HE CALLED MY BLUFF.

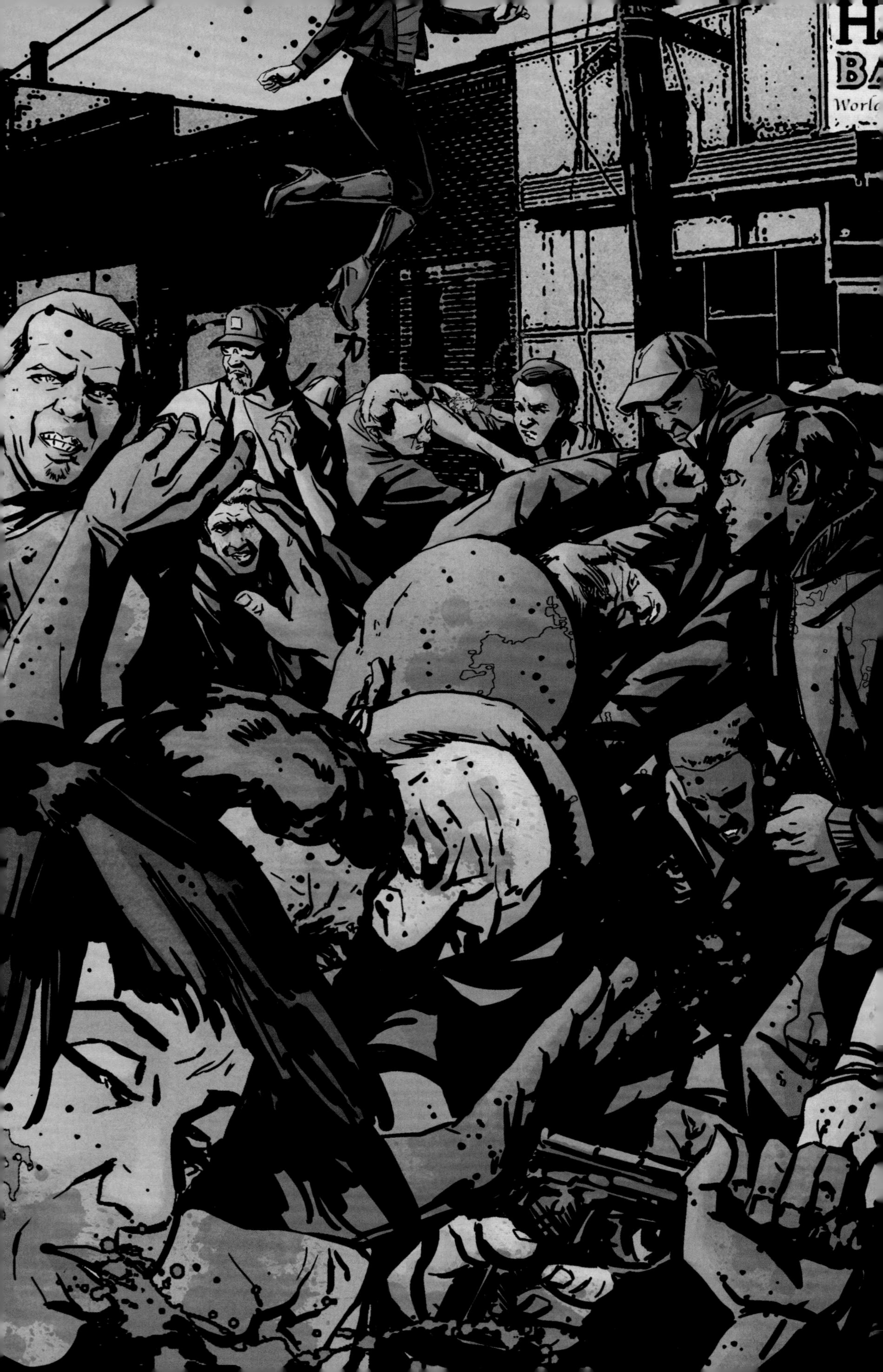

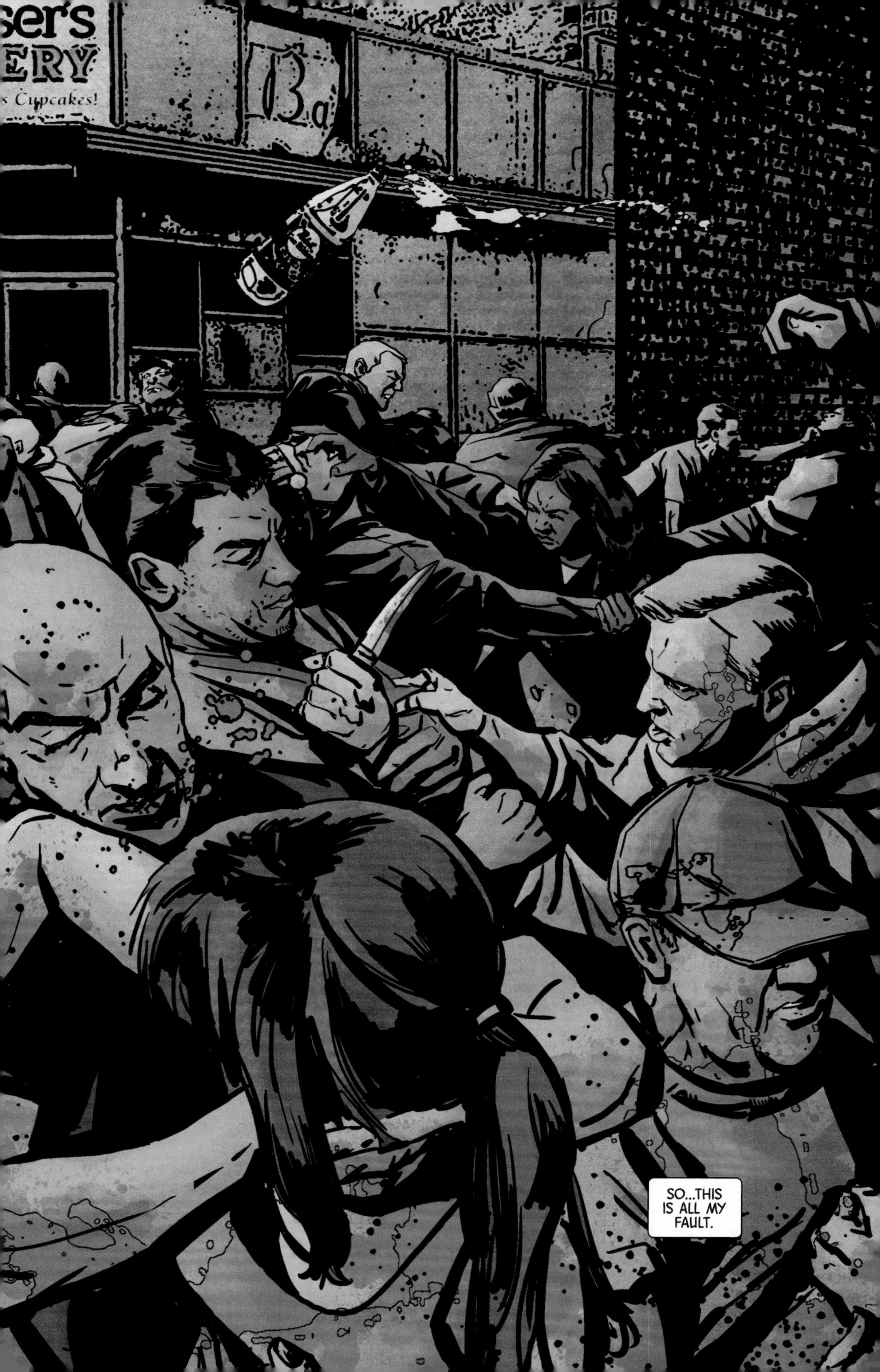
sers
ERY
s Cupcakes!
SO...THIS IS ALL MY FAULT.

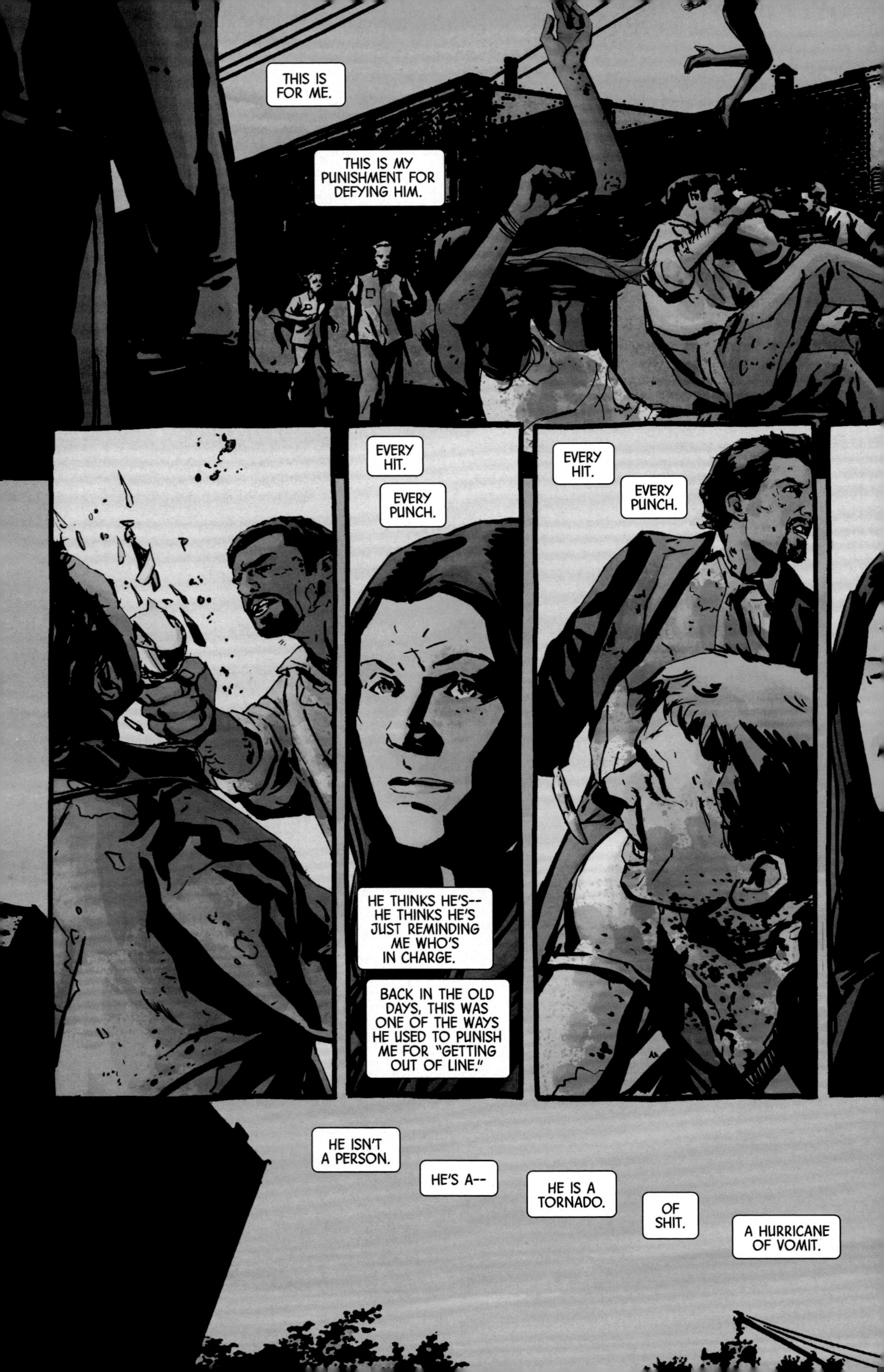
THIS IS FOR ME.
THIS IS MY PUNISHMENT FOR DEFYING HIM.
EVERY HIT.
EVERY PUNCH.
HE THINKS HE'S-- HE THINKS HE'S JUST REMINDING ME WHO'S IN CHARGE.
BACK IN THE OLD DAYS, THIS WAS ONE OF THE WAYS HE USED TO PUNISH ME FOR "GETTING OUT OF LINE."
EVERY HIT.
EVERY PUNCH.
HE ISN'T A PERSON.
HE'S A--
HE IS A TORNADO.
OF SHIT.
A HURRICANE OF VOMIT.

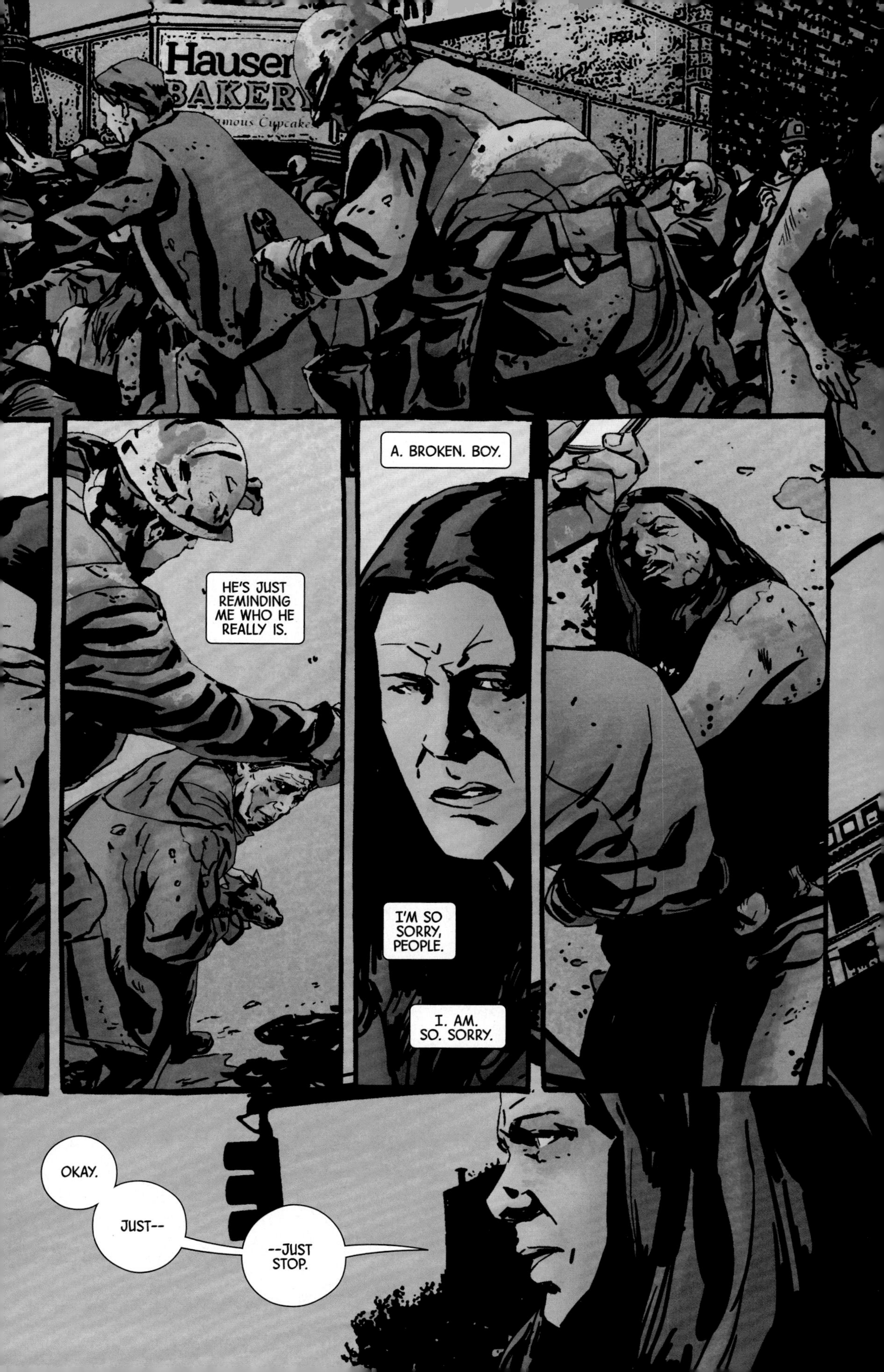
Hauser
BAKERY
Famous Cupcakes
HE'S JUST REMINDING ME WHO HE REALLY IS.
A. BROKEN. BOY.
I'M SO SORRY, PEOPLE.
I. AM. SO. SORRY.
OKAY.
JUST--
--JUST STOP.

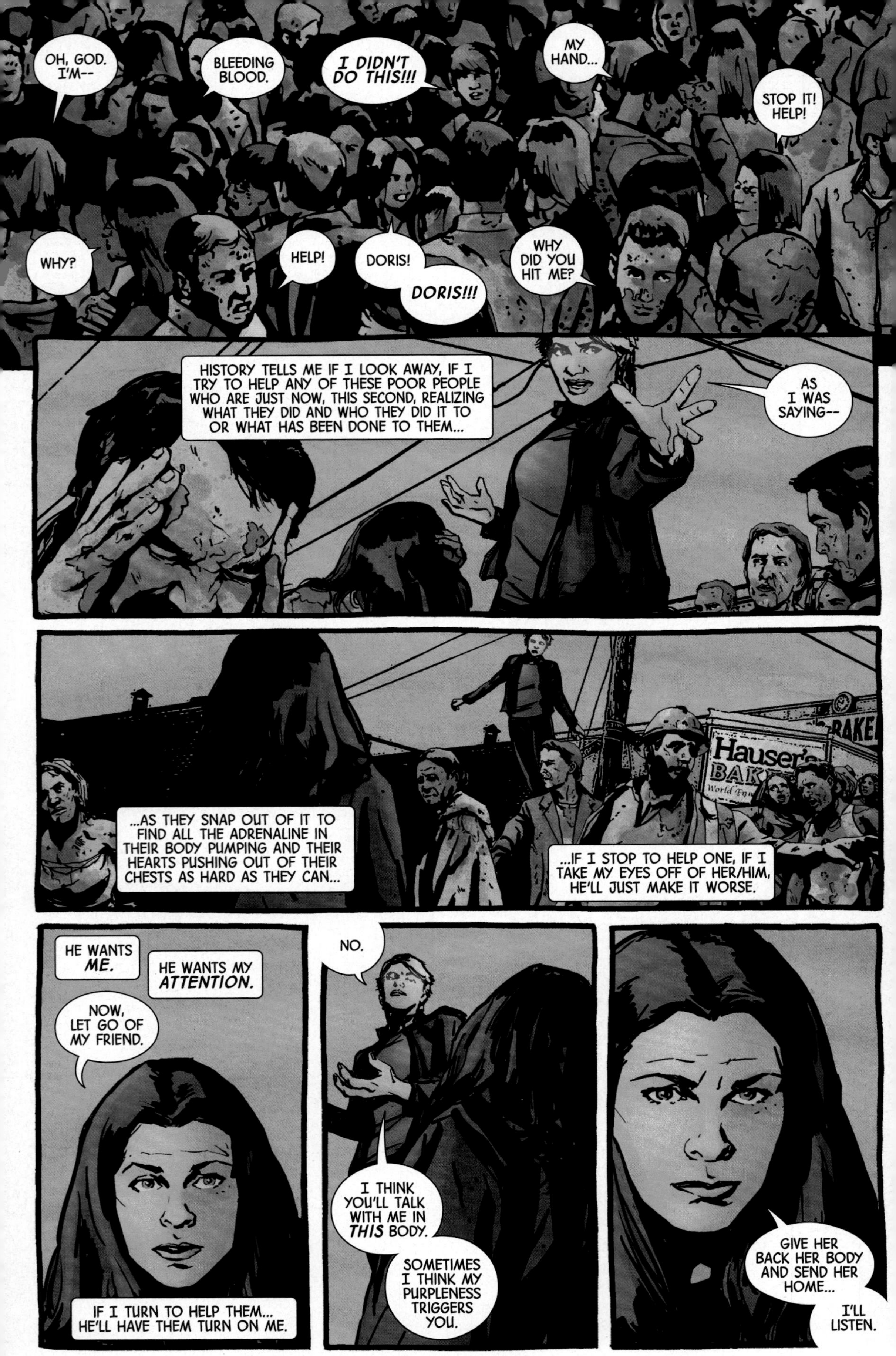
OH, GOD. I'M--
BLEEDING BLOOD.
I DIDN'T DO THIS!!!
MY HAND...
STOP IT! HELP!
WHY?
HELP!
DORIS!
DORIS!!!
WHY DID YOU HIT ME?
HISTORY TELLS ME IF I LOOK AWAY, IF I TRY TO HELP ANY OF THESE POOR PEOPLE WHO ARE JUST NOW, THIS SECOND, REALIZING WHAT THEY DID AND WHO THEY DID IT TO OR WHAT HAS BEEN DONE TO THEM...
AS I WAS SAYING--
...AS THEY SNAP OUT OF IT TO FIND ALL THE ADRENALINE IN THEIR BODY PUMPING AND THEIR HEARTS PUSHING OUT OF THEIR CHESTS AS HARD AS THEY CAN...
...IF I STOP TO HELP ONE, IF I TAKE MY EYES OFF OF HER/HIM, HE'LL JUST MAKE IT WORSE.
HE WANTS ME.
HE WANTS MY ATTENTION.
NOW, LET GO OF MY FRIEND.
IF I TURN TO HELP THEM... HE'LL HAVE THEM TURN ON ME.
NO.
I THINK YOU'LL TALK WITH ME IN THIS BODY.
SOMETIMES I THINK MY PURPLENESS TRIGGERS YOU.
GIVE HER BACK HER BODY AND SEND HER HOME...
I'LL LISTEN.

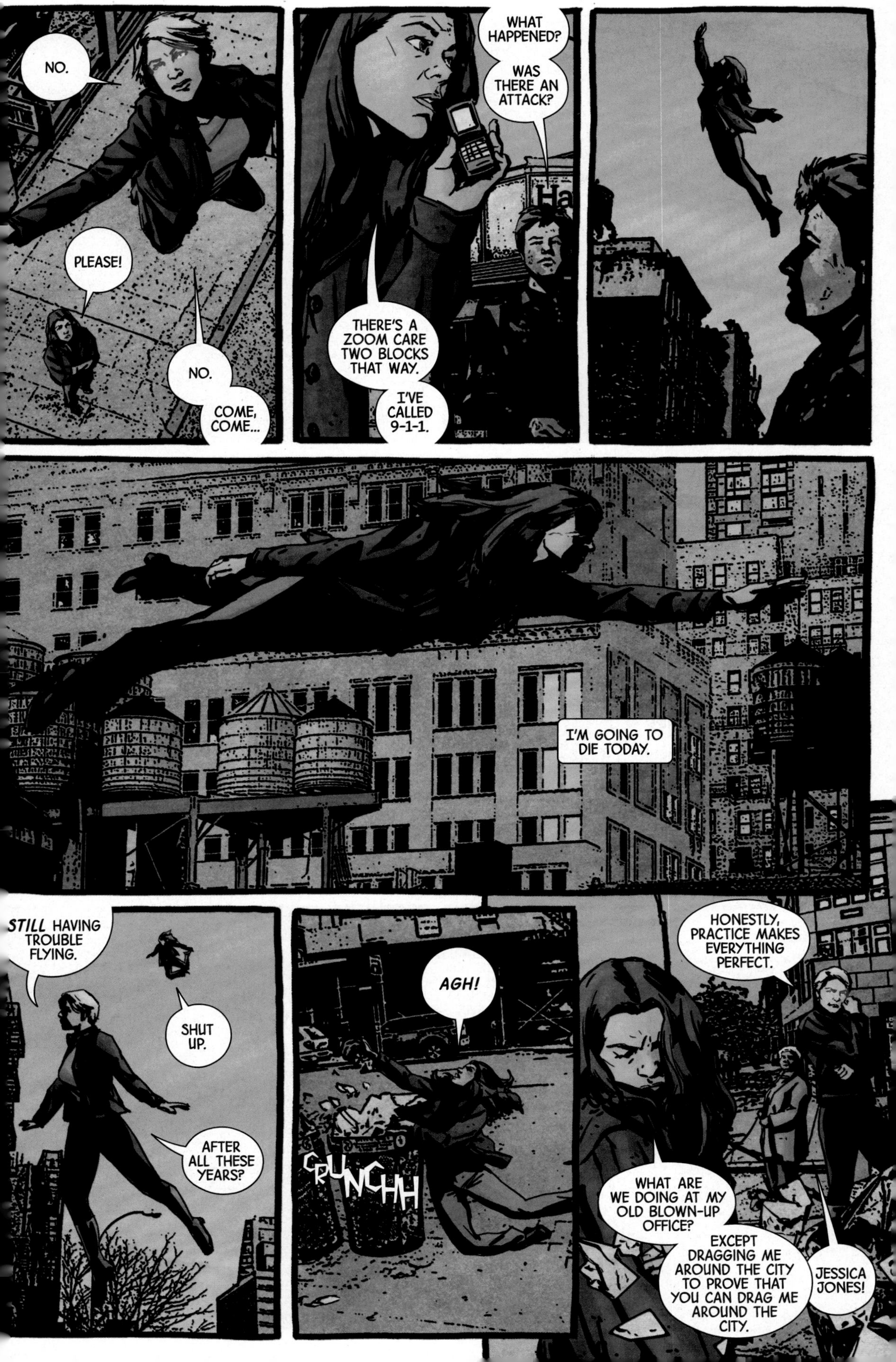
NO.
PLEASE!
NO.
COME, COME...
WHAT HAPPENED?
WAS THERE AN ATTACK?
THERE'S A ZOOM CARE TWO BLOCKS THAT WAY.
I'VE CALLED 9-1-1.
I'M GOING TO DIE TODAY.
STILL HAVING TROUBLE FLYING.
SHUT UP.
AFTER ALL THESE YEARS?
AGH!
CRUNCHH
HONESTLY, PRACTICE MAKES EVERYTHING PERFECT.
WHAT ARE WE DOING AT MY OLD BLOWN-UP OFFICE?
EXCEPT DRAGGING ME AROUND THE CITY TO PROVE THAT YOU CAN DRAG ME AROUND THE CITY.
JESSICA JONES!

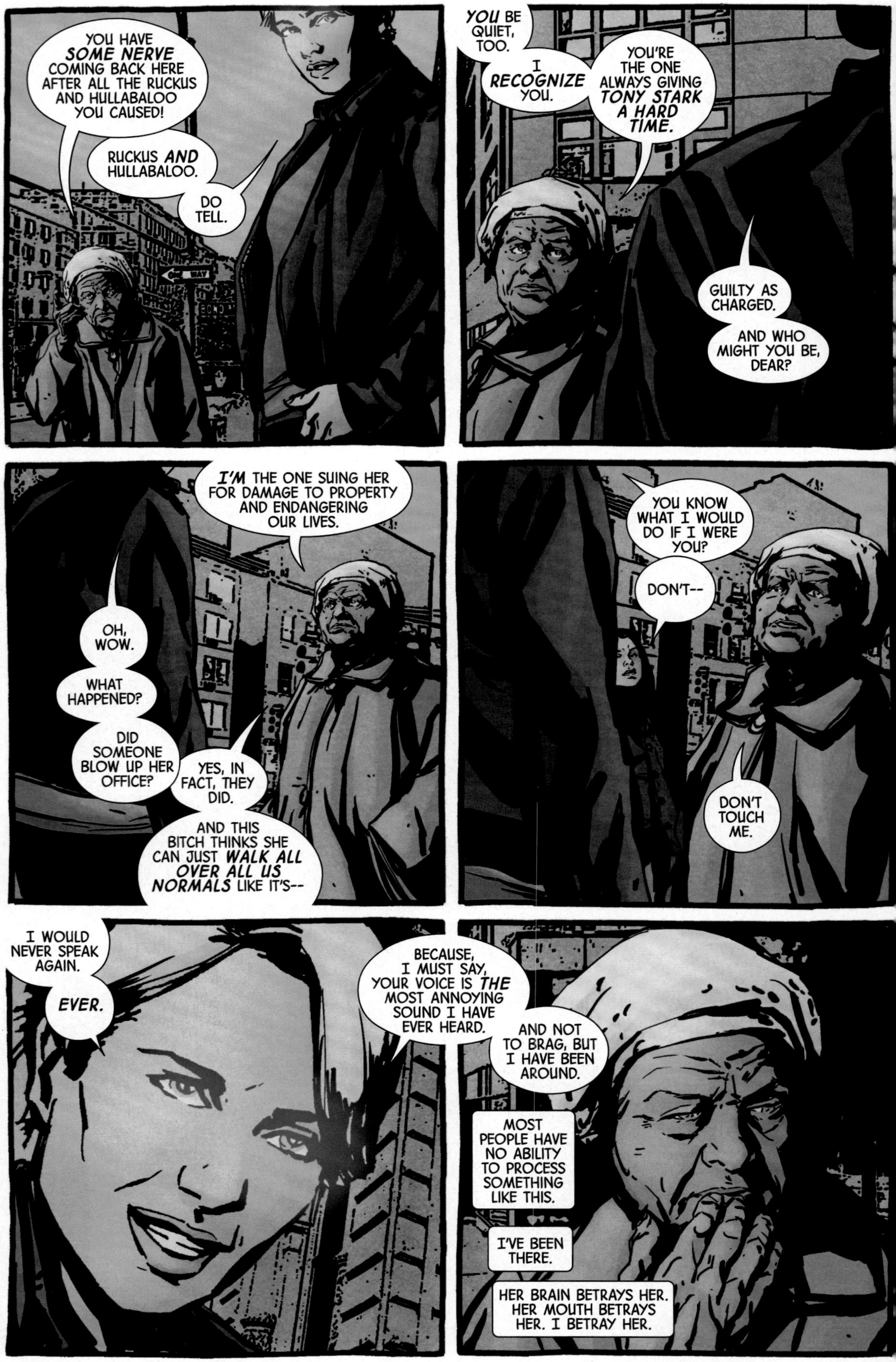
YOU HAVE SOME NERVE COMING BACK HERE AFTER ALL THE RUCKUS AND HULLABALOO YOU CAUSED!
RUCKUS AND HULLABALOO.
DO TELL.
ONE WAY
YOU BE QUIET, TOO.
I RECOGNIZE YOU.
YOU'RE THE ONE ALWAYS GIVING TONY STARK A HARD TIME.
GUILTY AS CHARGED.
AND WHO MIGHT YOU BE, DEAR?
I'M THE ONE SUING HER FOR DAMAGE TO PROPERTY AND ENDANGERING OUR LIVES.
OH, WOW.
WHAT HAPPENED?
DID SOMEONE BLOW UP HER OFFICE?
YES, IN FACT, THEY DID.
AND THIS BITCH THINKS SHE CAN JUST WALK ALL OVER ALL US NORMALS LIKE IT'S--
YOU KNOW WHAT I WOULD DO IF I WERE YOU?
DON'T--
DON'T TOUCH ME.
I WOULD NEVER SPEAK AGAIN.
EVER.
BECAUSE, I MUST SAY, YOUR VOICE IS THE MOST ANNOYING SOUND I HAVE EVER HEARD.
AND NOT TO BRAG, BUT I HAVE BEEN AROUND.
MOST PEOPLE HAVE NO ABILITY TO PROCESS SOMETHING LIKE THIS.
I'VE BEEN THERE.
HER BRAIN BETRAYS HER. HER MOUTH BETRAYS HER. I BETRAY HER.

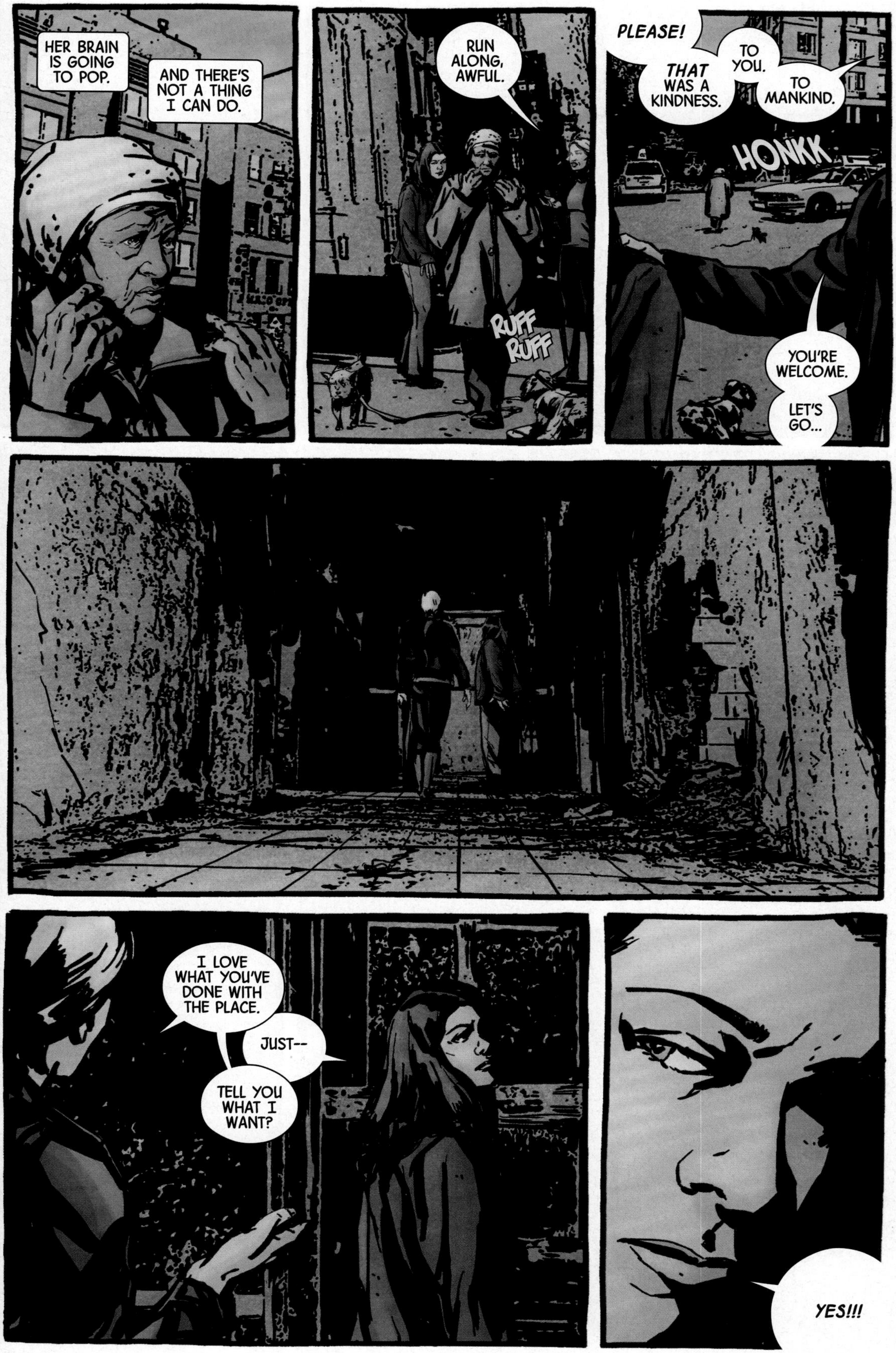
HER BRAIN IS GOING TO POP.
AND THERE'S NOT A THING I CAN DO.
RUN ALONG, AWFUL.
RUFF RUFF
PLEASE!
THAT WAS A KINDNESS.
TO YOU.
TO MANKIND.
HONKK
YOU'RE WELCOME.
LET'S GO...
I LOVE WHAT YOU'VE DONE WITH THE PLACE.
JUST--
TELL YOU WHAT I WANT?
YES!!!

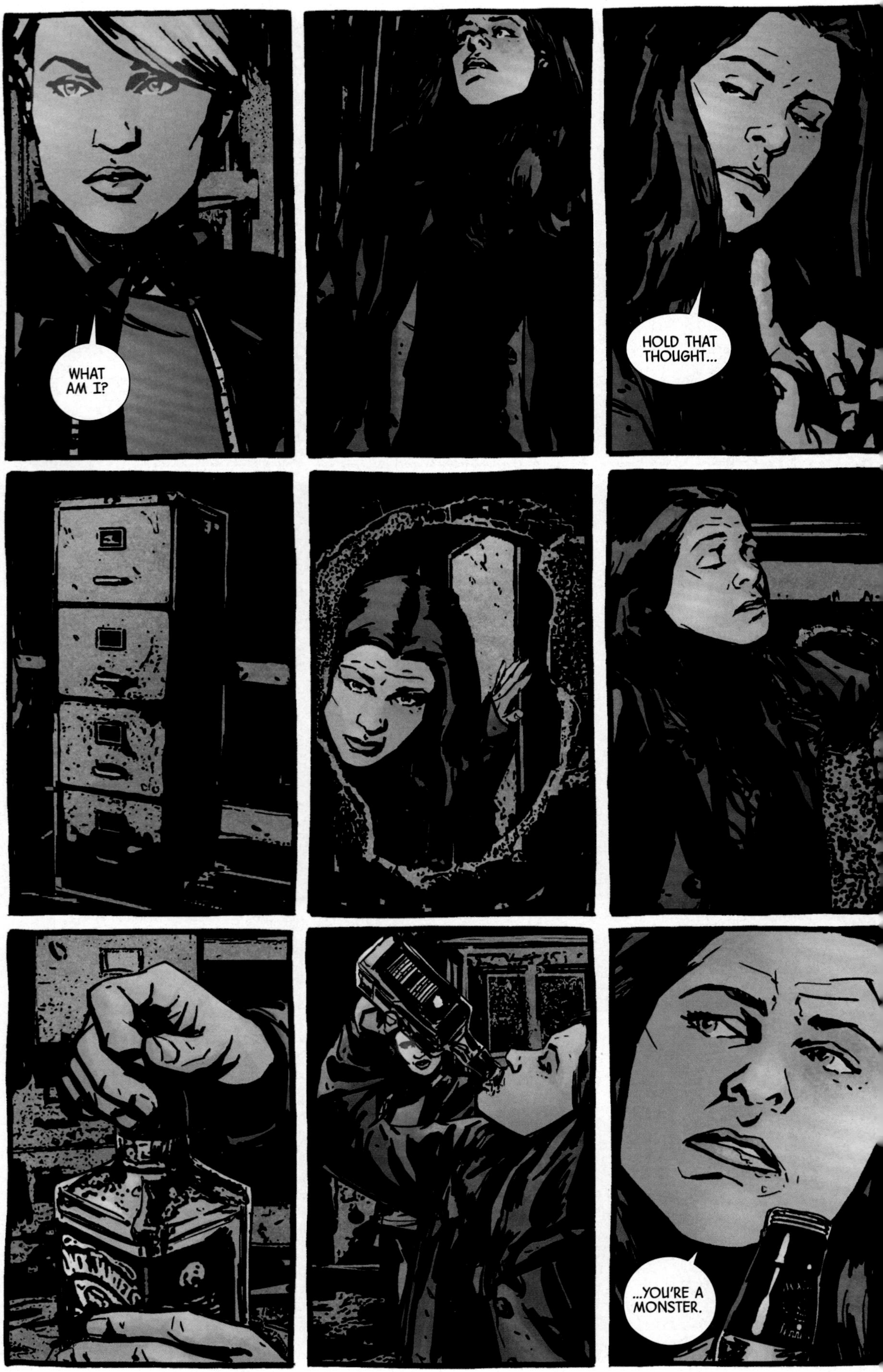
WHAT AM I?
HOLD THAT THOUGHT...
...YOU'RE A MONSTER.

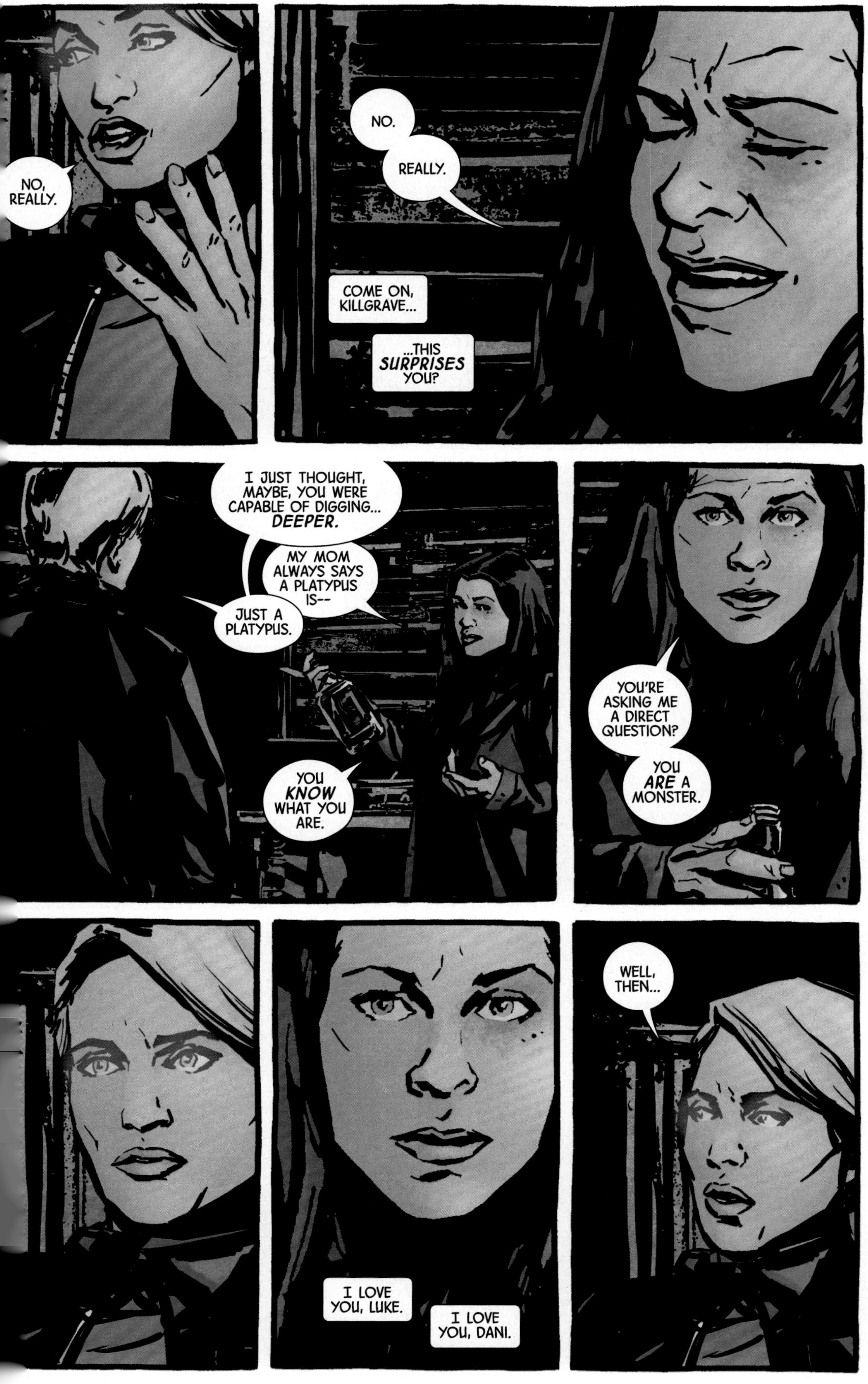
NO, REALLY.
NO.
REALLY.
COME ON, KILLGRAVE...
...THIS SURPRISES YOU?
I JUST THOUGHT, MAYBE, YOU WERE CAPABLE OF DIGGING... DEEPER.
MY MOM ALWAYS SAYS A PLATYPUS IS--
JUST A PLATYPUS.
YOU KNOW WHAT YOU ARE.
YOU'RE ASKING ME A DIRECT QUESTION?
YOU ARE A MONSTER.
WELL, THEN...
I LOVE YOU, LUKE.
I LOVE YOU, DANI.

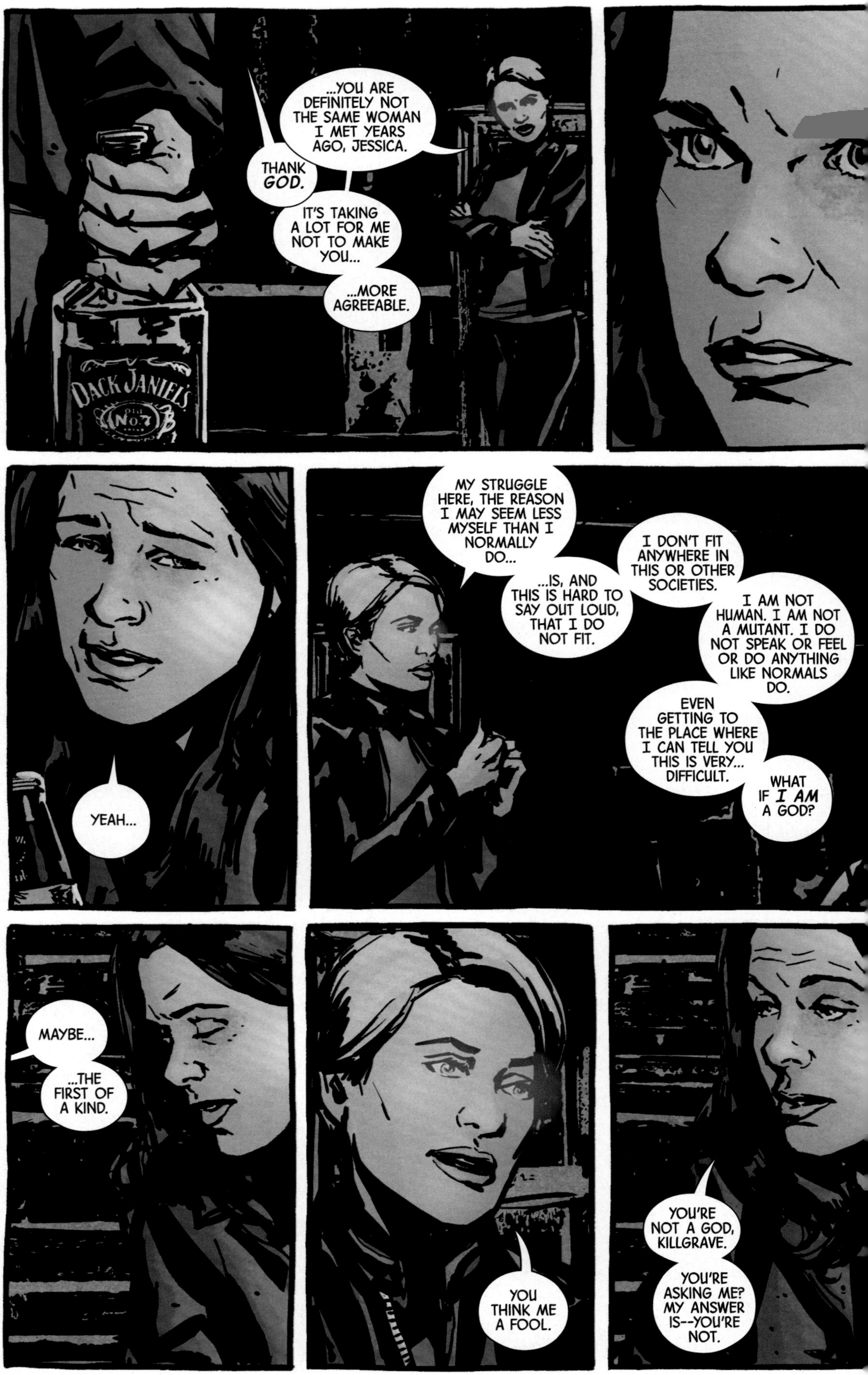
...YOU ARE DEFINITELY NOT THE SAME WOMAN I MET YEARS AGO, JESSICA.
THANK GOD.
IT'S TAKING A LOT FOR ME NOT TO MAKE YOU...
...MORE AGREEABLE.
JACK DANIEL'S Old No.7
YEAH...
MY STRUGGLE HERE, THE REASON I MAY SEEM LESS MYSELF THAN I NORMALLY DO...
...IS, AND THIS IS HARD TO SAY OUT LOUD, THAT I DO NOT FIT.
I DON'T FIT ANYWHERE IN THIS OR OTHER SOCIETIES.
I AM NOT HUMAN. I AM NOT A MUTANT. I DO NOT SPEAK OR FEEL OR DO ANYTHING LIKE NORMALS DO.
EVEN GETTING TO THE PLACE WHERE I CAN TELL YOU THIS IS VERY... DIFFICULT.
WHAT IF I AM A GOD?
MAYBE...
...THE FIRST OF A KIND.
YOU THINK ME A FOOL.
YOU'RE NOT A GOD, KILLGRAVE.
YOU'RE ASKING ME? MY ANSWER IS--YOU'RE NOT.

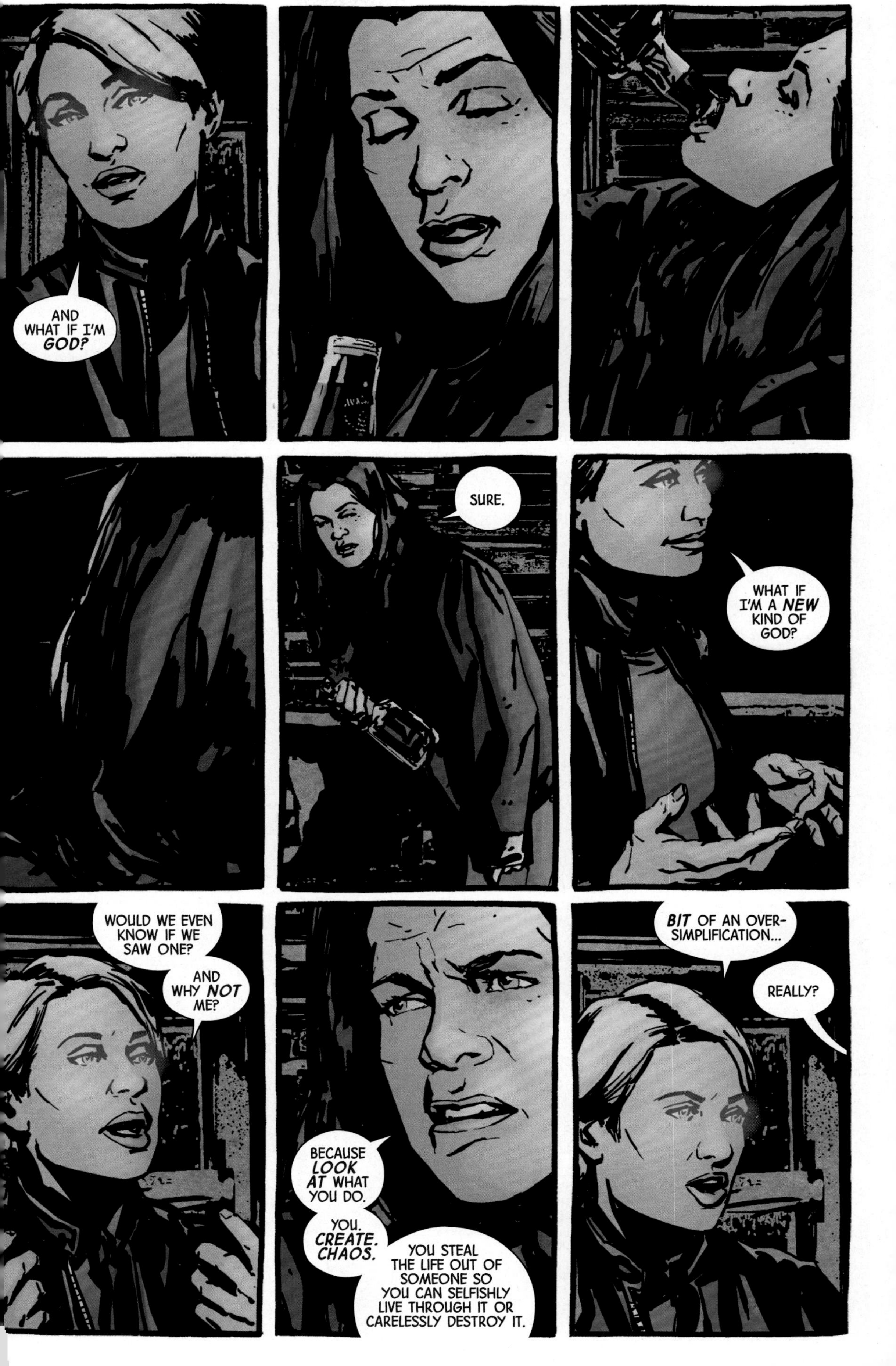
AND WHAT IF I'M *GOD?*
SURE.
WHAT IF I'M A ***NEW*** KIND OF GOD?
WOULD WE EVEN KNOW IF WE SAW ONE?
AND WHY ***NOT*** ME?
BECAUSE ***LOOK AT*** WHAT YOU DO.
YOU. ***CREATE. CHAOS.***
YOU STEAL THE LIFE OUT OF SOMEONE SO YOU CAN SELFISHLY LIVE THROUGH IT OR CARELESSLY DESTROY IT.
BIT OF AN OVER-SIMPLIFICATION...
REALLY?

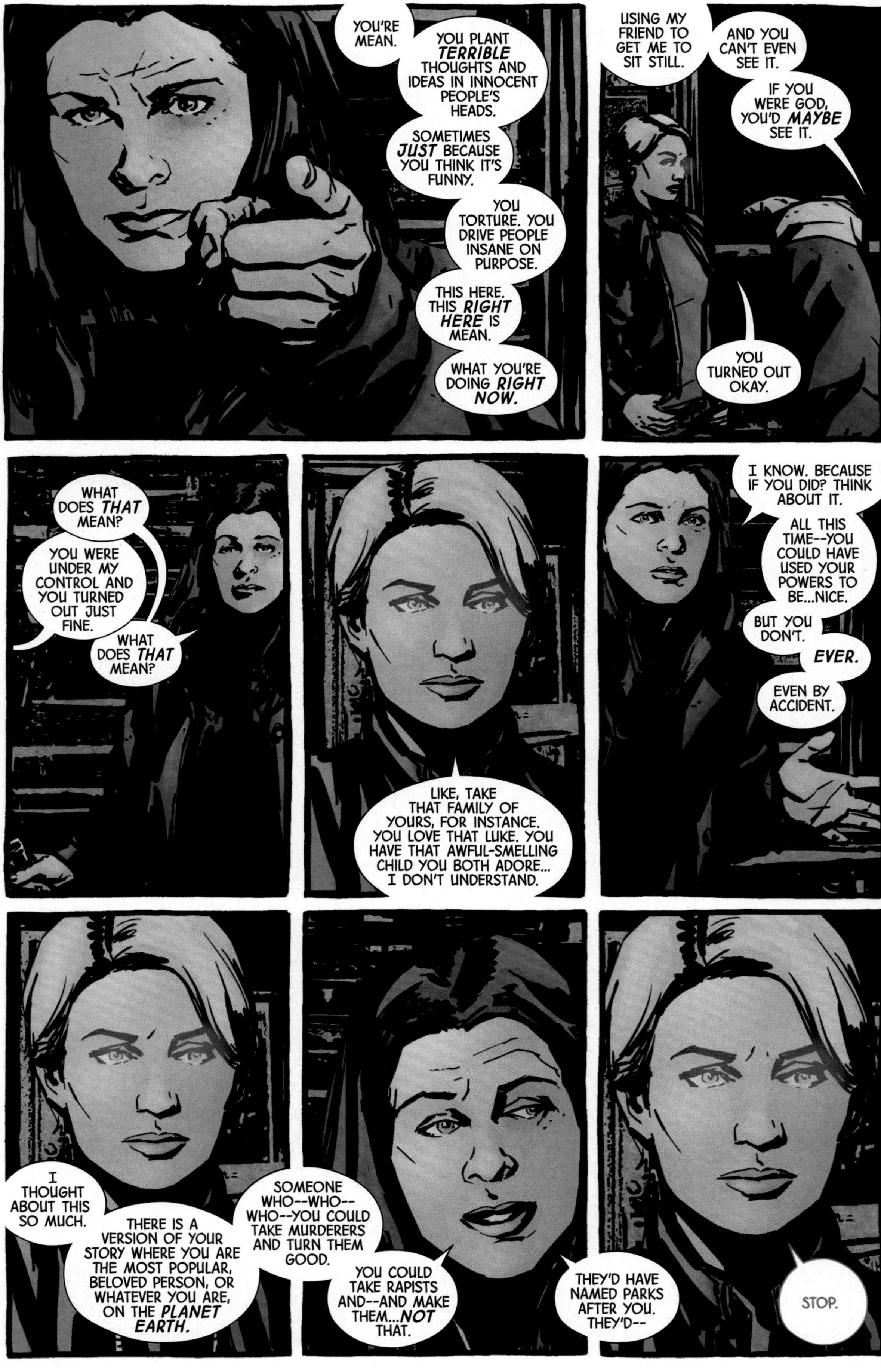

YOU'RE MEAN.
YOU PLANT *TERRIBLE* THOUGHTS AND IDEAS IN INNOCENT PEOPLE'S HEADS.
SOMETIMES *JUST* BECAUSE YOU THINK IT'S FUNNY.
YOU TORTURE. YOU DRIVE PEOPLE INSANE ON PURPOSE.
THIS HERE. THIS *RIGHT HERE* IS MEAN.
WHAT YOU'RE DOING *RIGHT NOW.*
USING MY FRIEND TO GET ME TO SIT STILL.
AND YOU CAN'T EVEN SEE IT.
IF YOU WERE GOD, YOU'D *MAYBE* SEE IT.
YOU TURNED OUT OKAY.
WHAT DOES *THAT* MEAN?
YOU WERE UNDER MY CONTROL AND YOU TURNED OUT JUST FINE.
WHAT DOES *THAT* MEAN?
LIKE, TAKE THAT FAMILY OF YOURS, FOR INSTANCE. YOU LOVE THAT LUKE. YOU HAVE THAT AWFUL-SMELLING CHILD YOU BOTH ADORE... I DON'T UNDERSTAND.
I KNOW. BECAUSE IF YOU DID? THINK ABOUT IT.
ALL THIS TIME--YOU COULD HAVE USED YOUR POWERS TO BE...NICE.
BUT YOU DON'T.
EVER.
EVEN BY ACCIDENT.
I THOUGHT ABOUT THIS SO MUCH.
THERE IS A VERSION OF YOUR STORY WHERE YOU ARE THE MOST POPULAR, BELOVED PERSON, OR WHATEVER YOU ARE, ON THE *PLANET EARTH.*
SOMEONE WHO--WHO--WHO--YOU COULD TAKE MURDERERS AND TURN THEM GOOD.
YOU COULD TAKE RAPISTS AND--AND MAKE THEM...*NOT* THAT.
THEY'D HAVE NAMED PARKS AFTER YOU. THEY'D--
STOP.

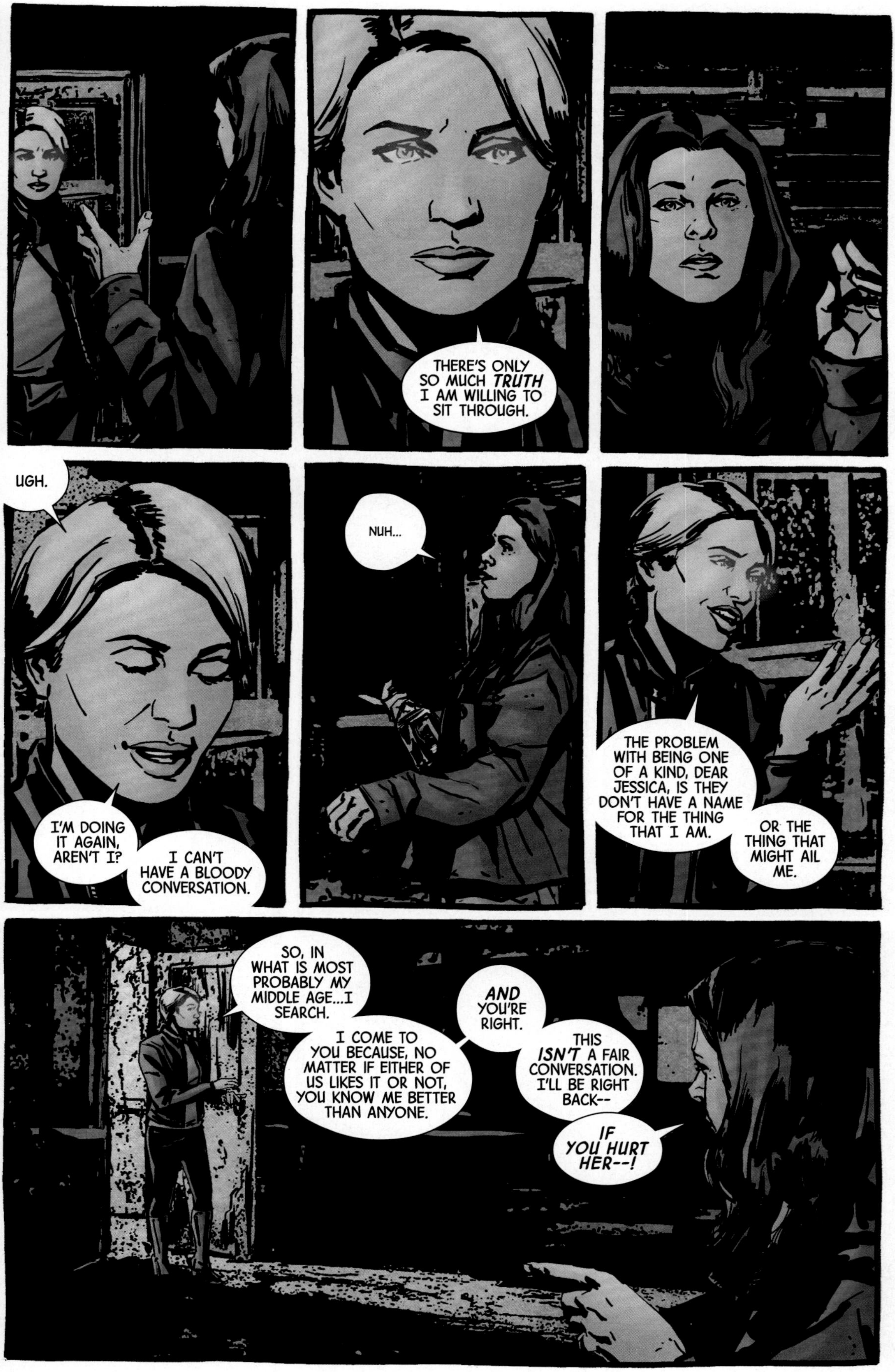
THERE'S ONLY SO MUCH *TRUTH* I AM WILLING TO SIT THROUGH.
UGH.
I'M DOING IT AGAIN, AREN'T I?
I CAN'T HAVE A BLOODY CONVERSATION.
NUH...
THE PROBLEM WITH BEING ONE OF A KIND, DEAR JESSICA, IS THEY DON'T HAVE A NAME FOR THE THING THAT I AM.
OR THE THING THAT MIGHT AIL ME.
SO, IN WHAT IS MOST PROBABLY MY MIDDLE AGE...I SEARCH.
I COME TO YOU BECAUSE, NO MATTER IF EITHER OF US LIKES IT OR NOT, YOU KNOW ME BETTER THAN ANYONE.
AND YOU'RE RIGHT.
THIS *ISN'T* A FAIR CONVERSATION. I'LL BE RIGHT BACK--
IF YOU HURT HER--!

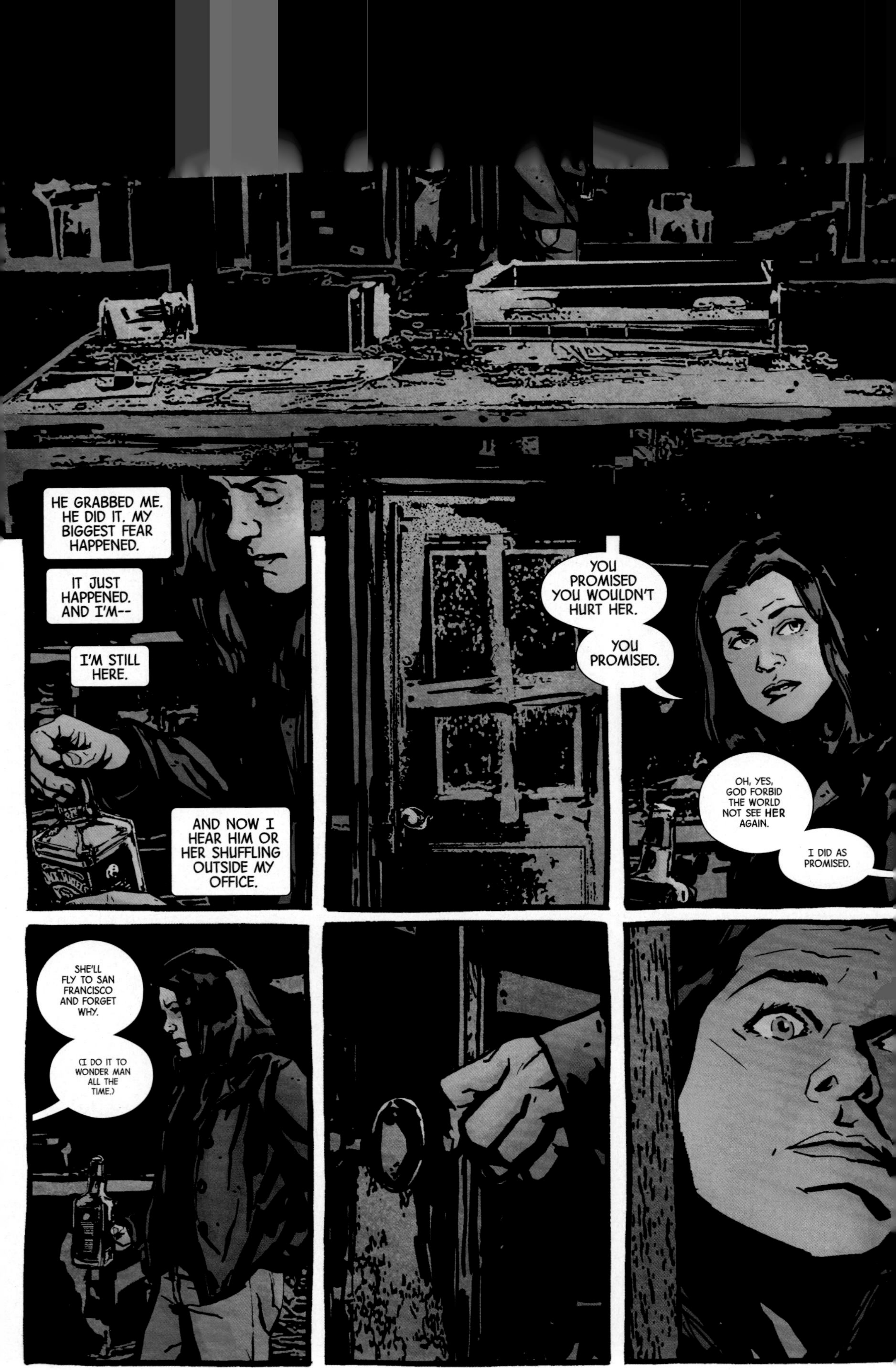
HE GRABBED ME. HE DID IT. MY BIGGEST FEAR HAPPENED.
IT JUST HAPPENED. AND I'M--
I'M STILL HERE.
AND NOW I HEAR HIM OR HER SHUFFLING OUTSIDE MY OFFICE.
YOU PROMISED YOU WOULDN'T HURT HER.
YOU PROMISED.
OH, YES, GOD FORBID THE WORLD NOT SEE HER AGAIN.
I DID AS PROMISED.
SHE'LL FLY TO SAN FRANCISCO AND FORGET WHY.
(I DO IT TO WONDER MAN ALL THE TIME.)

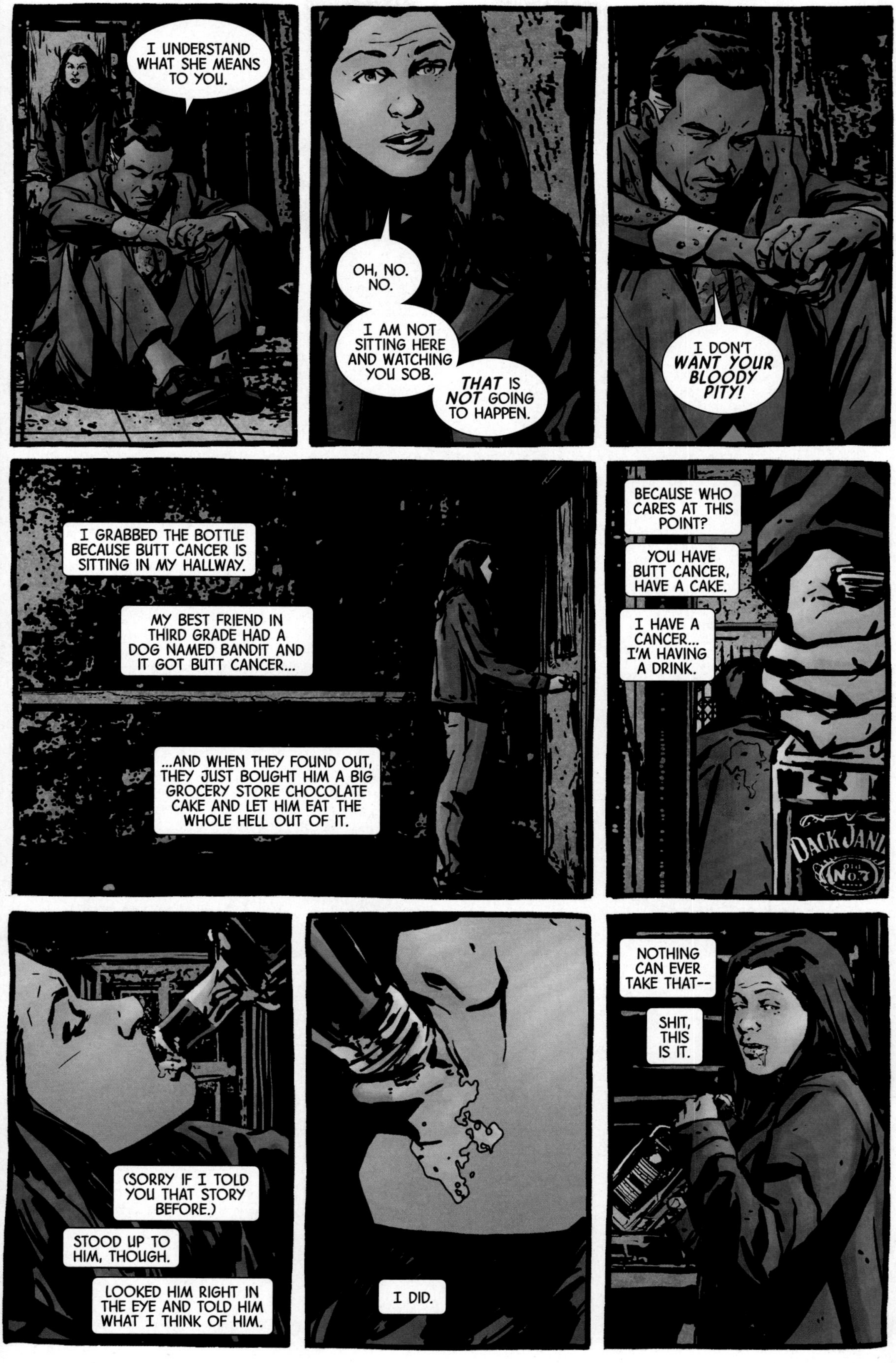

I UNDERSTAND WHAT SHE MEANS TO YOU.
OH, NO. NO.
I AM NOT SITTING HERE AND WATCHING YOU SOB.
THAT IS NOT GOING TO HAPPEN.
I DON'T WANT YOUR BLOODY PITY!
I GRABBED THE BOTTLE BECAUSE BUTT CANCER IS SITTING IN MY HALLWAY.
MY BEST FRIEND IN THIRD GRADE HAD A DOG NAMED BANDIT AND IT GOT BUTT CANCER...
...AND WHEN THEY FOUND OUT, THEY JUST BOUGHT HIM A BIG GROCERY STORE CHOCOLATE CAKE AND LET HIM EAT THE WHOLE HELL OUT OF IT.
BECAUSE WHO CARES AT THIS POINT?
YOU HAVE BUTT CANCER, HAVE A CAKE.
I HAVE A CANCER... I'M HAVING A DRINK.
(SORRY IF I TOLD YOU THAT STORY BEFORE.)
STOOD UP TO HIM, THOUGH.
LOOKED HIM RIGHT IN THE EYE AND TOLD HIM WHAT I THINK OF HIM.
I DID.
NOTHING CAN EVER TAKE THAT--
SHIT, THIS IS IT.

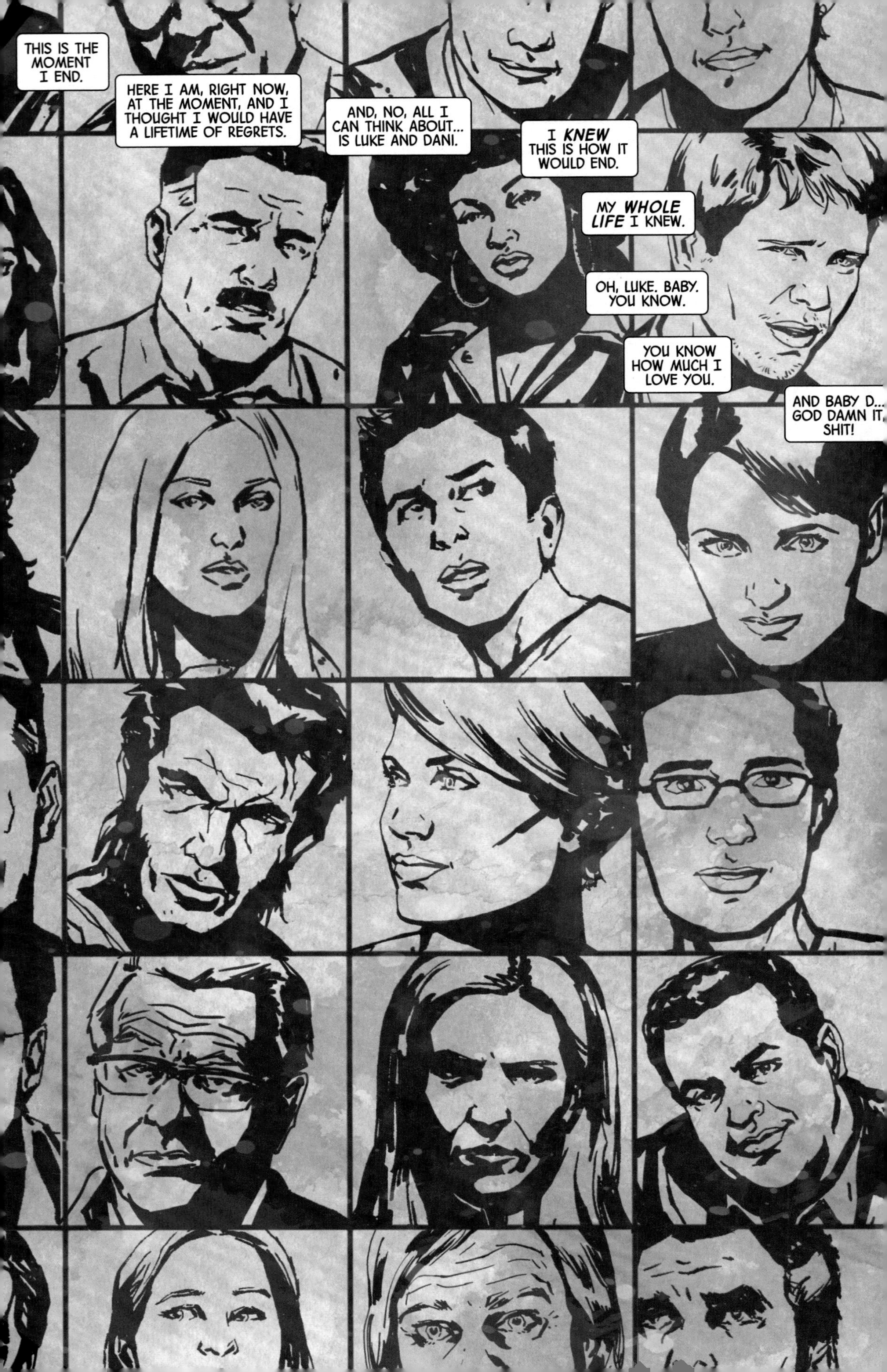

THIS IS THE MOMENT I END.
HERE I AM, RIGHT NOW, AT THE MOMENT, AND I THOUGHT I WOULD HAVE A LIFETIME OF REGRETS.
AND, NO, ALL I CAN THINK ABOUT... IS LUKE AND DANI.
I KNEW THIS IS HOW IT WOULD END.
MY WHOLE LIFE I KNEW.
OH, LUKE. BABY. YOU KNOW.
YOU KNOW HOW MUCH I LOVE YOU.
AND BABY D... GOD DAMN IT. SHIT!

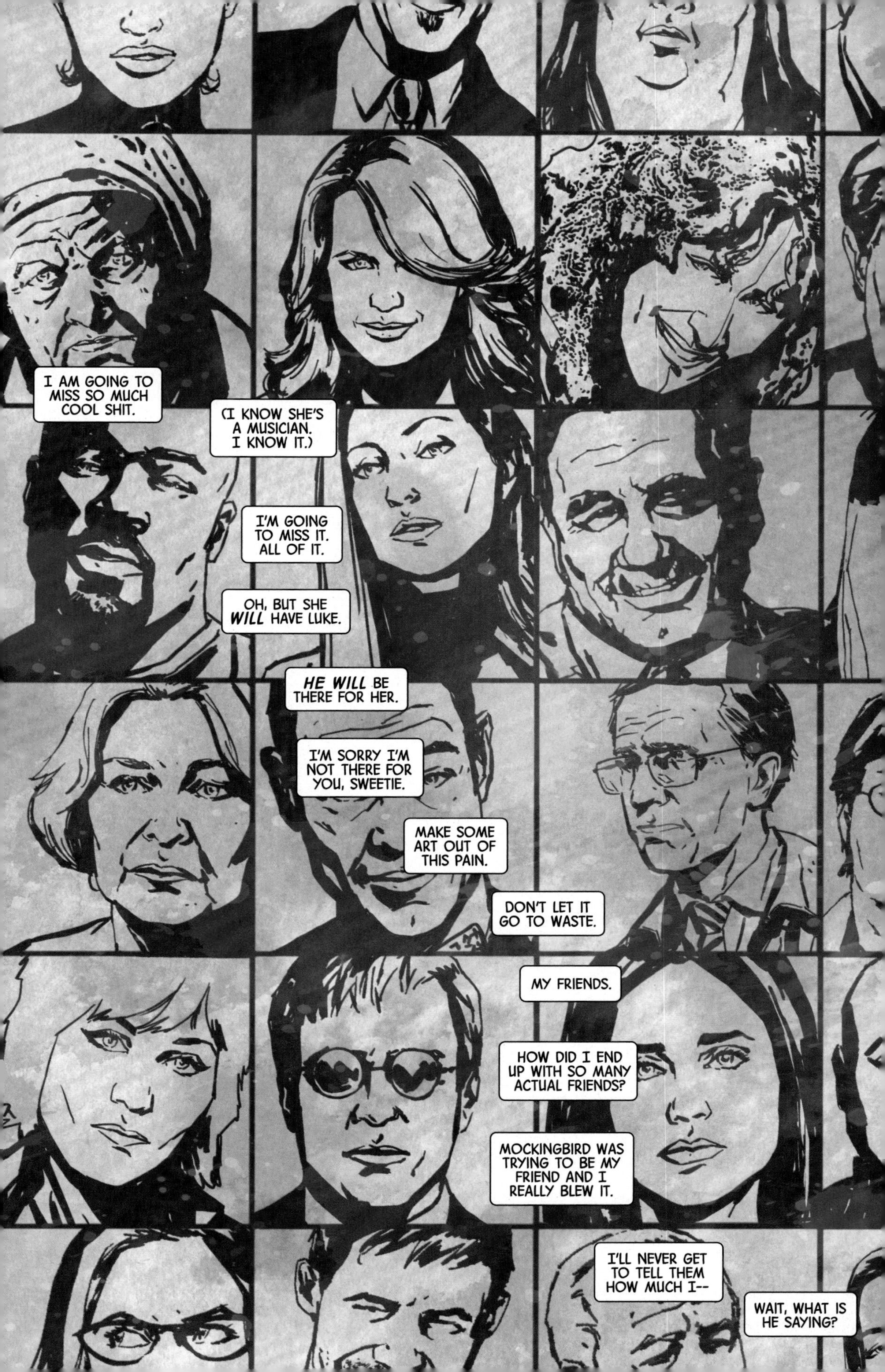
I AM GOING TO MISS SO MUCH COOL SHIT.
(I KNOW SHE'S A MUSICIAN. I KNOW IT.)
I'M GOING TO MISS IT. ALL OF IT.
OH, BUT SHE *WILL* HAVE LUKE.
HE WILL BE THERE FOR HER.
I'M SORRY I'M NOT THERE FOR YOU, SWEETIE.
MAKE SOME ART OUT OF THIS PAIN.
DON'T LET IT GO TO WASTE.
MY FRIENDS.
HOW DID I END UP WITH SO MANY ACTUAL FRIENDS?
MOCKINGBIRD WAS TRYING TO BE MY FRIEND AND I REALLY BLEW IT.
I'LL NEVER GET TO TELL THEM HOW MUCH I--
WAIT, WHAT IS HE SAYING?

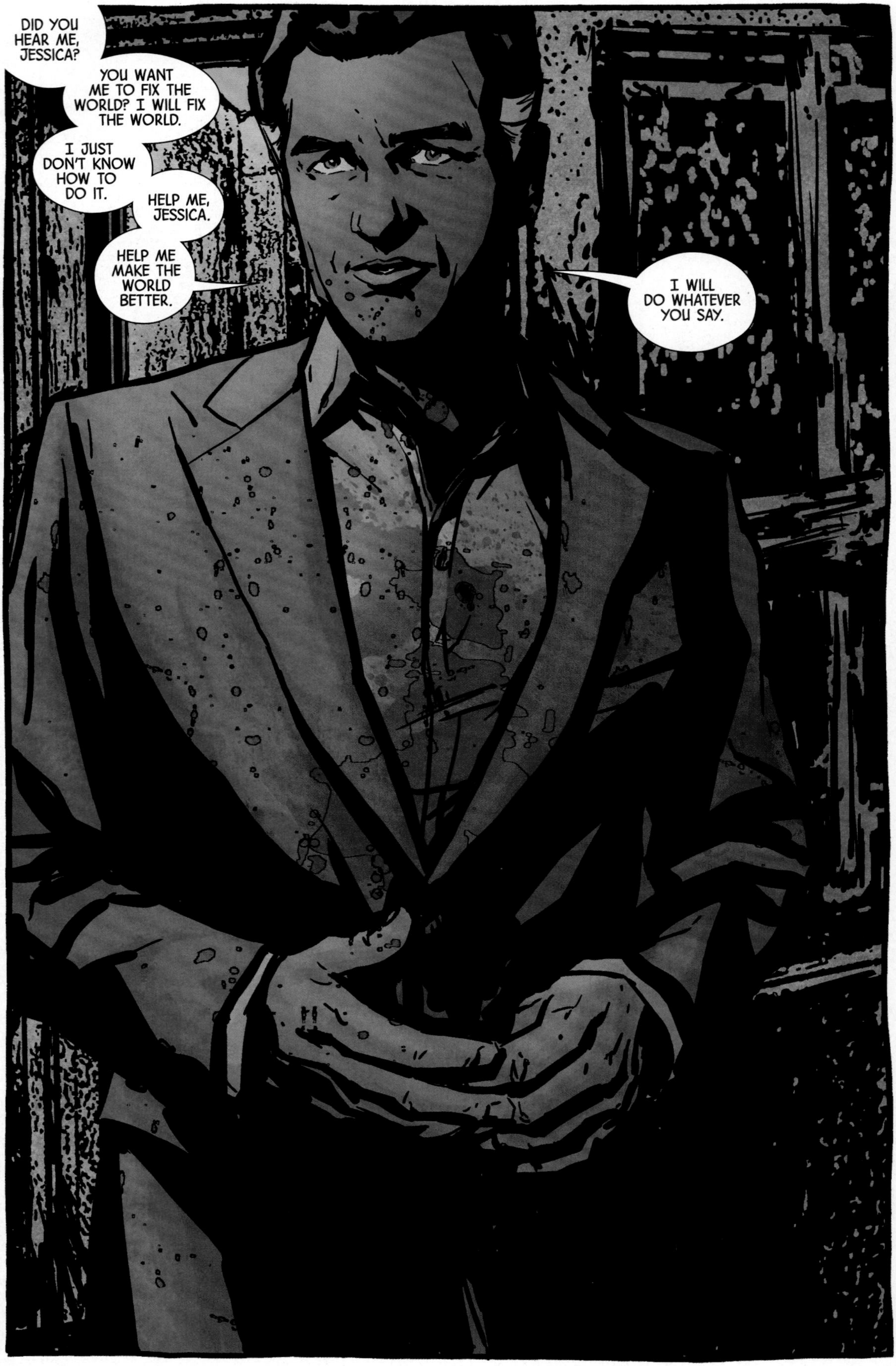
DID YOU HEAR ME, JESSICA?
YOU WANT ME TO FIX THE WORLD? I WILL FIX THE WORLD.
I JUST DON'T KNOW HOW TO DO IT.
HELP ME, JESSICA.
HELP ME MAKE THE WORLD BETTER.
I WILL DO WHATEVER YOU SAY.

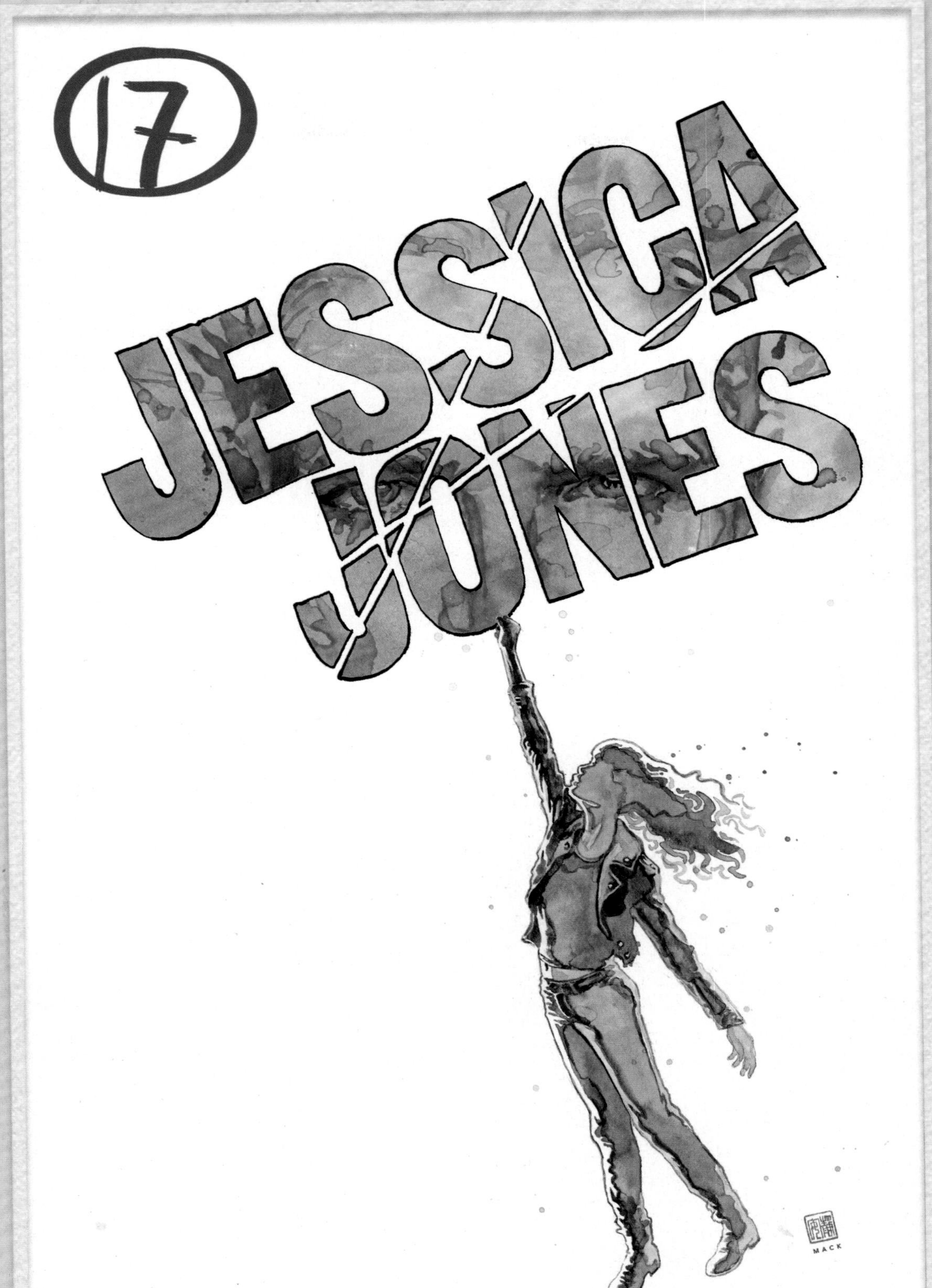
17
JESSICA
JONES
MACK

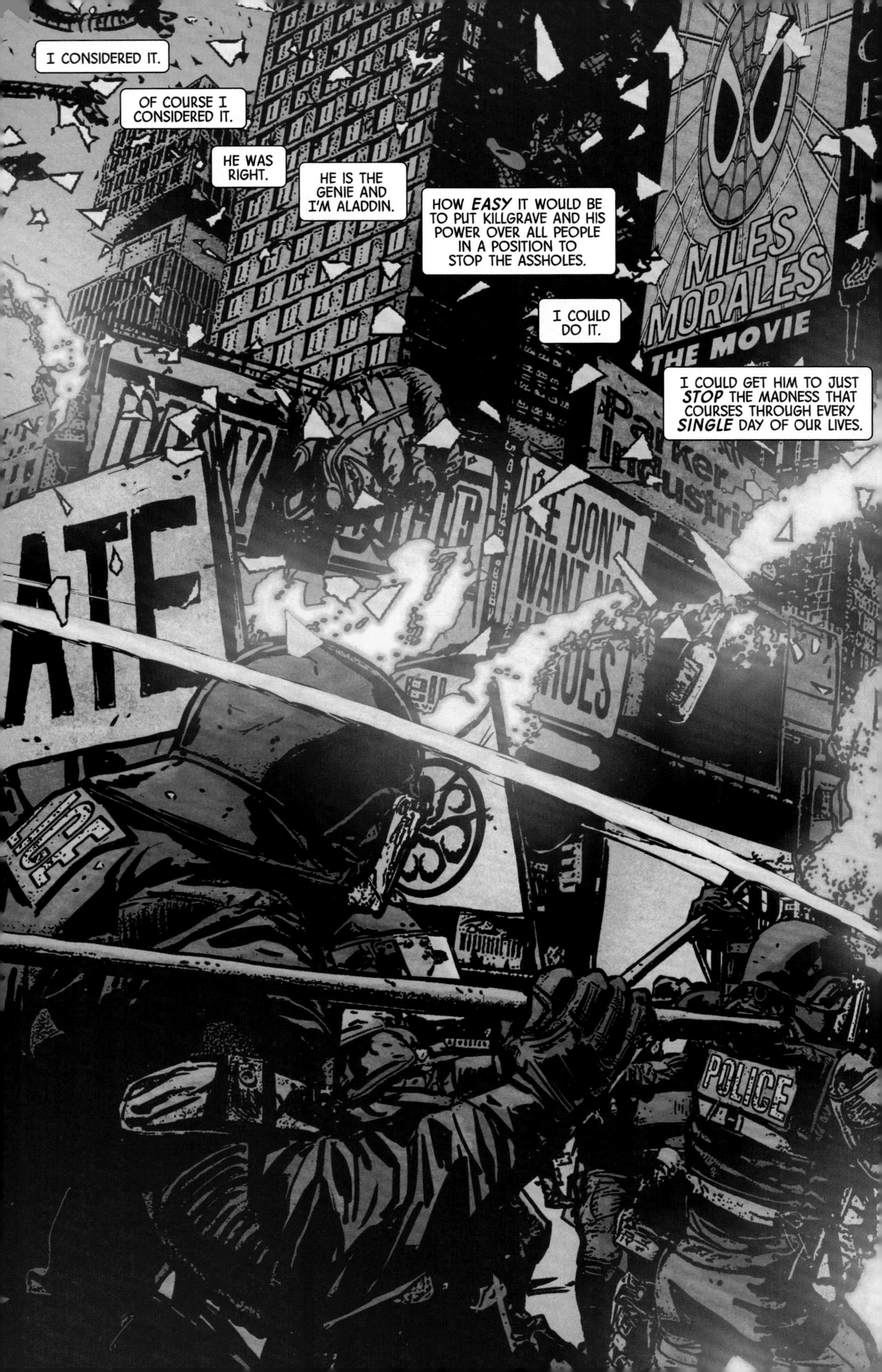
I CONSIDERED IT.
OF COURSE I CONSIDERED IT.
HE WAS RIGHT.
HE IS THE GENIE AND I'M ALADDIN.
HOW *EASY* IT WOULD BE TO PUT KILLGRAVE AND HIS POWER OVER ALL PEOPLE IN A POSITION TO STOP THE ASSHOLES.
I COULD DO IT.
I COULD GET HIM TO JUST *STOP* THE MADNESS THAT COURSES THROUGH EVERY *SINGLE* DAY OF OUR LIVES.
MILES MORALES
THE MOVIE
POLICE

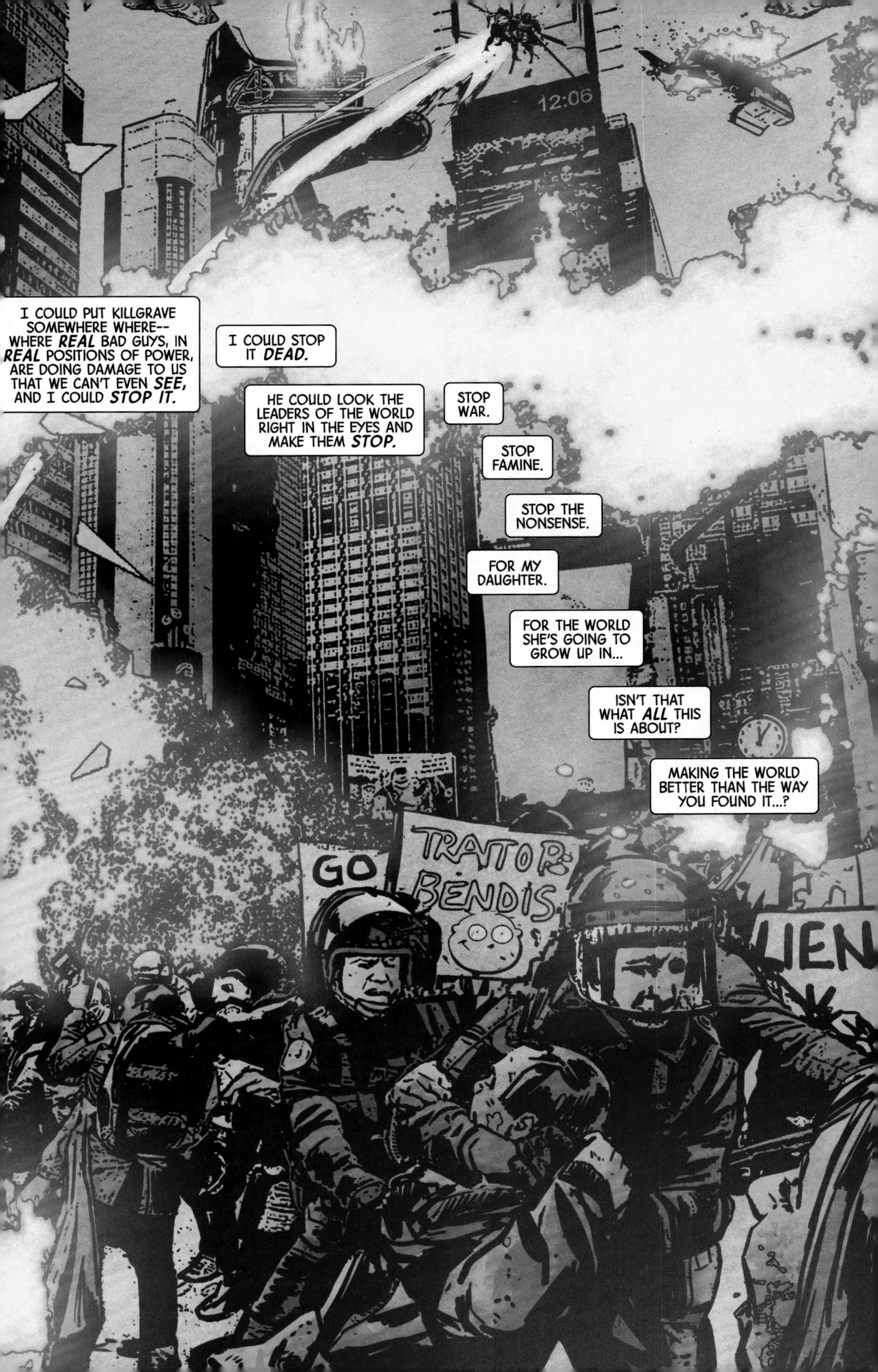

12:06
I COULD PUT KILLGRAVE SOMEWHERE WHERE-- WHERE REAL BAD GUYS, IN REAL POSITIONS OF POWER, ARE DOING DAMAGE TO US THAT WE CAN'T EVEN SEE, AND I COULD STOP IT.
I COULD STOP IT DEAD.
HE COULD LOOK THE LEADERS OF THE WORLD RIGHT IN THE EYES AND MAKE THEM STOP.
STOP WAR.
STOP FAMINE.
STOP THE NONSENSE.
FOR MY DAUGHTER.
FOR THE WORLD SHE'S GOING TO GROW UP IN...
ISN'T THAT WHAT ALL THIS IS ABOUT?
MAKING THE WORLD BETTER THAN THE WAY YOU FOUND IT...?
GO
TRAITOR: BENDIS
LIEN

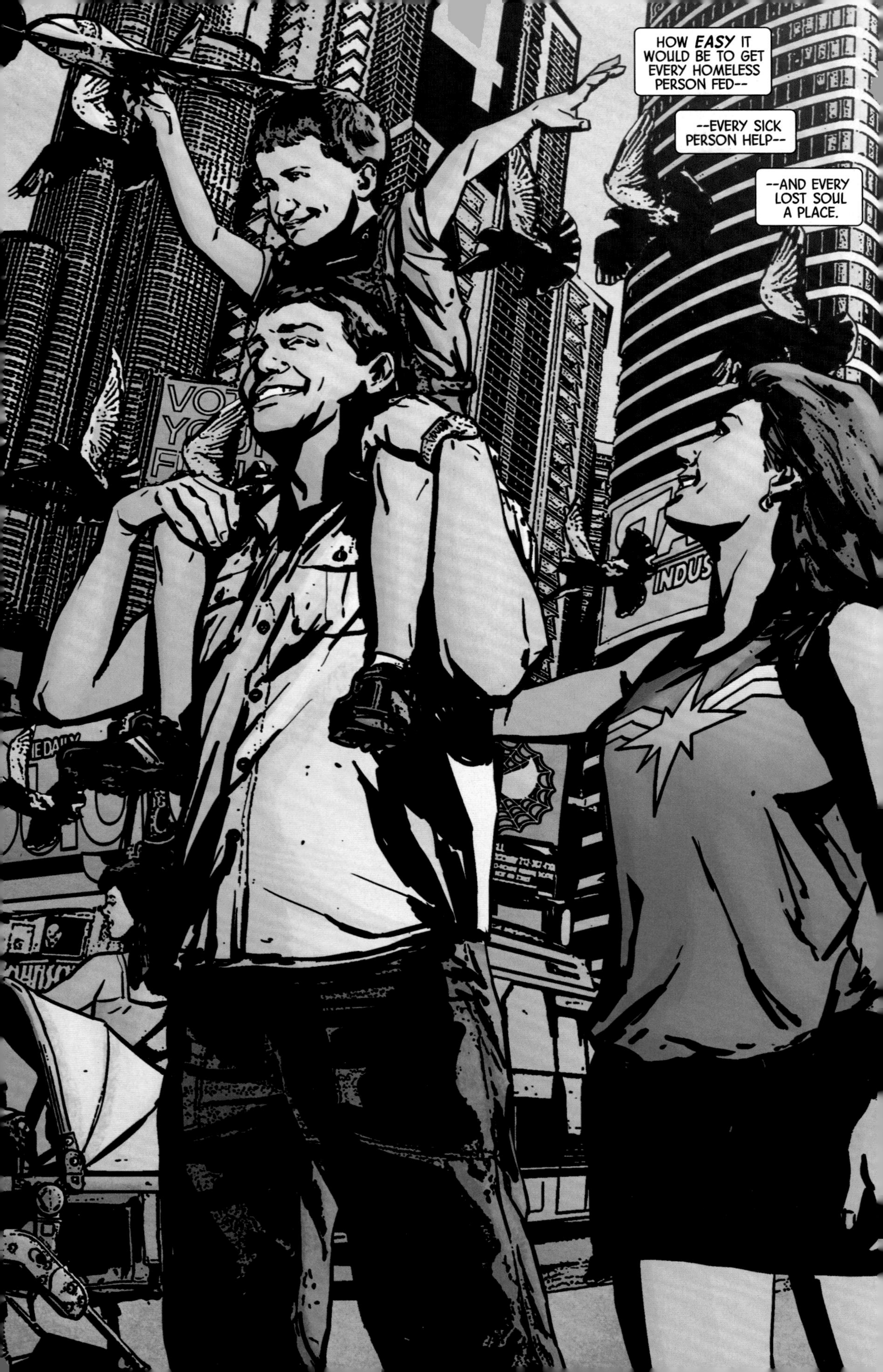
HOW EASY IT WOULD BE TO GET EVERY HOMELESS PERSON FED--
--EVERY SICK PERSON HELP--
--AND EVERY LOST SOUL A PLACE.

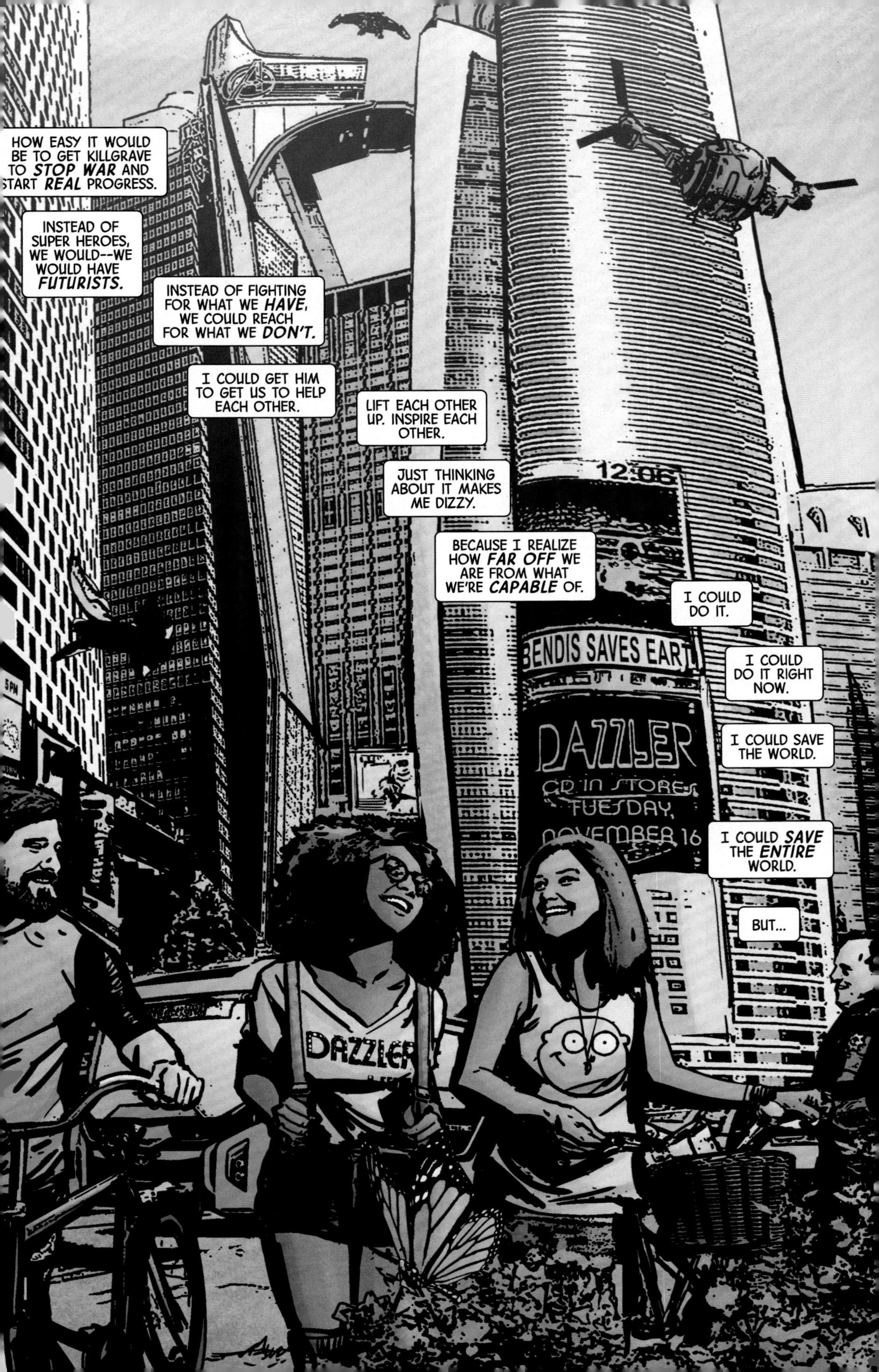

HOW EASY IT WOULD BE TO GET KILLGRAVE TO *STOP WAR* AND START *REAL* PROGRESS.
INSTEAD OF SUPER HEROES, WE WOULD--WE WOULD HAVE *FUTURISTS.*
INSTEAD OF FIGHTING FOR WHAT WE *HAVE*, WE COULD REACH FOR WHAT WE *DON'T.*
I COULD GET HIM TO GET US TO HELP EACH OTHER.
LIFT EACH OTHER UP. INSPIRE EACH OTHER.
JUST THINKING ABOUT IT MAKES ME DIZZY.
BECAUSE I REALIZE HOW *FAR OFF* WE ARE FROM WHAT WE'RE *CAPABLE* OF.
12:06
BENDIS SAVES EART
DAZZLER
CD IN STORES TUESDAY, NOVEMBER 16
I COULD DO IT.
I COULD DO IT RIGHT NOW.
I COULD SAVE THE WORLD.
I COULD *SAVE* THE *ENTIRE* WORLD.
BUT...
DAZZLER

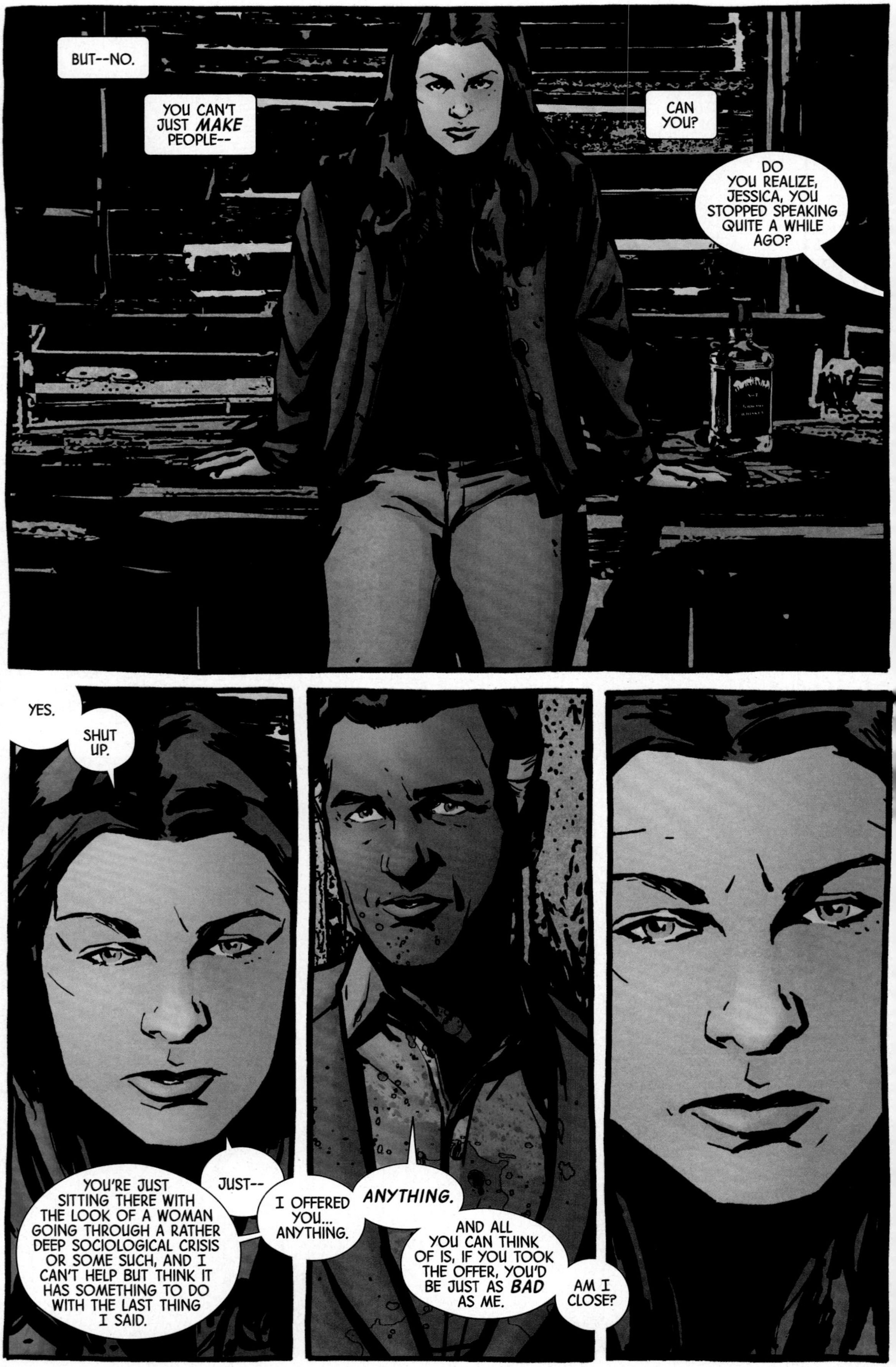
BUT--NO.
YOU CAN'T JUST *MAKE* PEOPLE--
CAN YOU?
DO YOU REALIZE, JESSICA, YOU STOPPED SPEAKING QUITE A WHILE AGO?
YES.
SHUT UP.
YOU'RE JUST SITTING THERE WITH THE LOOK OF A WOMAN GOING THROUGH A RATHER DEEP SOCIOLOGICAL CRISIS OR SOME SUCH, AND I CAN'T HELP BUT THINK IT HAS SOMETHING TO DO WITH THE LAST THING I SAID.
JUST--
I OFFERED YOU... ANYTHING.
ANYTHING.
AND ALL YOU CAN THINK OF IS, IF YOU TOOK THE OFFER, YOU'D BE JUST AS *BAD* AS ME.
AM I CLOSE?

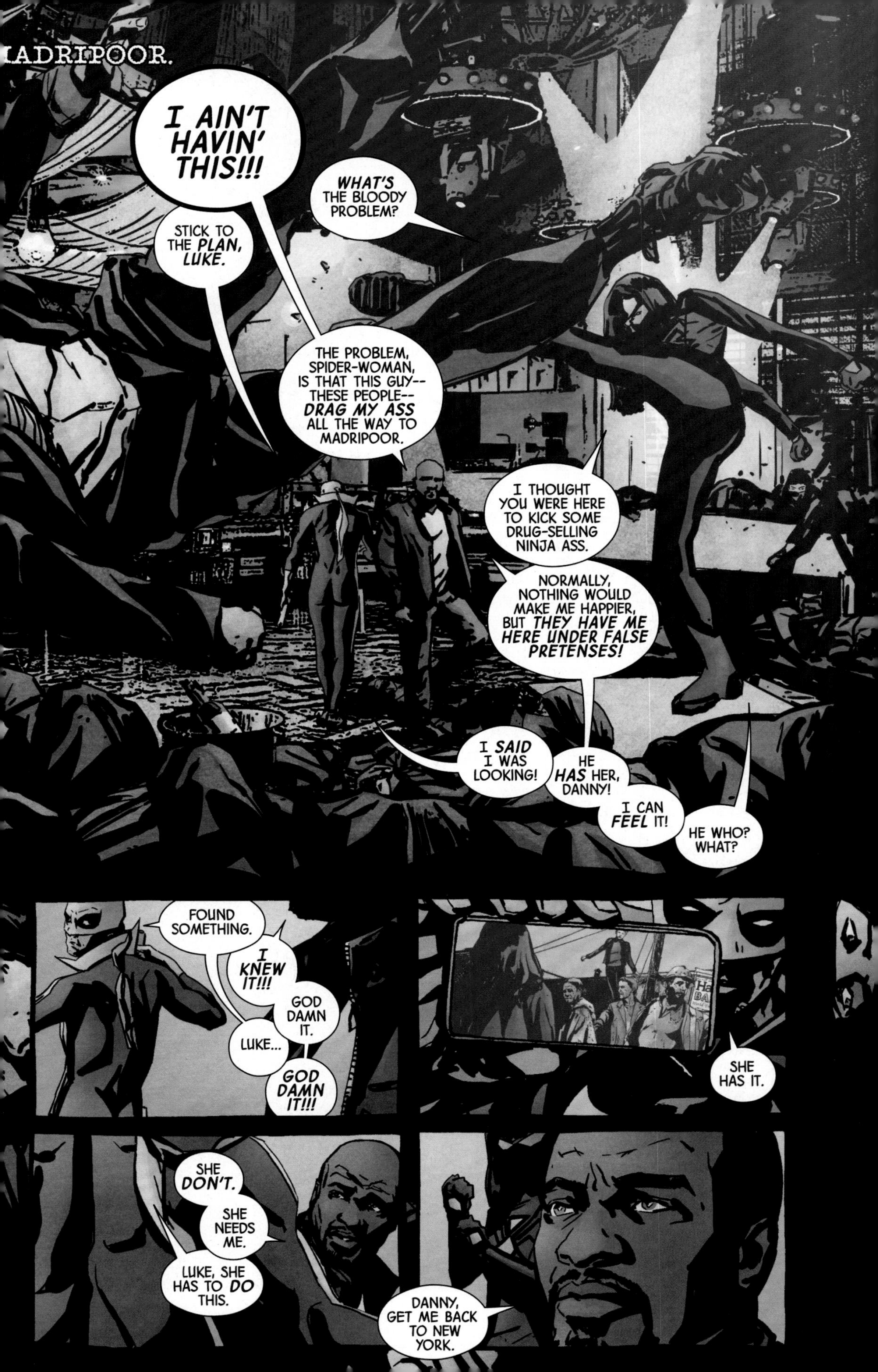
MADRIPOOR.
I AIN'T HAVIN' THIS!!!
STICK TO THE PLAN, LUKE.
WHAT'S THE BLOODY PROBLEM?
THE PROBLEM, SPIDER-WOMAN, IS THAT THIS GUY-- THESE PEOPLE-- DRAG MY ASS ALL THE WAY TO MADRIPOOR.
I THOUGHT YOU WERE HERE TO KICK SOME DRUG-SELLING NINJA ASS.
NORMALLY, NOTHING WOULD MAKE ME HAPPIER, BUT THEY HAVE ME HERE UNDER FALSE PRETENSES!
I SAID I WAS LOOKING!
HE HAS HER, DANNY!
I CAN FEEL IT!
HE WHO? WHAT?
FOUND SOMETHING.
I KNEW IT!!!
GOD DAMN IT.
LUKE...
GOD DAMN IT!!!
SHE HAS IT.
SHE DON'T.
SHE NEEDS ME.
LUKE, SHE HAS TO DO THIS.
DANNY, GET ME BACK TO NEW YORK.

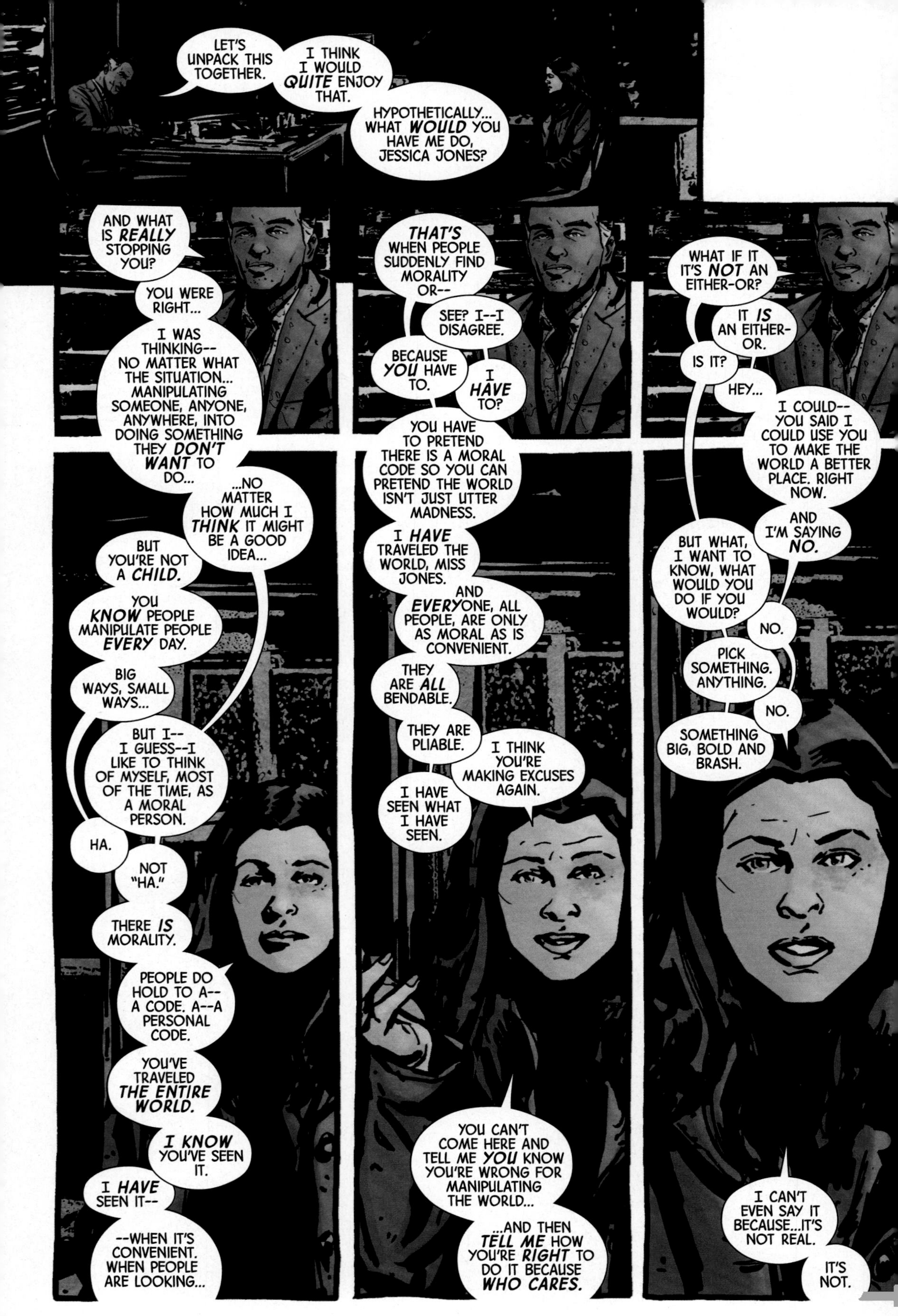
LET'S UNPACK THIS TOGETHER.
I THINK I WOULD QUITE ENJOY THAT.
HYPOTHETICALLY... WHAT WOULD YOU HAVE ME DO, JESSICA JONES?
AND WHAT IS REALLY STOPPING YOU?
YOU WERE RIGHT...
I WAS THINKING-- NO MATTER WHAT THE SITUATION... MANIPULATING SOMEONE, ANYONE, ANYWHERE, INTO DOING SOMETHING THEY DON'T WANT TO DO...
...NO MATTER HOW MUCH I THINK IT MIGHT BE A GOOD IDEA...
BUT YOU'RE NOT A CHILD.
YOU KNOW PEOPLE MANIPULATE PEOPLE EVERY DAY.
BIG WAYS, SMALL WAYS...
BUT I-- I GUESS--I LIKE TO THINK OF MYSELF, MOST OF THE TIME, AS A MORAL PERSON.
HA.
NOT "HA."
THERE IS MORALITY.
PEOPLE DO HOLD TO A-- A CODE. A--A PERSONAL CODE.
YOU'VE TRAVELED THE ENTIRE WORLD.
I KNOW YOU'VE SEEN IT.
I HAVE SEEN IT--
--WHEN IT'S CONVENIENT. WHEN PEOPLE ARE LOOKING...
THAT'S WHEN PEOPLE SUDDENLY FIND MORALITY OR--
SEE? I--I DISAGREE.
BECAUSE YOU HAVE TO.
I HAVE TO?
YOU HAVE TO PRETEND THERE IS A MORAL CODE SO YOU CAN PRETEND THE WORLD ISN'T JUST UTTER MADNESS.
I HAVE TRAVELED THE WORLD, MISS JONES.
AND EVERYONE, ALL PEOPLE, ARE ONLY AS MORAL AS IS CONVENIENT.
THEY ARE ALL BENDABLE.
THEY ARE PLIABLE.
I THINK YOU'RE MAKING EXCUSES AGAIN.
I HAVE SEEN WHAT I HAVE SEEN.
YOU CAN'T COME HERE AND TELL ME YOU KNOW YOU'RE WRONG FOR MANIPULATING THE WORLD...
...AND THEN TELL ME HOW YOU'RE RIGHT TO DO IT BECAUSE WHO CARES.
WHAT IF IT IT'S NOT AN EITHER-OR?
IT IS AN EITHER-OR.
IS IT?
HEY...
I COULD-- YOU SAID I COULD USE YOU TO MAKE THE WORLD A BETTER PLACE. RIGHT NOW.
AND I'M SAYING NO.
BUT WHAT, I WANT TO KNOW, WHAT WOULD YOU DO IF YOU WOULD?
NO.
PICK SOMETHING. ANYTHING.
NO.
SOMETHING BIG, BOLD AND BRASH.
I CAN'T EVEN SAY IT BECAUSE...IT'S NOT REAL.
IT'S NOT.

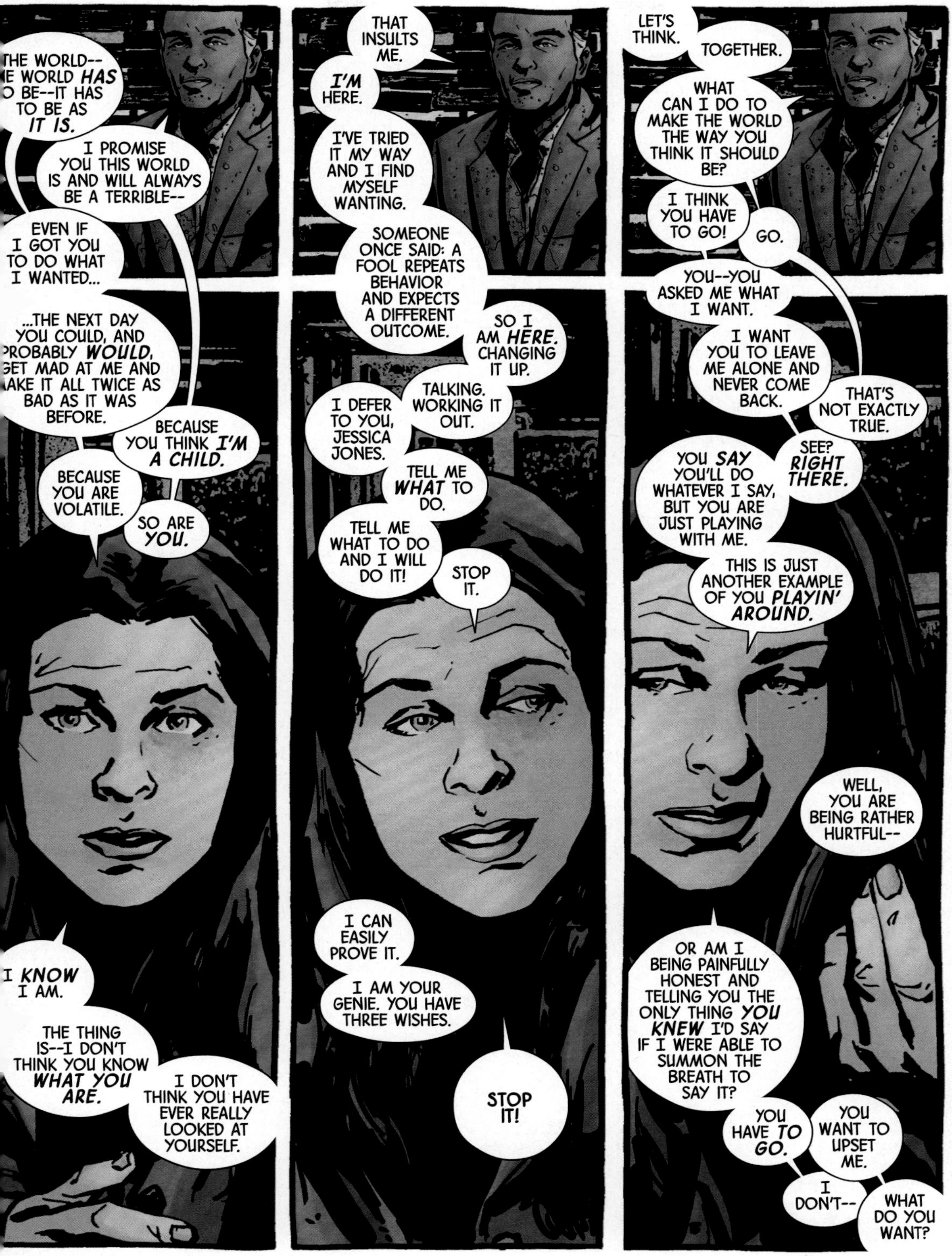

THE WORLD-- E WORLD HAS O BE--IT HAS TO BE AS IT IS.
I PROMISE YOU THIS WORLD IS AND WILL ALWAYS BE A TERRIBLE--
EVEN IF I GOT YOU TO DO WHAT I WANTED...
...THE NEXT DAY YOU COULD, AND PROBABLY WOULD, GET MAD AT ME AND AKE IT ALL TWICE AS BAD AS IT WAS BEFORE.
BECAUSE YOU THINK I'M A CHILD.
BECAUSE YOU ARE VOLATILE.
SO ARE YOU.
I KNOW I AM.
THE THING IS--I DON'T THINK YOU KNOW WHAT YOU ARE.
I DON'T THINK YOU HAVE EVER REALLY LOOKED AT YOURSELF.
THAT INSULTS ME.
I'M HERE.
I'VE TRIED IT MY WAY AND I FIND MYSELF WANTING.
SOMEONE ONCE SAID: A FOOL REPEATS BEHAVIOR AND EXPECTS A DIFFERENT OUTCOME.
SO I AM HERE. CHANGING IT UP.
TALKING. WORKING IT OUT.
I DEFER TO YOU, JESSICA JONES.
TELL ME WHAT TO DO.
TELL ME WHAT TO DO AND I WILL DO IT!
STOP IT.
I CAN EASILY PROVE IT.
I AM YOUR GENIE. YOU HAVE THREE WISHES.
STOP IT!
LET'S THINK.
TOGETHER.
WHAT CAN I DO TO MAKE THE WORLD THE WAY YOU THINK IT SHOULD BE?
I THINK YOU HAVE TO GO!
GO.
YOU--YOU ASKED ME WHAT I WANT.
I WANT YOU TO LEAVE ME ALONE AND NEVER COME BACK.
THAT'S NOT EXACTLY TRUE.
SEE? RIGHT THERE.
YOU SAY YOU'LL DO WHATEVER I SAY, BUT YOU ARE JUST PLAYING WITH ME.
THIS IS JUST ANOTHER EXAMPLE OF YOU PLAYIN' AROUND.
WELL, YOU ARE BEING RATHER HURTFUL--
OR AM I BEING PAINFULLY HONEST AND TELLING YOU THE ONLY THING YOU KNEW I'D SAY IF I WERE ABLE TO SUMMON THE BREATH TO SAY IT?
YOU HAVE TO GO.
YOU WANT TO UPSET ME.
I DON'T--
WHAT DO YOU WANT?

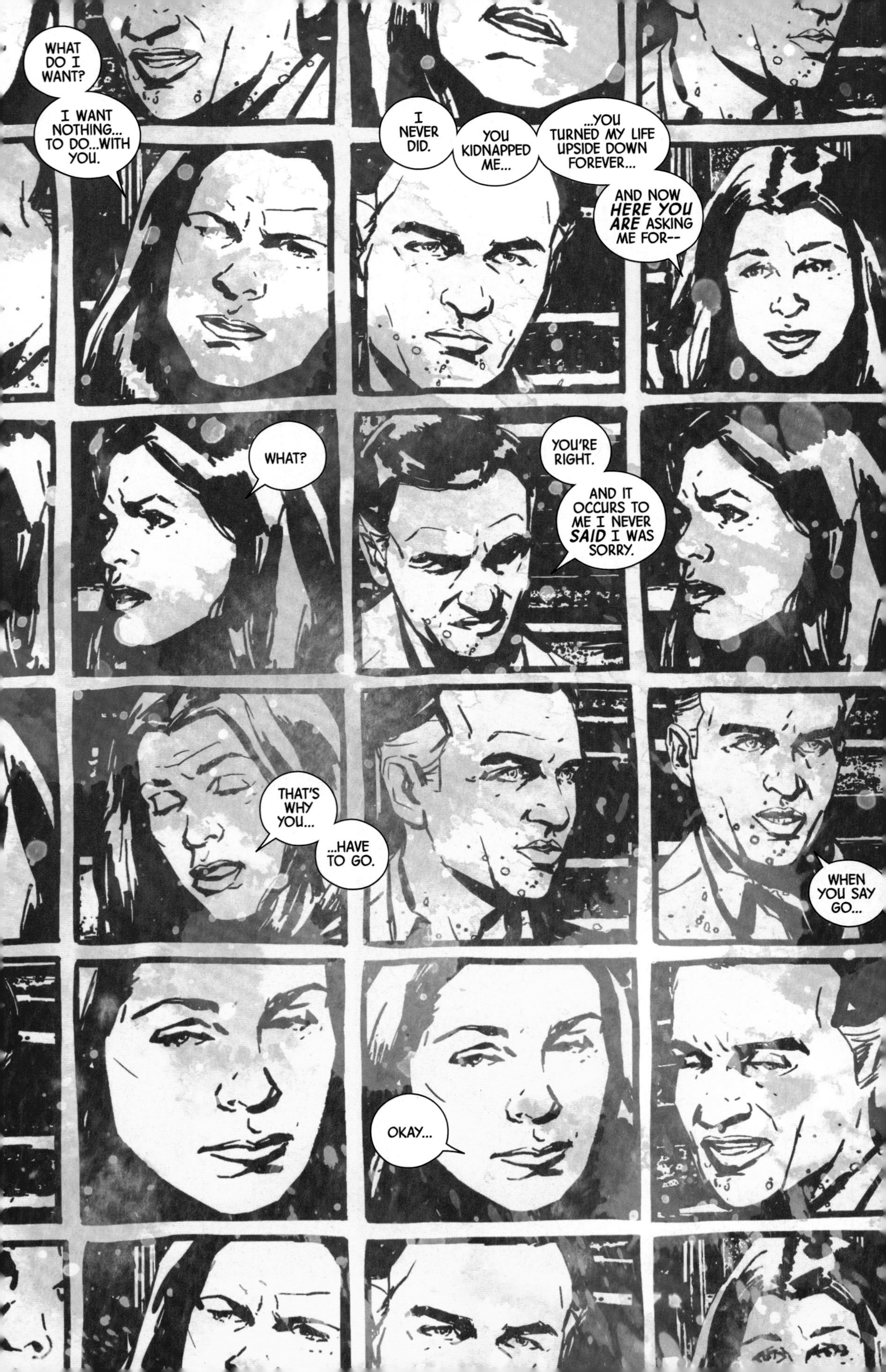
WHAT DO I WANT?
I WANT NOTHING... TO DO...WITH YOU.
I NEVER DID.
YOU KIDNAPPED ME...
...YOU TURNED MY LIFE UPSIDE DOWN FOREVER...
AND NOW HERE YOU ARE ASKING ME FOR--
WHAT?
YOU'RE RIGHT.
AND IT OCCURS TO ME I NEVER SAID I WAS SORRY.
THAT'S WHY YOU...
...HAVE TO GO.
WHEN YOU SAY GO...
OKAY...

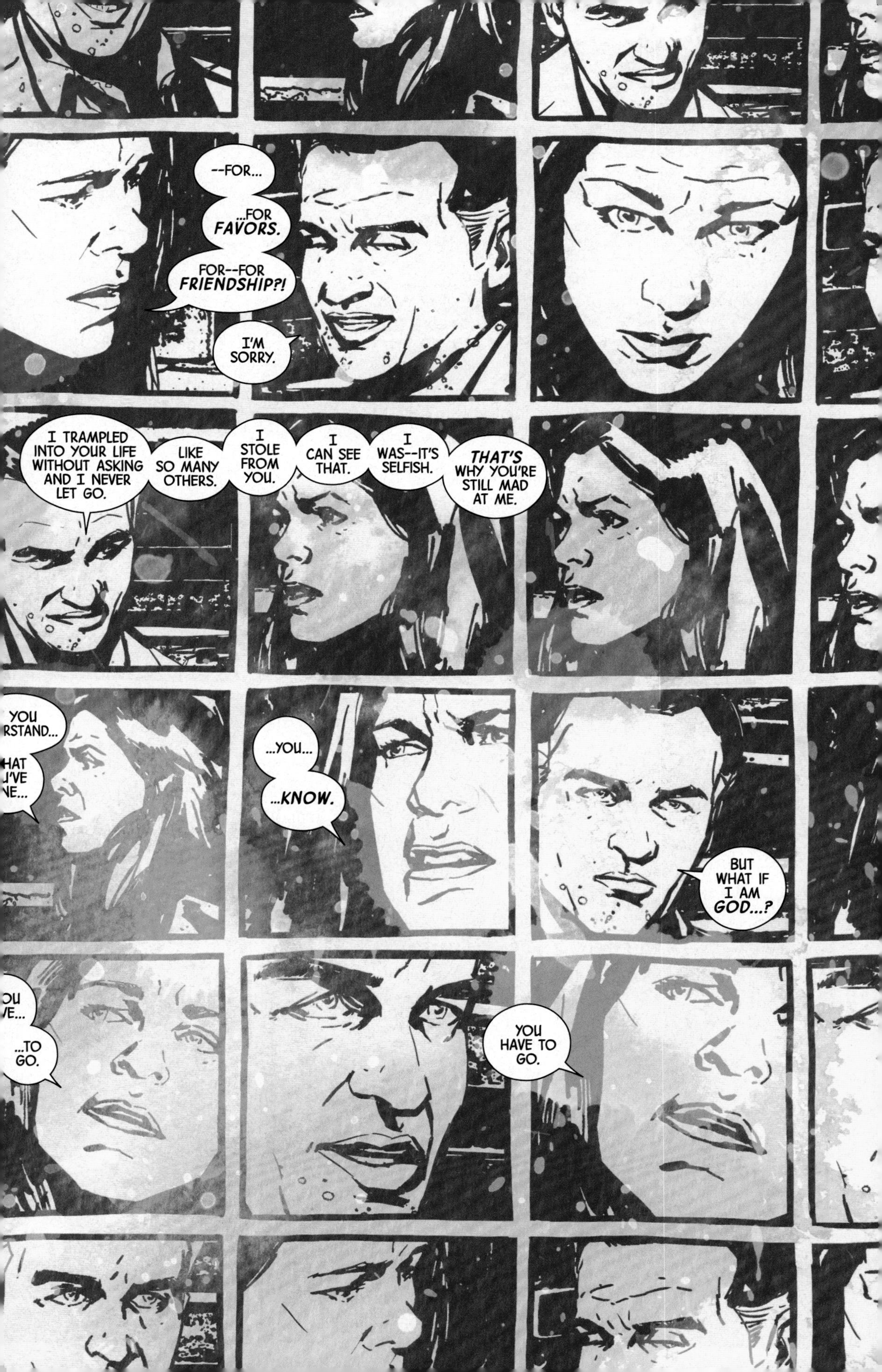
--FOR...
...FOR FAVORS.
FOR--FOR FRIENDSHIP?!
I'M SORRY.
I TRAMPLED INTO YOUR LIFE WITHOUT ASKING AND I NEVER LET GO.
LIKE SO MANY OTHERS.
I STOLE FROM YOU.
I CAN SEE THAT.
I WAS--IT'S SELFISH.
THAT'S WHY YOU'RE STILL MAD AT ME.
YOU RSTAND...
HAT U'VE NE...
...YOU...
...KNOW.
BUT WHAT IF I AM GOD...?
OU VE...
...TO GO.
YOU HAVE TO GO.

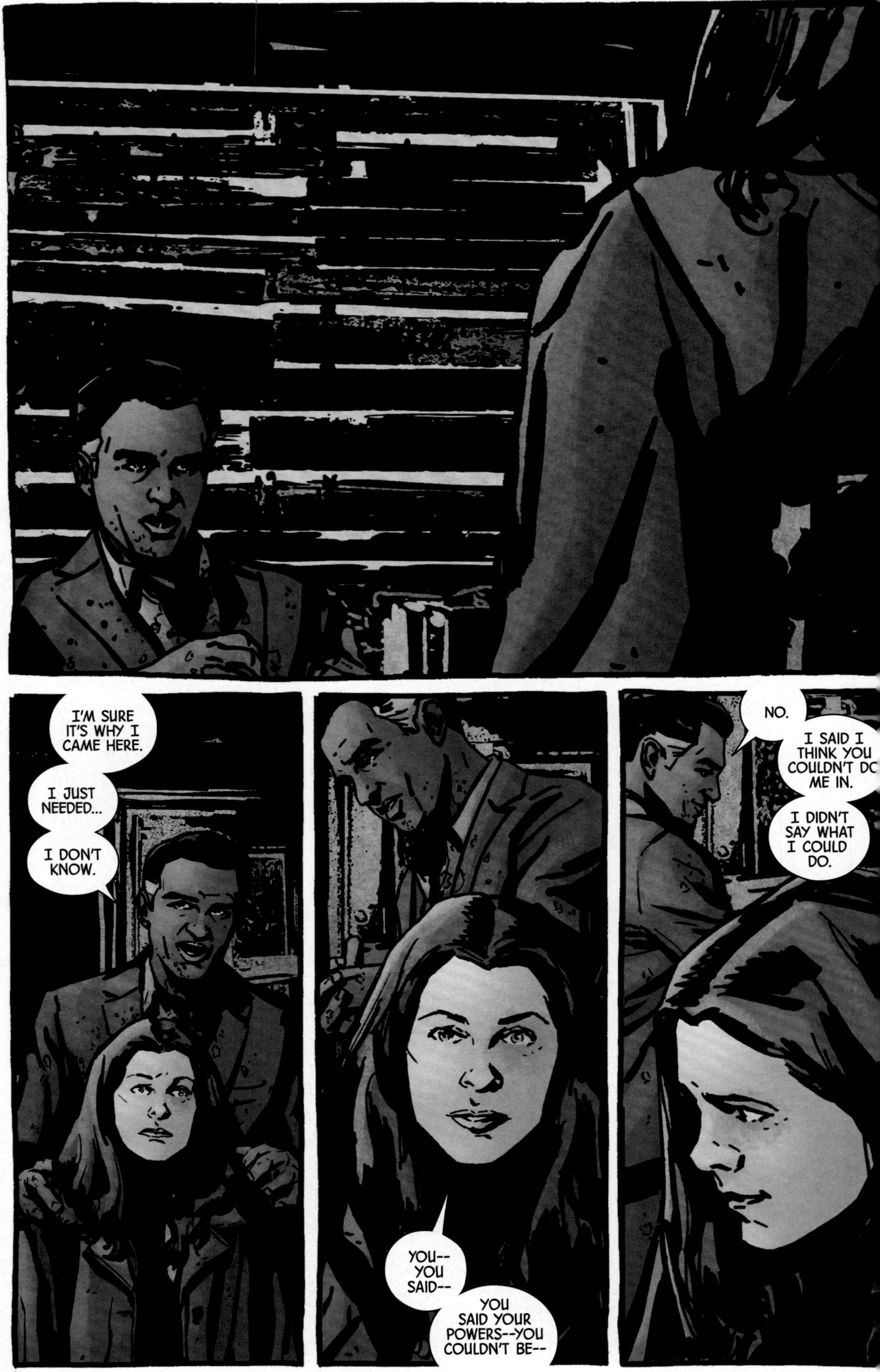
I'M SURE IT'S WHY I CAME HERE.
I JUST NEEDED...
I DON'T KNOW.
YOU-- YOU SAID--
YOU SAID YOUR POWERS--YOU COULDN'T BE--
NO.
I SAID I THINK YOU COULDN'T DO ME IN.
I DIDN'T SAY WHAT I COULD DO.

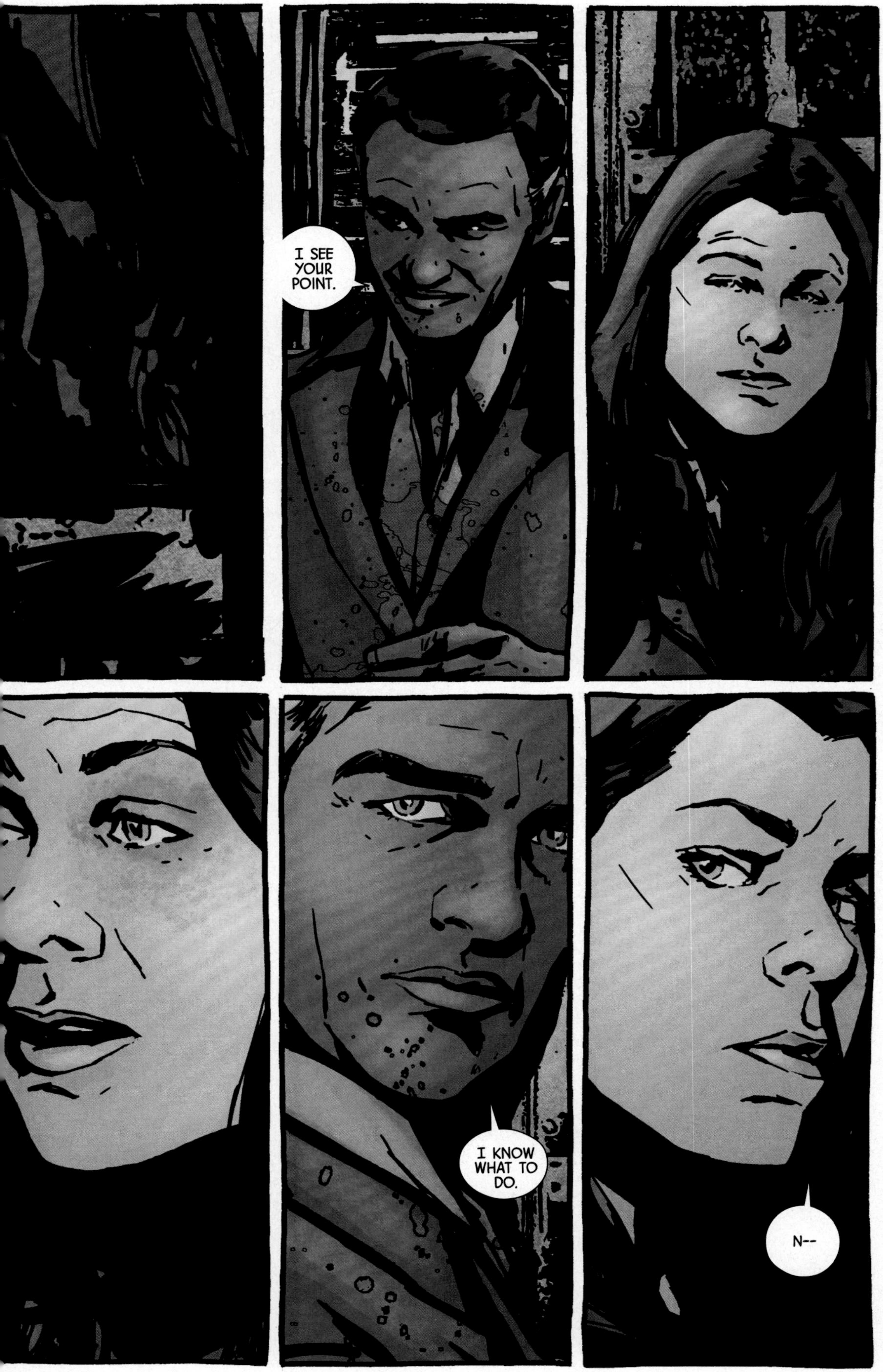
I SEE YOUR POINT.
I KNOW WHAT TO DO.
N--

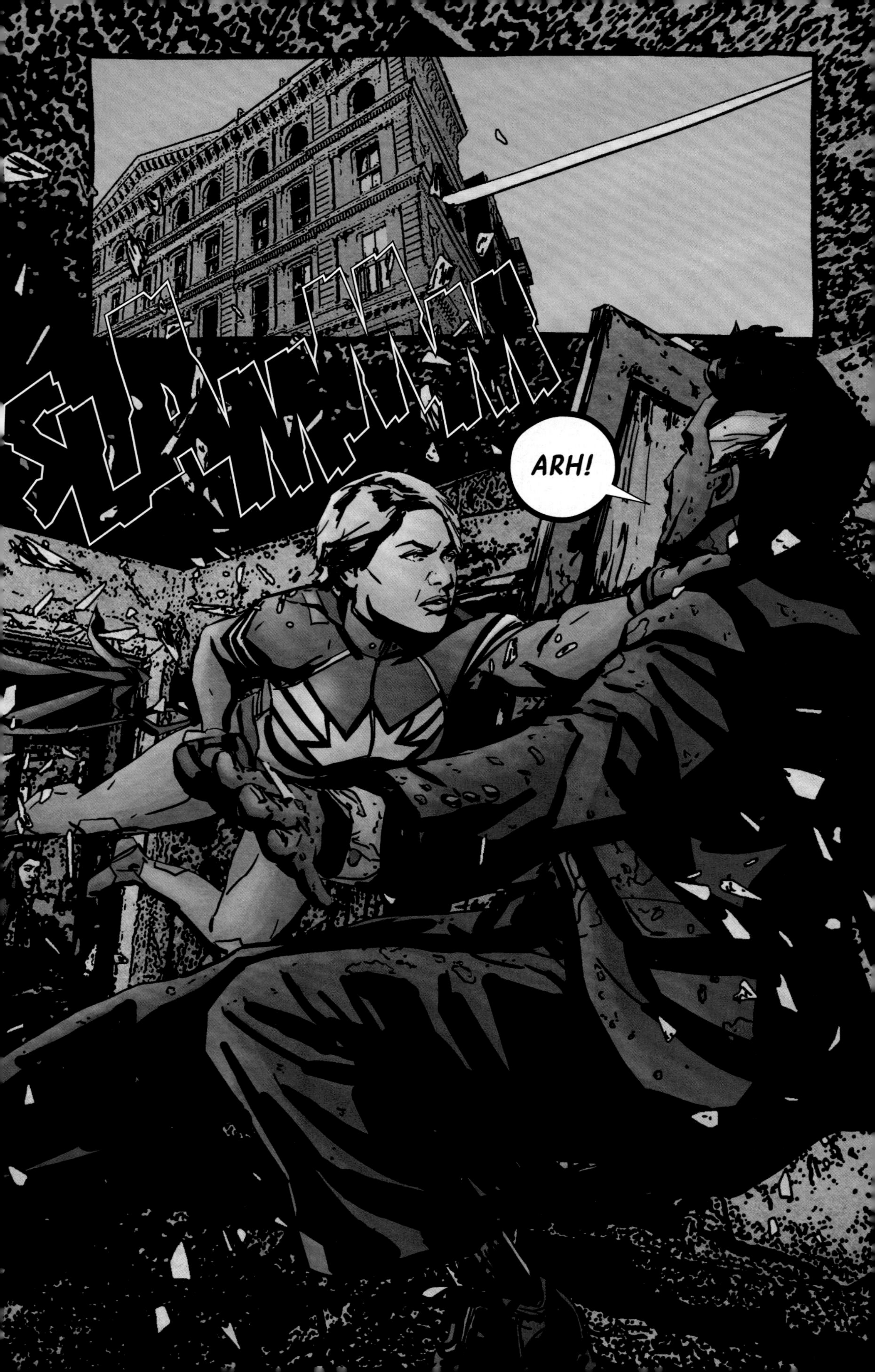
ARH!

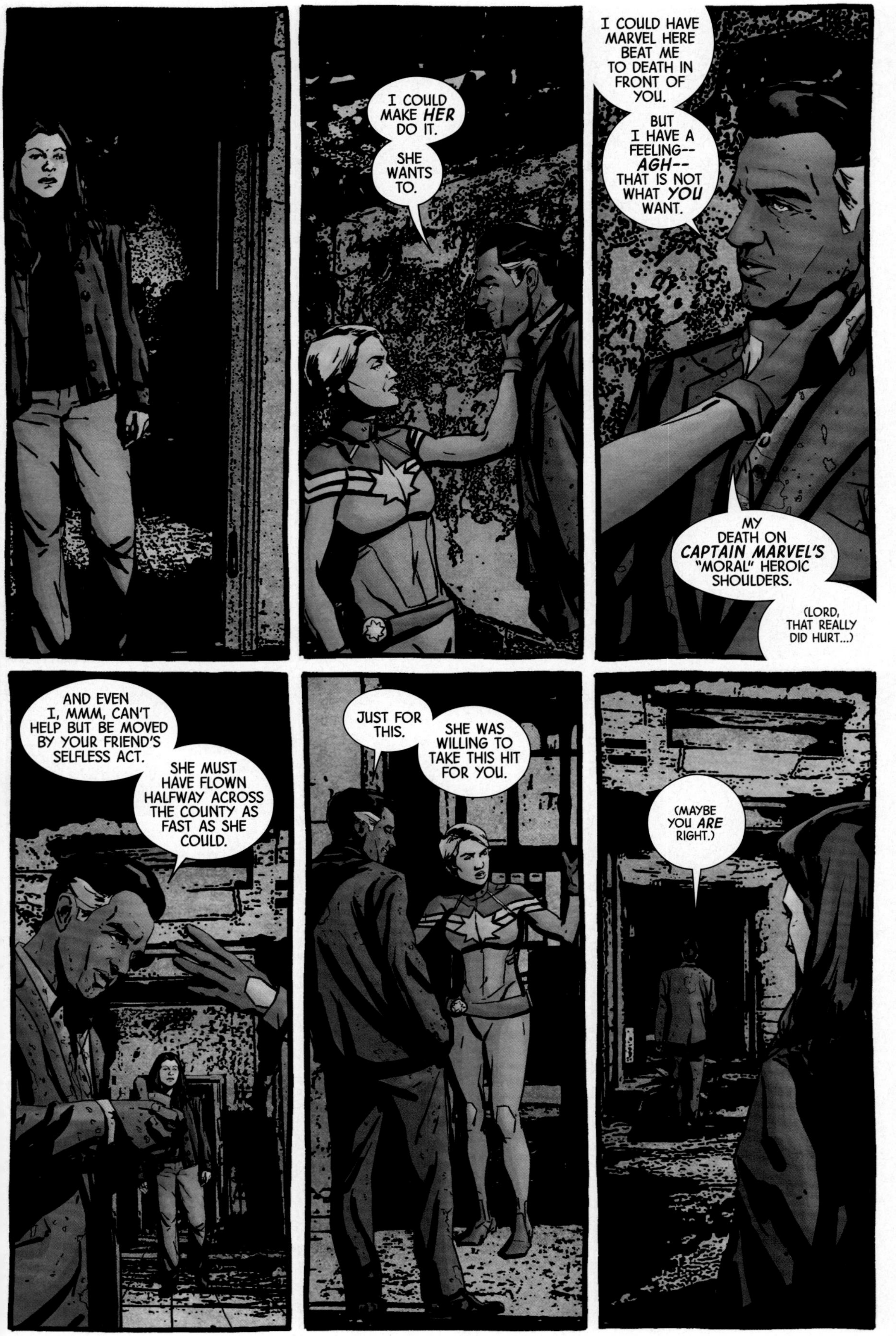
I COULD MAKE HER DO IT.
SHE WANTS TO.
I COULD HAVE MARVEL HERE BEAT ME TO DEATH IN FRONT OF YOU.
BUT I HAVE A FEELING-- AGH-- THAT IS NOT WHAT YOU WANT.
MY DEATH ON CAPTAIN MARVEL'S "MORAL" HEROIC SHOULDERS.
(LORD, THAT REALLY DID HURT...)
AND EVEN I, MMM, CAN'T HELP BUT BE MOVED BY YOUR FRIEND'S SELFLESS ACT.
SHE MUST HAVE FLOWN HALFWAY ACROSS THE COUNTY AS FAST AS SHE COULD.
JUST FOR THIS.
SHE WAS WILLING TO TAKE THIS HIT FOR YOU.
(MAYBE YOU ARE RIGHT.)

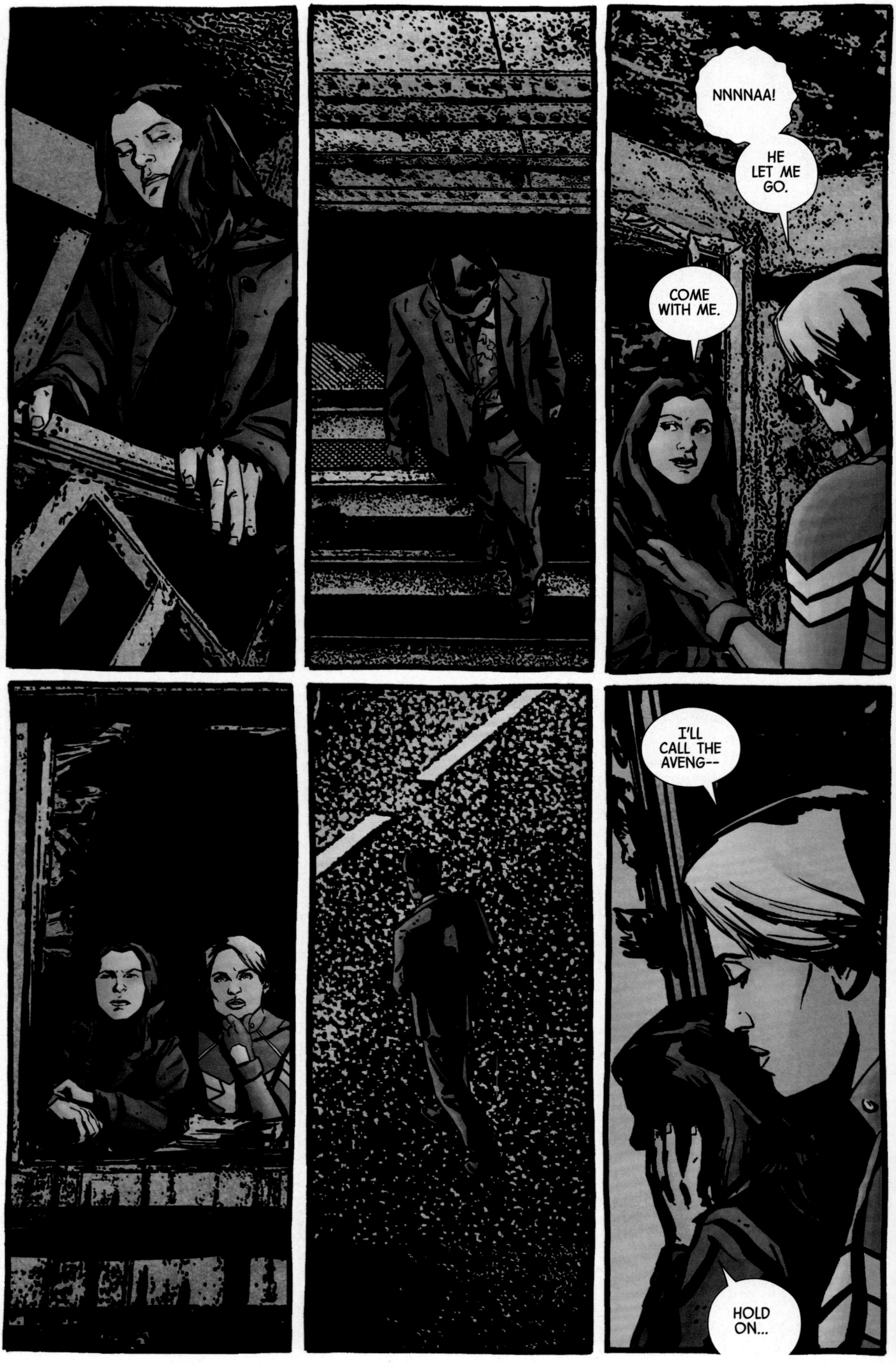
NNNNAA!
HE LET ME GO.
COME WITH ME.
I'LL CALL THE AVENG--
HOLD ON...

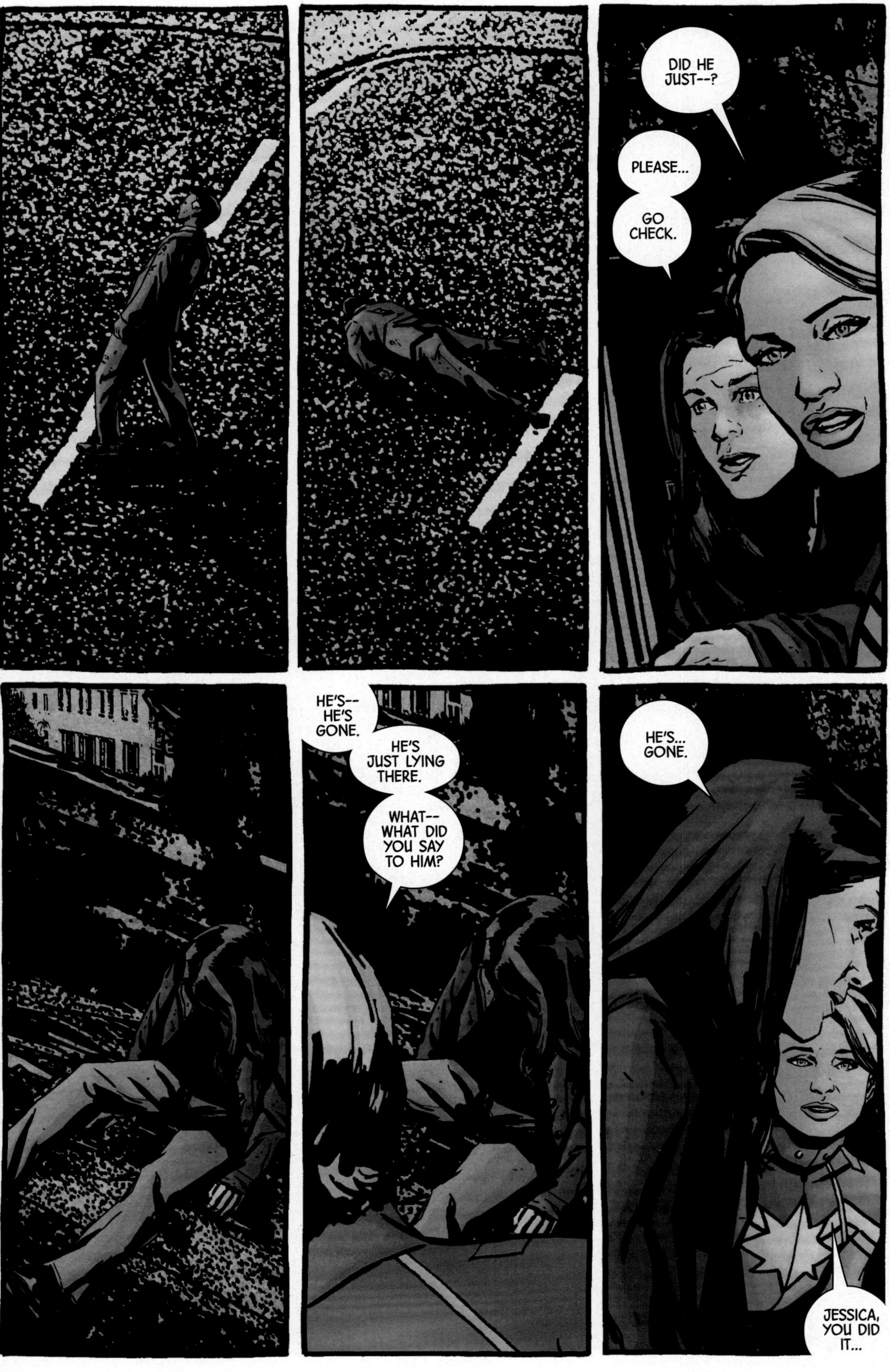
DID HE JUST--?
PLEASE...
GO CHECK.
HE'S-- HE'S GONE.
HE'S JUST LYING THERE.
WHAT-- WHAT DID YOU SAY TO HIM?
HE'S... GONE.
JESSICA, YOU DID IT...

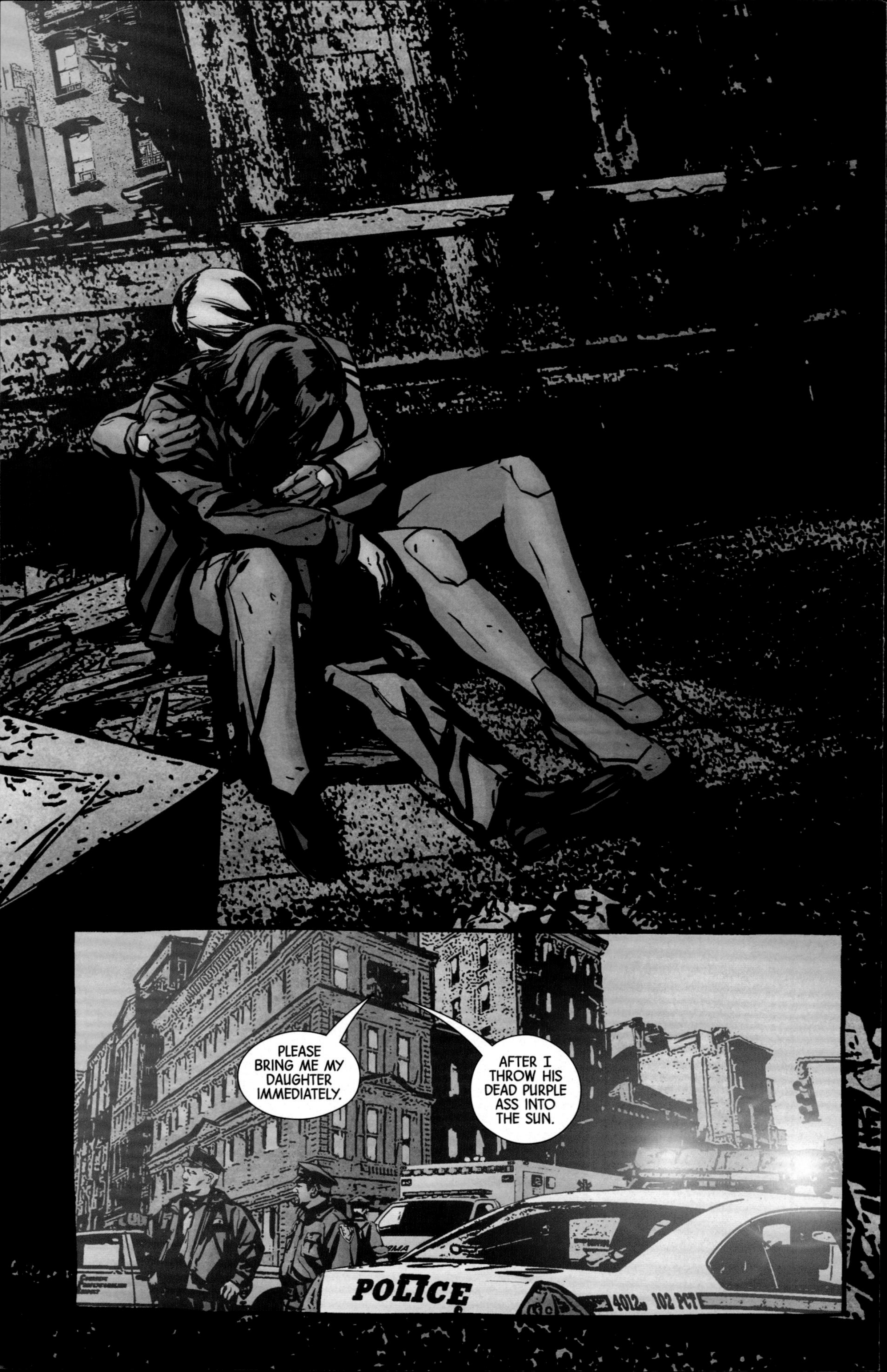
PLEASE BRING ME MY DAUGHTER IMMEDIATELY.
AFTER I THROW HIS DEAD PURPLE ASS INTO THE SUN.
POLICE
102 PCT

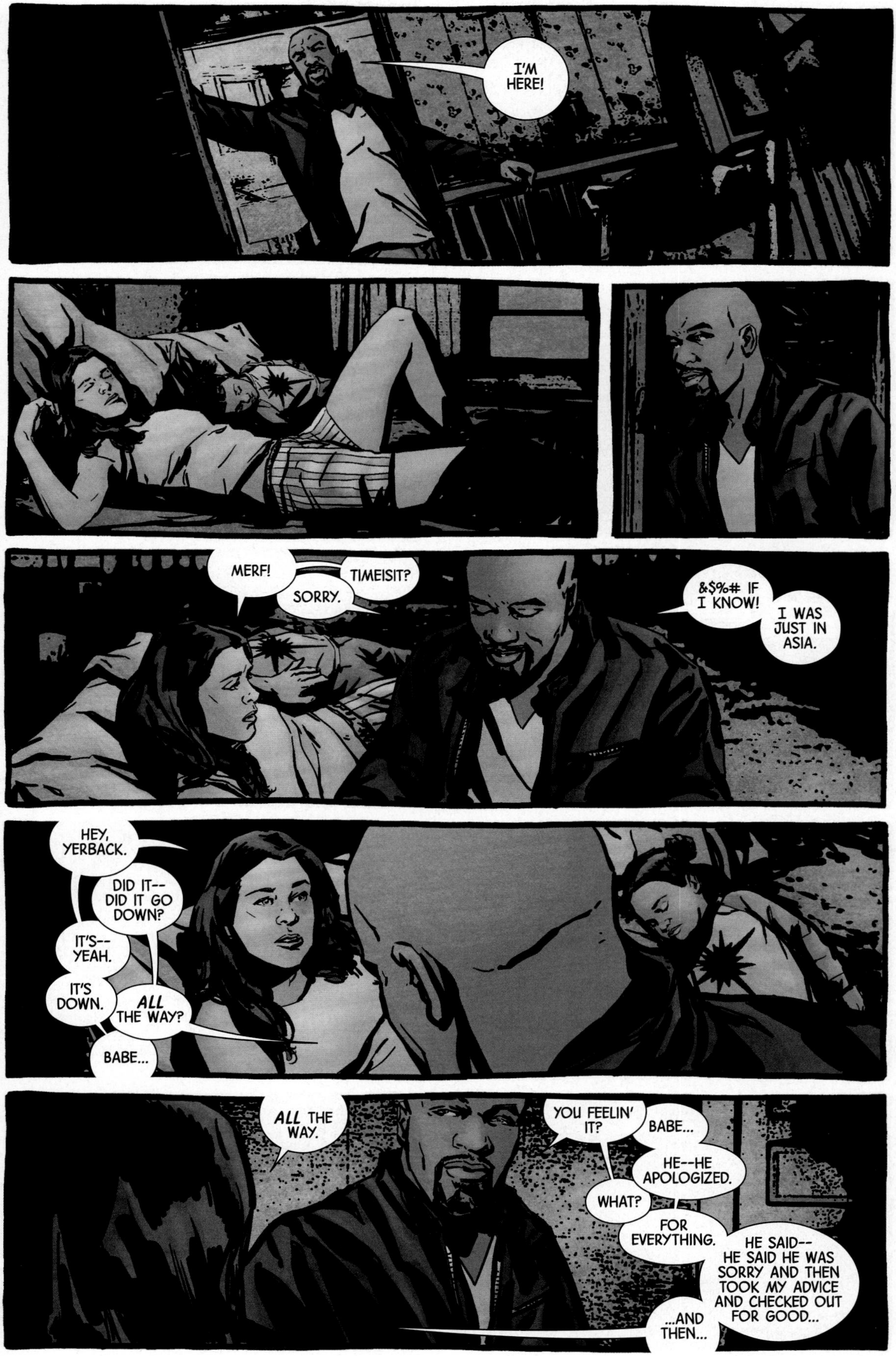

I'M HERE!
MERF!
TIMEISIT?
SORRY.
&$%# IF I KNOW!
I WAS JUST IN ASIA.
HEY, YERBACK.
DID IT-- DID IT GO DOWN?
IT'S-- YEAH.
IT'S DOWN.
ALL THE WAY?
BABE...
ALL THE WAY.
YOU FEELIN' IT?
BABE...
HE--HE APOLOGIZED.
WHAT?
FOR EVERYTHING.
HE SAID-- HE SAID HE WAS SORRY AND THEN TOOK MY ADVICE AND CHECKED OUT FOR GOOD...
...AND THEN...

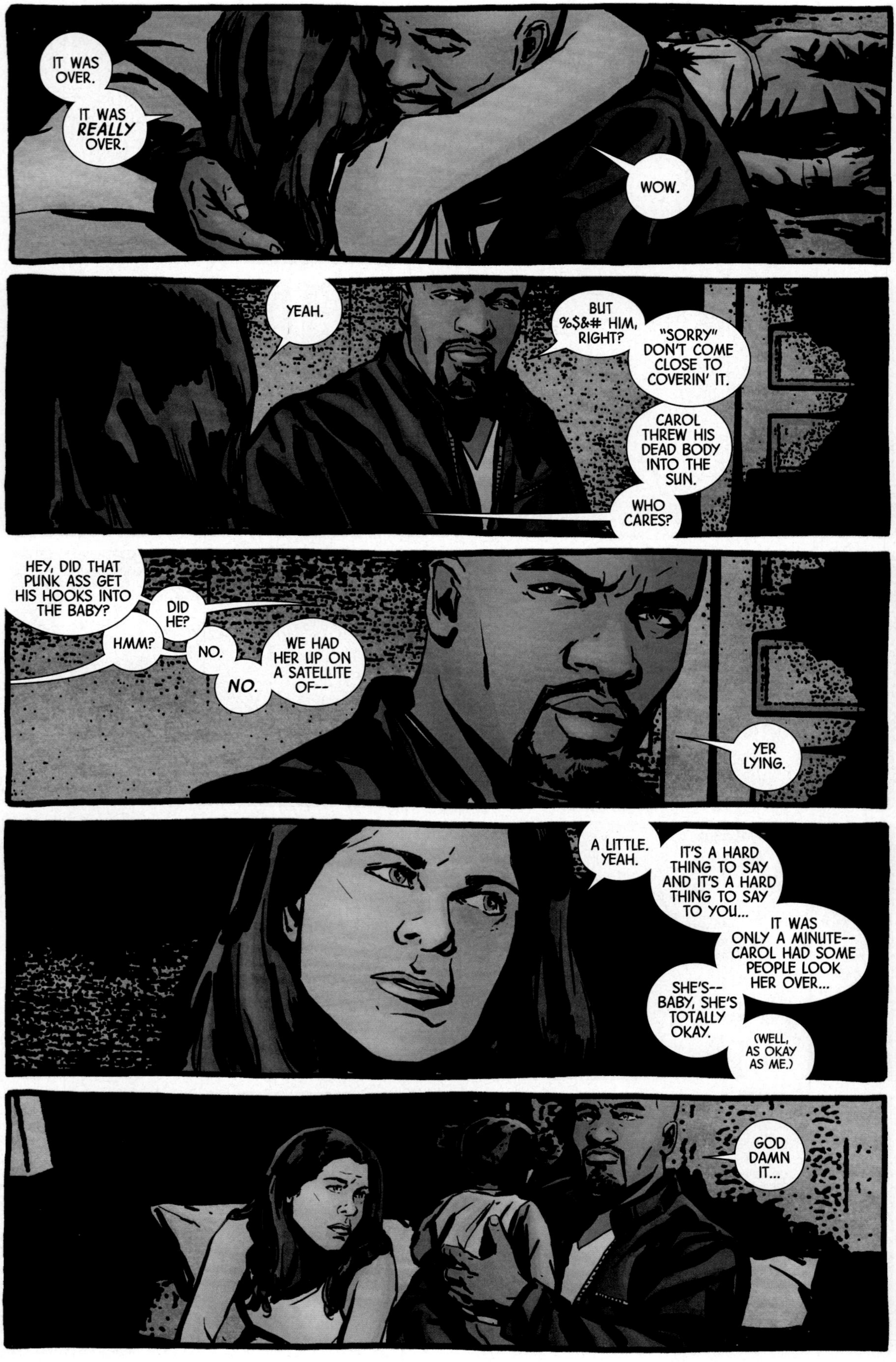
IT WAS OVER.
IT WAS *REALLY* OVER.
WOW.
YEAH.
BUT %$&# HIM, RIGHT?
"SORRY" DON'T COME CLOSE TO COVERIN' IT.
CAROL THREW HIS DEAD BODY INTO THE SUN.
WHO CARES?
HEY, DID THAT PUNK ASS GET HIS HOOKS INTO THE BABY?
DID HE?
HMM?
NO.
NO.
WE HAD HER UP ON A SATELLITE OF--
YER LYING.
A LITTLE. YEAH.
IT'S A HARD THING TO SAY AND IT'S A HARD THING TO SAY TO YOU...
IT WAS ONLY A MINUTE-- CAROL HAD SOME PEOPLE LOOK HER OVER...
SHE'S-- BABY, SHE'S TOTALLY OKAY.
(WELL, AS OKAY AS ME.)
GOD DAMN IT...

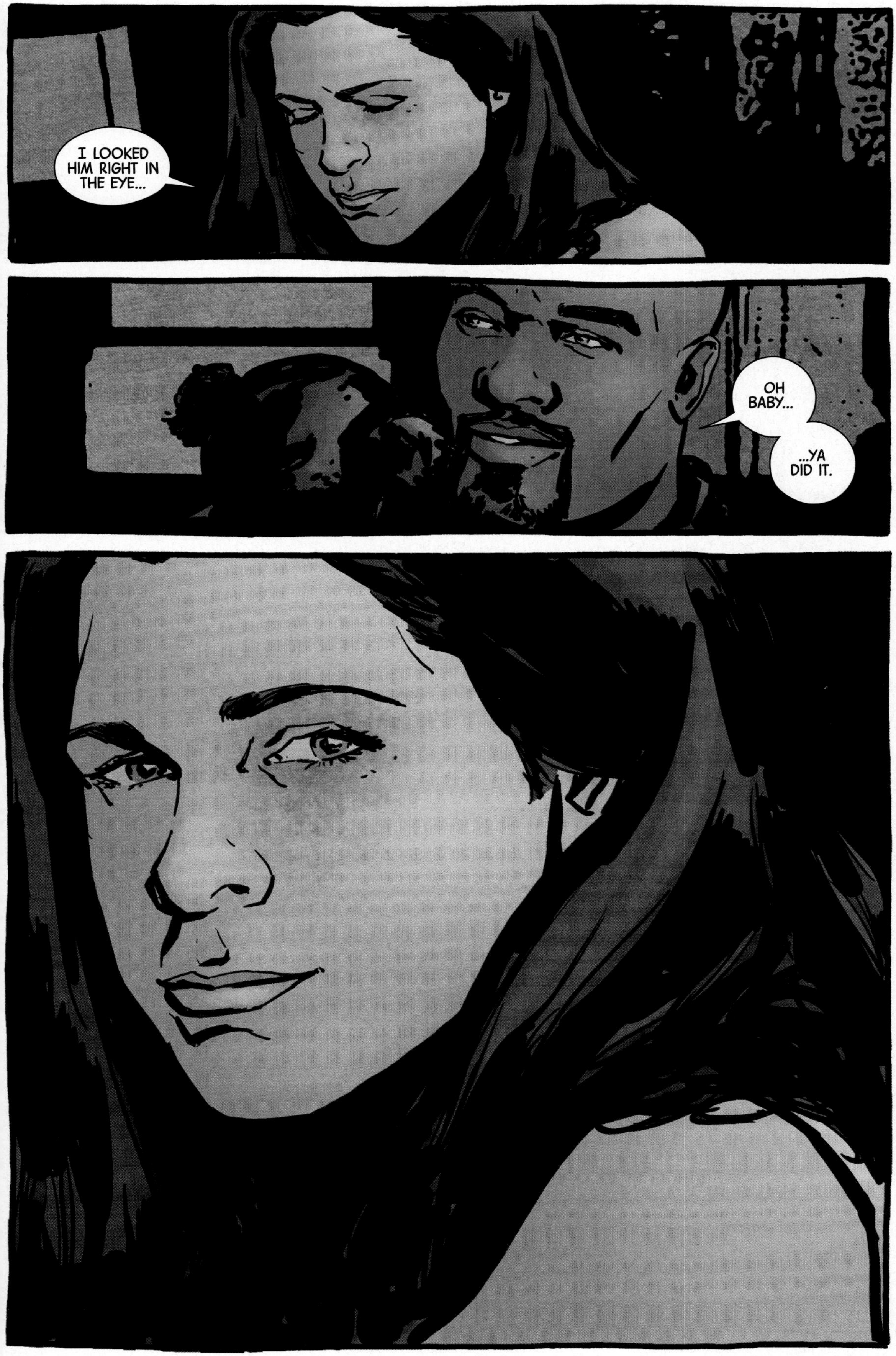
I LOOKED HIM RIGHT IN THE EYE...
OH BABY...
...YA DID IT.

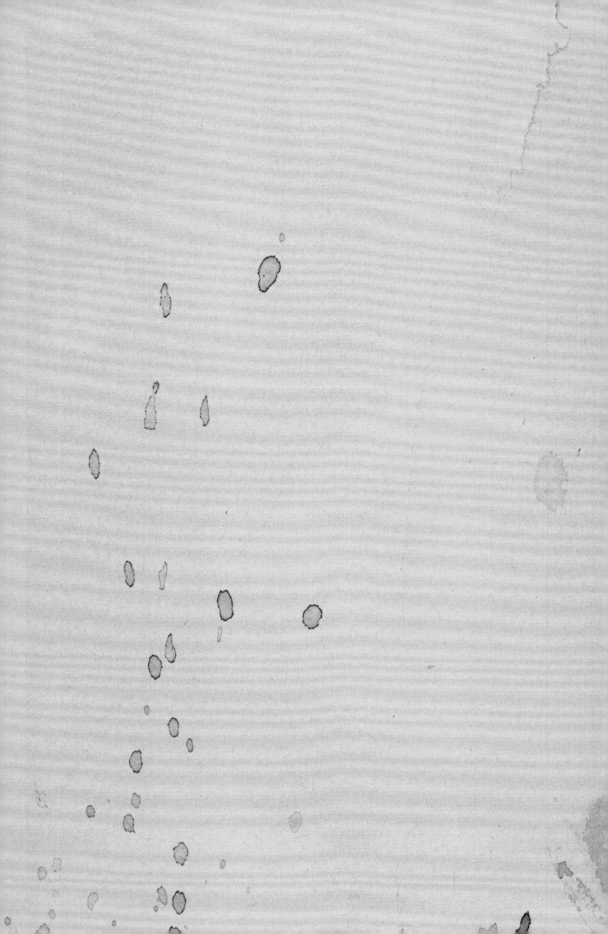

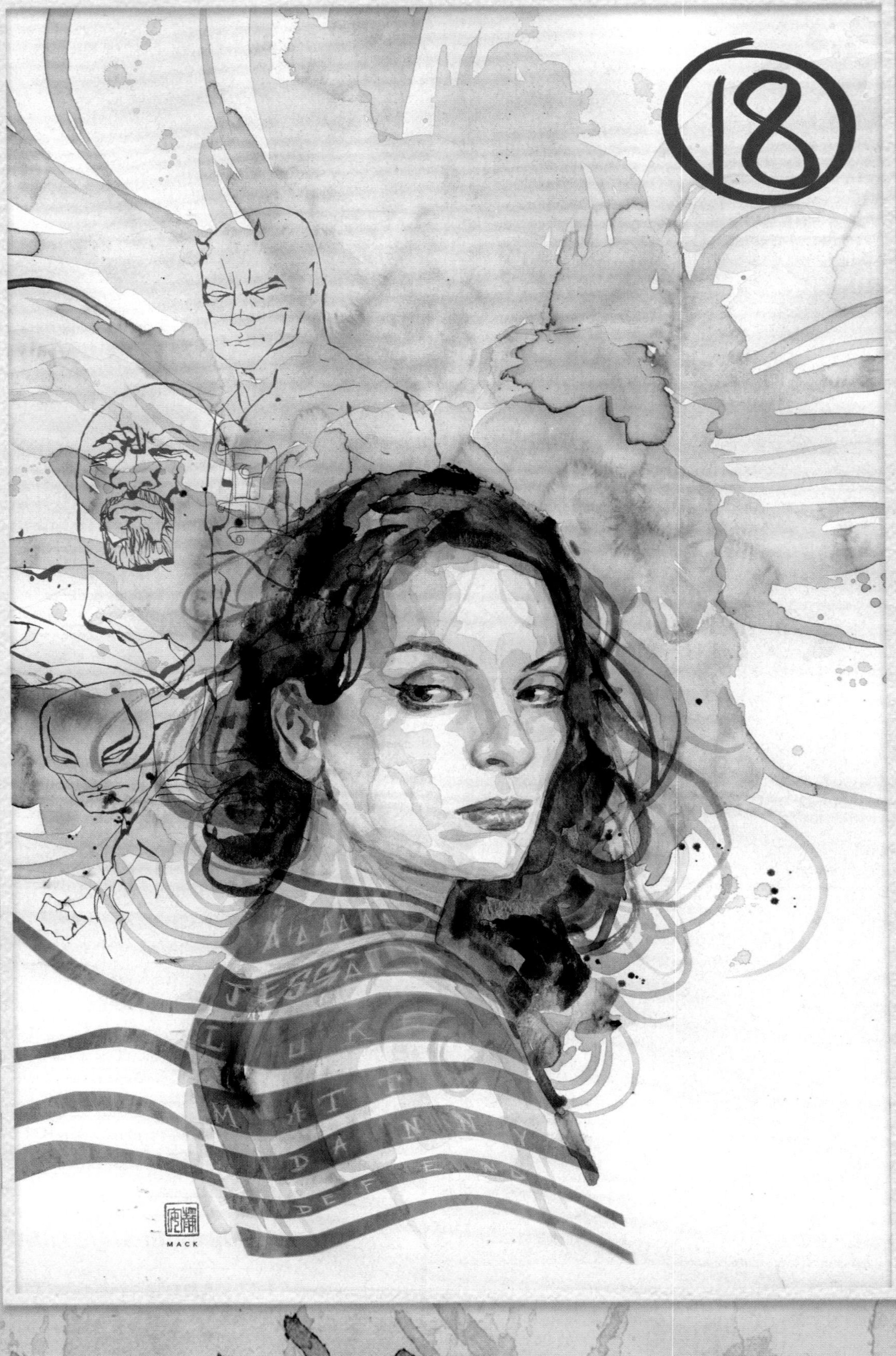
18
LUKE
MATT
DANNY
MACK

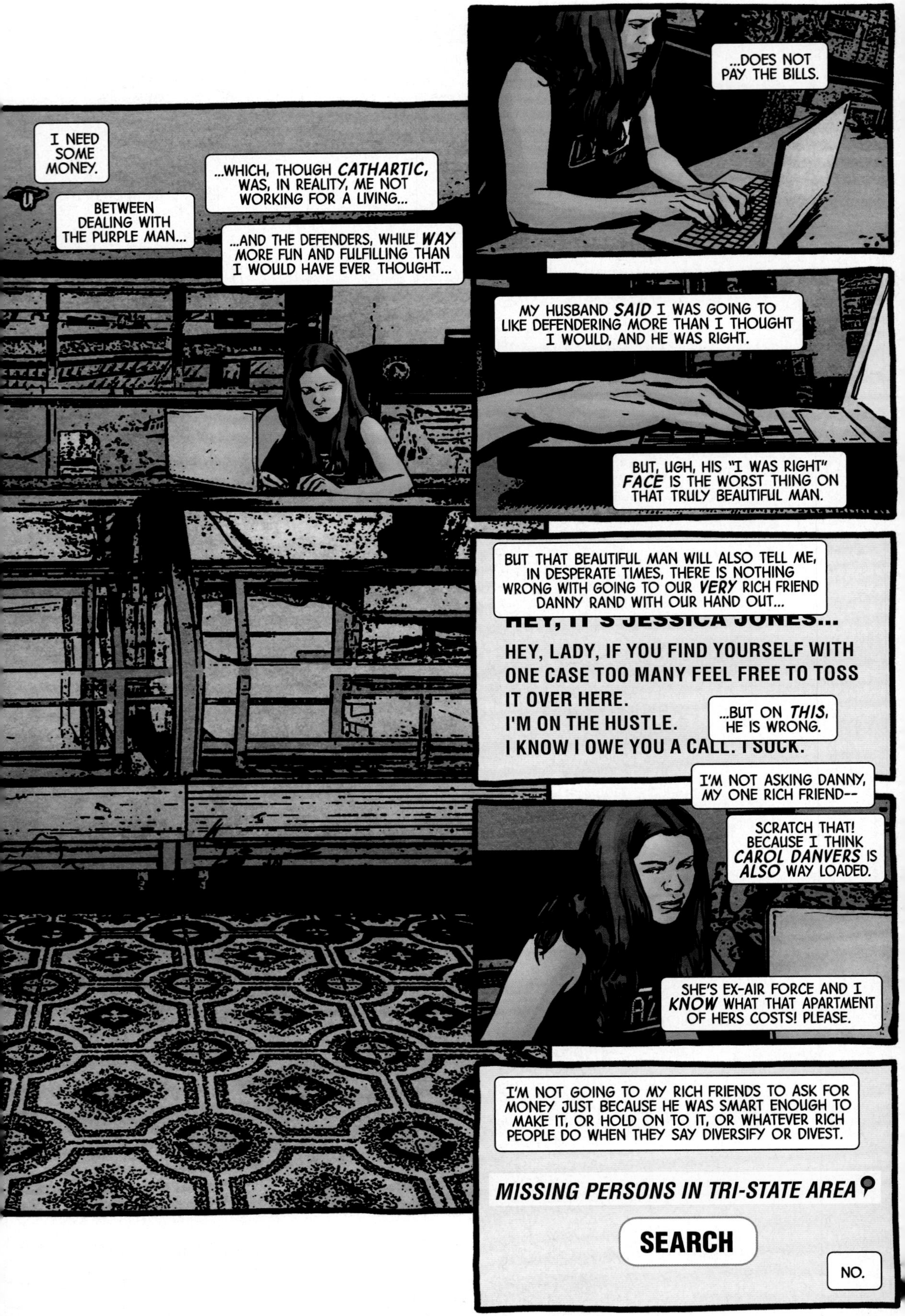
I NEED SOME MONEY.
BETWEEN DEALING WITH THE PURPLE MAN...
...WHICH, THOUGH CATHARTIC, WAS, IN REALITY, ME NOT WORKING FOR A LIVING...
...AND THE DEFENDERS, WHILE WAY MORE FUN AND FULFILLING THAN I WOULD HAVE EVER THOUGHT...
...DOES NOT PAY THE BILLS.
MY HUSBAND SAID I WAS GOING TO LIKE DEFENDERING MORE THAN I THOUGHT I WOULD, AND HE WAS RIGHT.
BUT, UGH, HIS "I WAS RIGHT" FACE IS THE WORST THING ON THAT TRULY BEAUTIFUL MAN.
BUT THAT BEAUTIFUL MAN WILL ALSO TELL ME, IN DESPERATE TIMES, THERE IS NOTHING WRONG WITH GOING TO OUR VERY RICH FRIEND DANNY RAND WITH OUR HAND OUT...
HEY, LADY, IF YOU FIND YOURSELF WITH ONE CASE TOO MANY FEEL FREE TO TOSS IT OVER HERE.
I'M ON THE HUSTLE.
...BUT ON THIS, HE IS WRONG.
I'M NOT ASKING DANNY, MY ONE RICH FRIEND--
SCRATCH THAT! BECAUSE I THINK CAROL DANVERS IS ALSO WAY LOADED.
SHE'S EX-AIR FORCE AND I KNOW WHAT THAT APARTMENT OF HERS COSTS! PLEASE.
I'M NOT GOING TO MY RICH FRIENDS TO ASK FOR MONEY JUST BECAUSE HE WAS SMART ENOUGH TO MAKE IT, OR HOLD ON TO IT, OR WHATEVER RICH PEOPLE DO WHEN THEY SAY DIVERSIFY OR DIVEST.
MISSING PERSONS IN TRI-STATE AREA
SEARCH
NO.

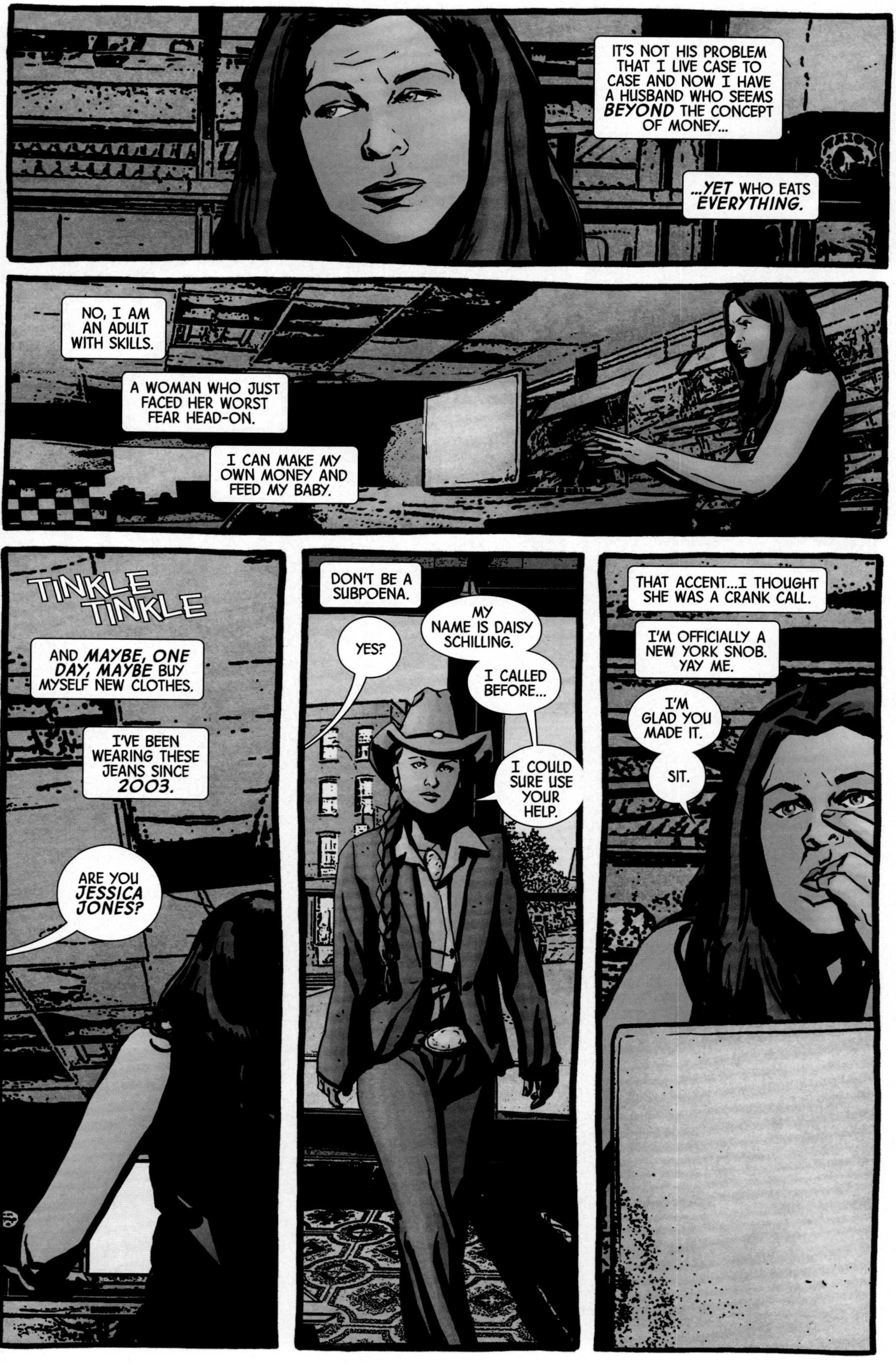
IT'S NOT HIS PROBLEM THAT I LIVE CASE TO CASE AND NOW I HAVE A HUSBAND WHO SEEMS BEYOND THE CONCEPT OF MONEY...
...YET WHO EATS EVERYTHING.
NO, I AM AN ADULT WITH SKILLS.
A WOMAN WHO JUST FACED HER WORST FEAR HEAD-ON.
I CAN MAKE MY OWN MONEY AND FEED MY BABY.
TINKLE TINKLE
AND MAYBE, ONE DAY, MAYBE BUY MYSELF NEW CLOTHES.
I'VE BEEN WEARING THESE JEANS SINCE 2003.
ARE YOU JESSICA JONES?
DON'T BE A SUBPOENA.
YES?
MY NAME IS DAISY SCHILLING.
I CALLED BEFORE...
I COULD SURE USE YOUR HELP.
THAT ACCENT...I THOUGHT SHE WAS A CRANK CALL.
I'M OFFICIALLY A NEW YORK SNOB. YAY ME.
I'M GLAD YOU MADE IT.
SIT.

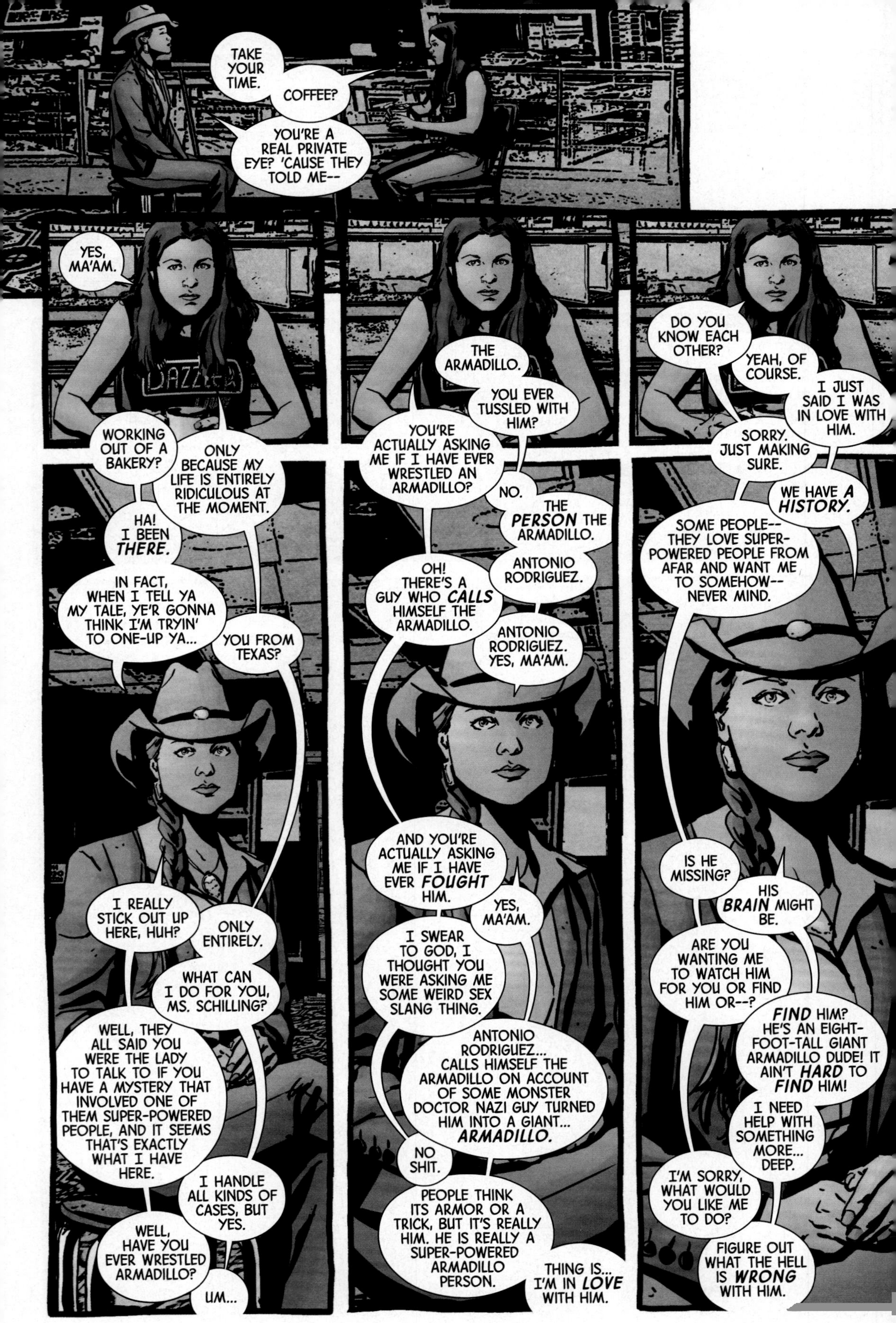
TAKE YOUR TIME.
COFFEE?
YOU'RE A REAL PRIVATE EYE? 'CAUSE THEY TOLD ME--
YES, MA'AM.
WORKING OUT OF A BAKERY?
ONLY BECAUSE MY LIFE IS ENTIRELY RIDICULOUS AT THE MOMENT.
HA! I BEEN THERE.
IN FACT, WHEN I TELL YA MY TALE, YE'R GONNA THINK I'M TRYIN' TO ONE-UP YA...
YOU FROM TEXAS?
I REALLY STICK OUT UP HERE, HUH?
ONLY ENTIRELY.
WHAT CAN I DO FOR YOU, MS. SCHILLING?
WELL, THEY ALL SAID YOU WERE THE LADY TO TALK TO IF YOU HAVE A MYSTERY THAT INVOLVED ONE OF THEM SUPER-POWERED PEOPLE, AND IT SEEMS THAT'S EXACTLY WHAT I HAVE HERE.
I HANDLE ALL KINDS OF CASES, BUT YES.
WELL, HAVE YOU EVER WRESTLED ARMADILLO?
UM...
THE ARMADILLO.
YOU EVER TUSSLED WITH HIM?
YOU'RE ACTUALLY ASKING ME IF I HAVE EVER WRESTLED AN ARMADILLO?
NO.
THE PERSON THE ARMADILLO.
ANTONIO RODRIGUEZ.
OH! THERE'S A GUY WHO CALLS HIMSELF THE ARMADILLO.
ANTONIO RODRIGUEZ. YES, MA'AM.
AND YOU'RE ACTUALLY ASKING ME IF I HAVE EVER FOUGHT HIM.
YES, MA'AM.
I SWEAR TO GOD, I THOUGHT YOU WERE ASKING ME SOME WEIRD SEX SLANG THING.
ANTONIO RODRIGUEZ... CALLS HIMSELF THE ARMADILLO ON ACCOUNT OF SOME MONSTER DOCTOR NAZI GUY TURNED HIM INTO A GIANT... ARMADILLO.
NO SHIT.
PEOPLE THINK ITS ARMOR OR A TRICK, BUT IT'S REALLY HIM. HE IS REALLY A SUPER-POWERED ARMADILLO PERSON.
THING IS... I'M IN LOVE WITH HIM.
DO YOU KNOW EACH OTHER?
YEAH, OF COURSE.
I JUST SAID I WAS IN LOVE WITH HIM.
SORRY. JUST MAKING SURE.
WE HAVE A HISTORY.
SOME PEOPLE-- THEY LOVE SUPER-POWERED PEOPLE FROM AFAR AND WANT ME TO SOMEHOW-- NEVER MIND.
IS HE MISSING?
HIS BRAIN MIGHT BE.
ARE YOU WANTING ME TO WATCH HIM FOR YOU OR FIND HIM OR--?
FIND HIM? HE'S AN EIGHT-FOOT-TALL GIANT ARMADILLO DUDE! IT AIN'T HARD TO FIND HIM!
I NEED HELP WITH SOMETHING MORE... DEEP.
I'M SORRY, WHAT WOULD YOU LIKE ME TO DO?
FIGURE OUT WHAT THE HELL IS WRONG WITH HIM.

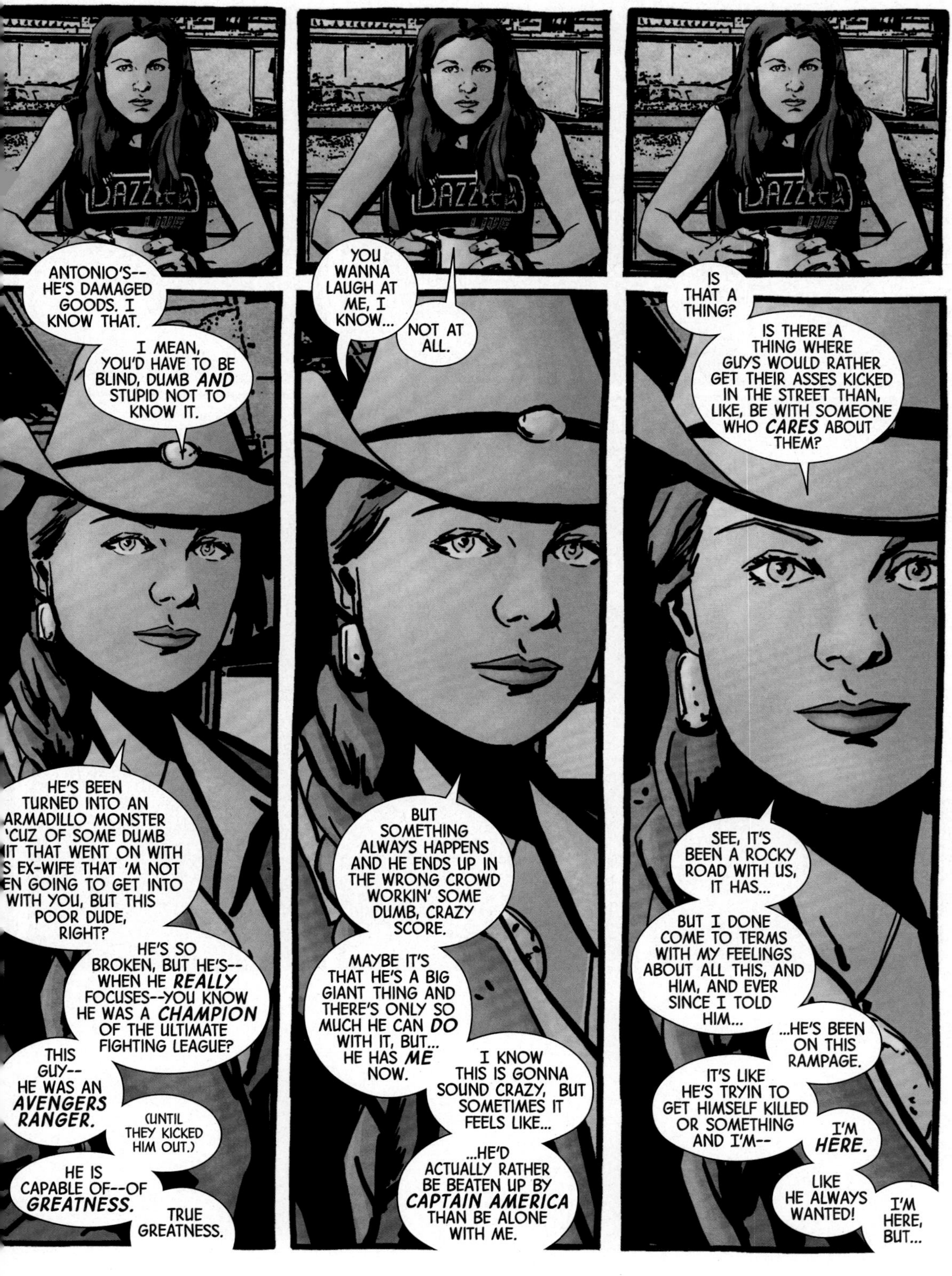
ANTONIO'S-- HE'S DAMAGED GOODS. I KNOW THAT.
I MEAN, YOU'D HAVE TO BE BLIND, DUMB AND STUPID NOT TO KNOW IT.
HE'S BEEN TURNED INTO AN ARMADILLO MONSTER 'CUZ OF SOME DUMB IT THAT WENT ON WITH S EX-WIFE THAT 'M NOT EN GOING TO GET INTO WITH YOU, BUT THIS POOR DUDE, RIGHT?
HE'S SO BROKEN, BUT HE'S-- WHEN HE REALLY FOCUSES--YOU KNOW HE WAS A CHAMPION OF THE ULTIMATE FIGHTING LEAGUE?
THIS GUY-- HE WAS AN AVENGERS RANGER.
(UNTIL THEY KICKED HIM OUT.)
HE IS CAPABLE OF--OF GREATNESS.
TRUE GREATNESS.
YOU WANNA LAUGH AT ME, I KNOW...
NOT AT ALL.
BUT SOMETHING ALWAYS HAPPENS AND HE ENDS UP IN THE WRONG CROWD WORKIN' SOME DUMB, CRAZY SCORE.
MAYBE IT'S THAT HE'S A BIG GIANT THING AND THERE'S ONLY SO MUCH HE CAN DO WITH IT, BUT... HE HAS ME NOW.
I KNOW THIS IS GONNA SOUND CRAZY, BUT SOMETIMES IT FEELS LIKE...
...HE'D ACTUALLY RATHER BE BEATEN UP BY CAPTAIN AMERICA THAN BE ALONE WITH ME.
IS THAT A THING?
IS THERE A THING WHERE GUYS WOULD RATHER GET THEIR ASSES KICKED IN THE STREET THAN, LIKE, BE WITH SOMEONE WHO CARES ABOUT THEM?
SEE, IT'S BEEN A ROCKY ROAD WITH US, IT HAS...
BUT I DONE COME TO TERMS WITH MY FEELINGS ABOUT ALL THIS, AND HIM, AND EVER SINCE I TOLD HIM...
...HE'S BEEN ON THIS RAMPAGE.
IT'S LIKE HE'S TRYIN TO GET HIMSELF KILLED OR SOMETHING AND I'M--
I'M HERE.
LIKE HE ALWAYS WANTED!
I'M HERE, BUT...

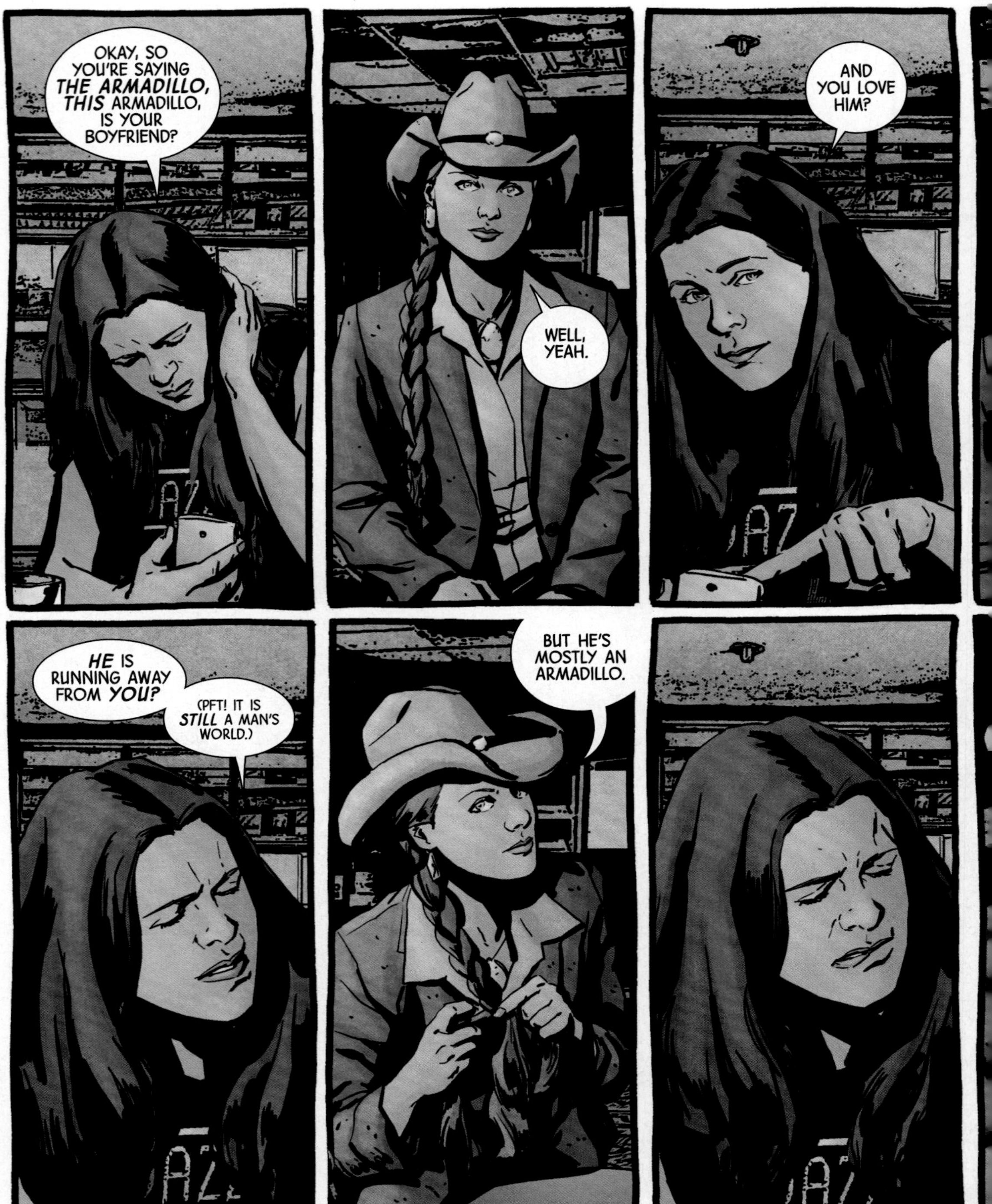
OKAY, SO YOU'RE SAYING *THE ARMADILLO, THIS* ARMADILLO, IS YOUR BOYFRIEND?
WELL, YEAH.
AND YOU LOVE HIM?
HE IS RUNNING AWAY FROM *YOU?*
(PFT! IT IS *STILL* A MAN'S WORLD.)
BUT HE'S MOSTLY AN ARMADILLO.

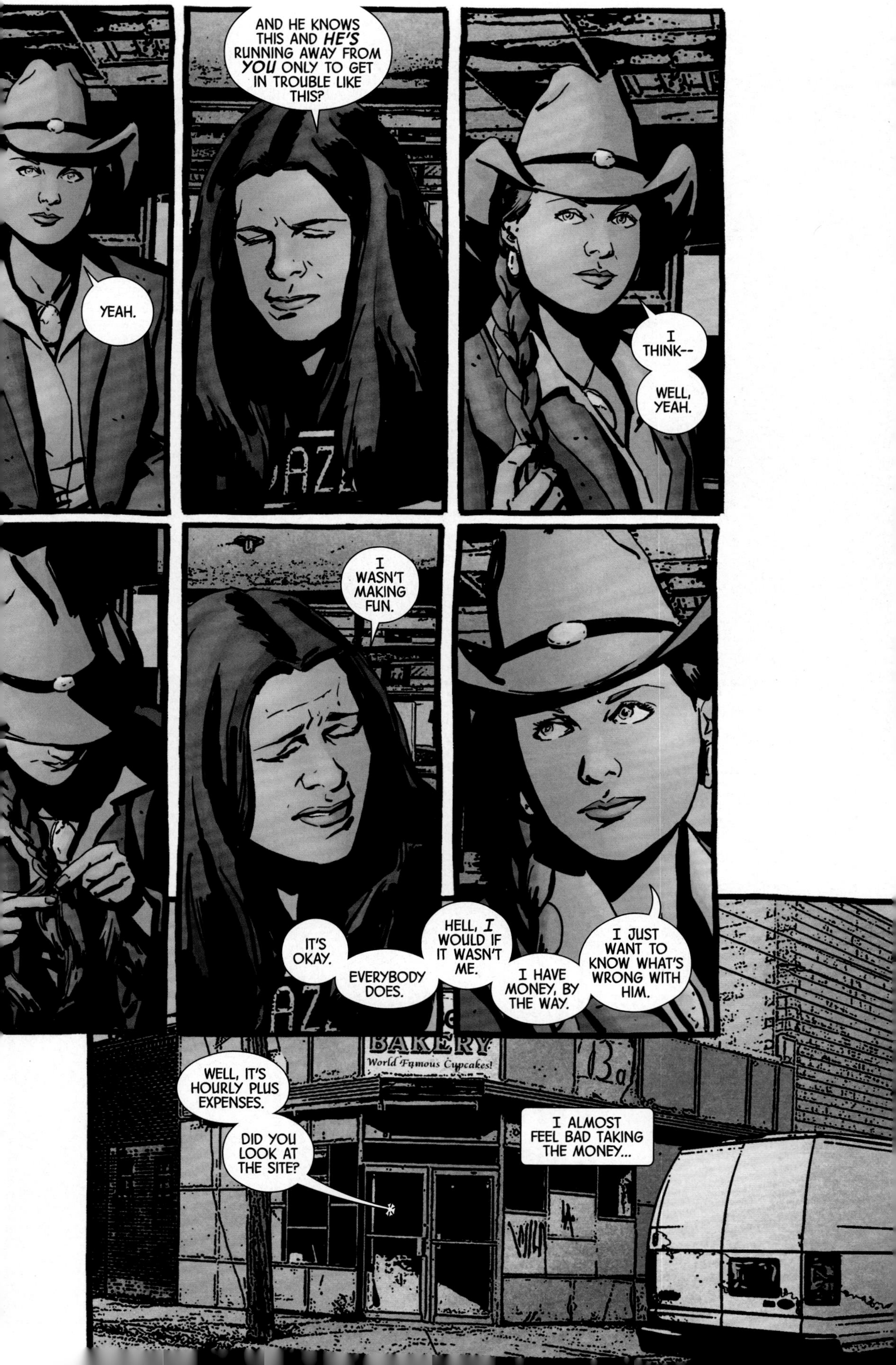
AND HE KNOWS THIS AND HE'S RUNNING AWAY FROM YOU ONLY TO GET IN TROUBLE LIKE THIS?
YEAH.
I THINK--
WELL, YEAH.
I WASN'T MAKING FUN.
IT'S OKAY.
EVERYBODY DOES.
HELL, I WOULD IF IT WASN'T ME.
I HAVE MONEY, BY THE WAY.
I JUST WANT TO KNOW WHAT'S WRONG WITH HIM.
BAKERY
World Famous Cupcakes!
WELL, IT'S HOURLY PLUS EXPENSES.
DID YOU LOOK AT THE SITE?
I ALMOST FEEL BAD TAKING THE MONEY...

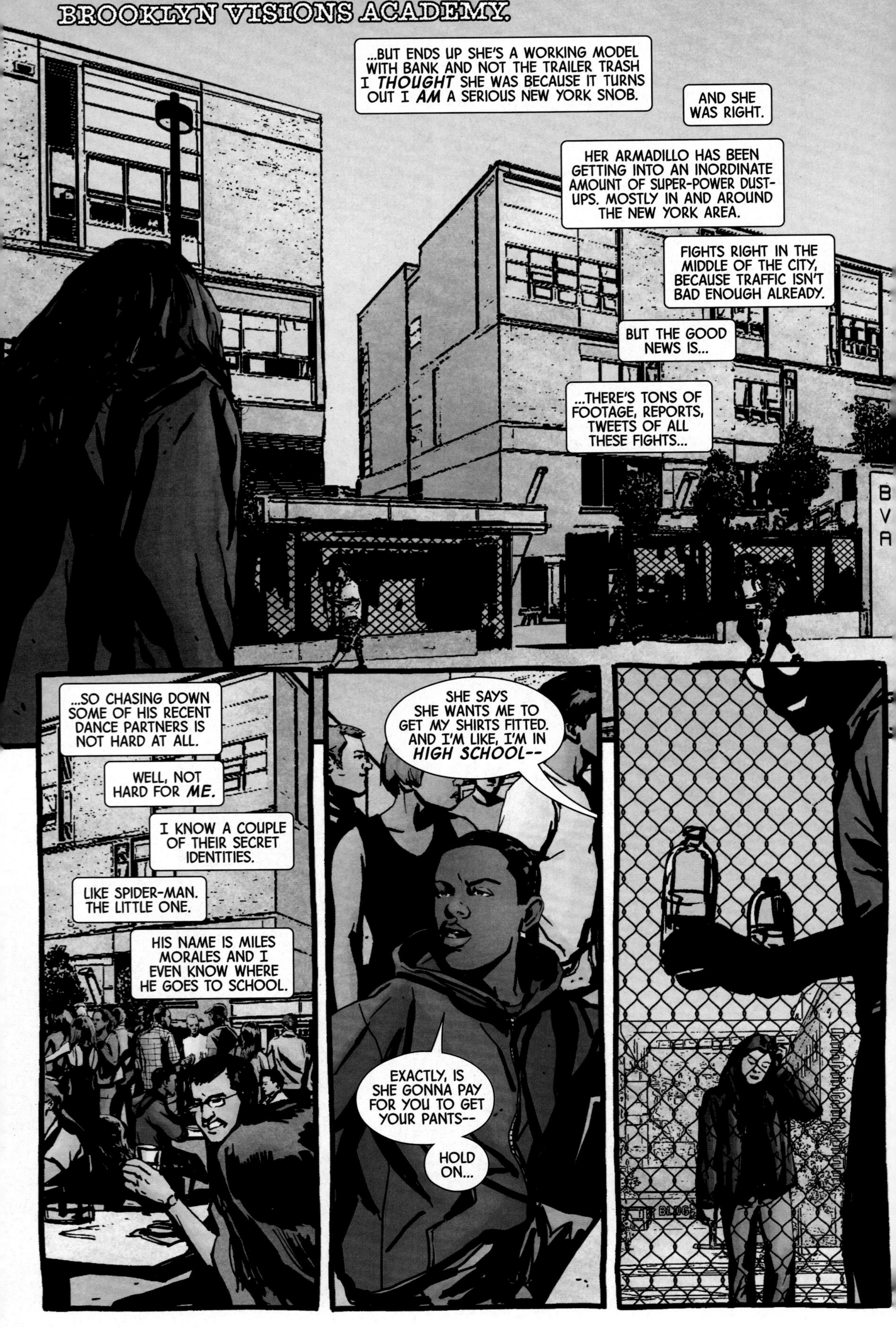
BROOKLYN VISIONS ACADEMY.
...BUT ENDS UP SHE'S A WORKING MODEL WITH BANK AND NOT THE TRAILER TRASH I THOUGHT SHE WAS BECAUSE IT TURNS OUT I AM A SERIOUS NEW YORK SNOB.
AND SHE WAS RIGHT.
HER ARMADILLO HAS BEEN GETTING INTO AN INORDINATE AMOUNT OF SUPER-POWER DUST-UPS. MOSTLY IN AND AROUND THE NEW YORK AREA.
FIGHTS RIGHT IN THE MIDDLE OF THE CITY, BECAUSE TRAFFIC ISN'T BAD ENOUGH ALREADY.
BUT THE GOOD NEWS IS...
...THERE'S TONS OF FOOTAGE, REPORTS, TWEETS OF ALL THESE FIGHTS...
BVA
...SO CHASING DOWN SOME OF HIS RECENT DANCE PARTNERS IS NOT HARD AT ALL.
WELL, NOT HARD FOR ME.
I KNOW A COUPLE OF THEIR SECRET IDENTITIES.
LIKE SPIDER-MAN. THE LITTLE ONE.
HIS NAME IS MILES MORALES AND I EVEN KNOW WHERE HE GOES TO SCHOOL.
SHE SAYS SHE WANTS ME TO GET MY SHIRTS FITTED. AND I'M LIKE, I'M IN HIGH SCHOOL--
EXACTLY, IS SHE GONNA PAY FOR YOU TO GET YOUR PANTS--
HOLD ON...

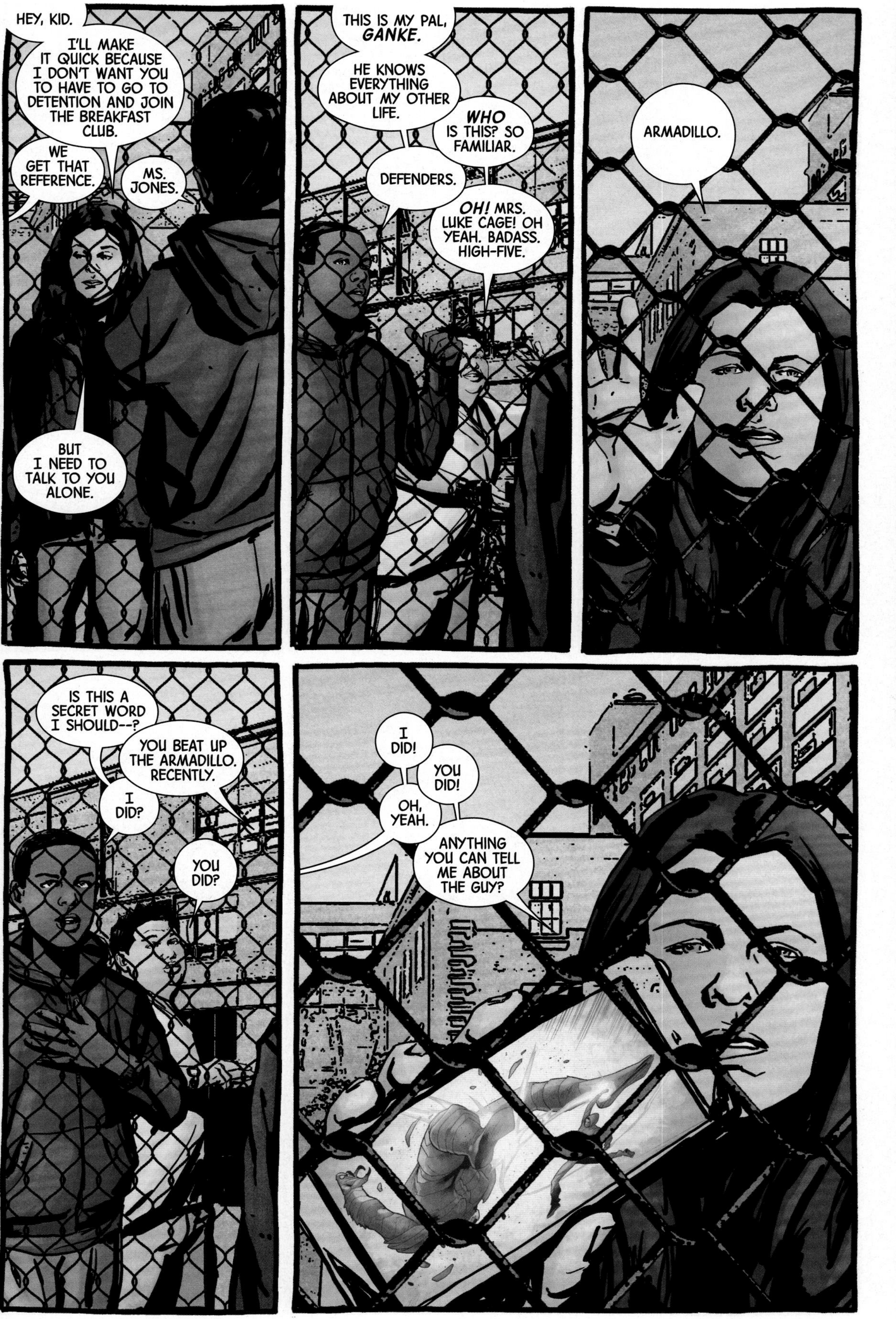

HEY, KID.
I'LL MAKE IT QUICK BECAUSE I DON'T WANT YOU TO HAVE TO GO TO DETENTION AND JOIN THE BREAKFAST CLUB.
WE GET THAT REFERENCE.
MS. JONES.
BUT I NEED TO TALK TO YOU ALONE.
THIS IS MY PAL, GANKE.
HE KNOWS EVERYTHING ABOUT MY OTHER LIFE.
WHO IS THIS? SO FAMILIAR.
DEFENDERS.
OH! MRS. LUKE CAGE! OH YEAH. BADASS. HIGH-FIVE.
ARMADILLO.
IS THIS A SECRET WORD I SHOULD--?
YOU BEAT UP THE ARMADILLO. RECENTLY.
I DID?
YOU DID?
I DID!
YOU DID!
OH, YEAH.
ANYTHING YOU CAN TELL ME ABOUT THE GUY?

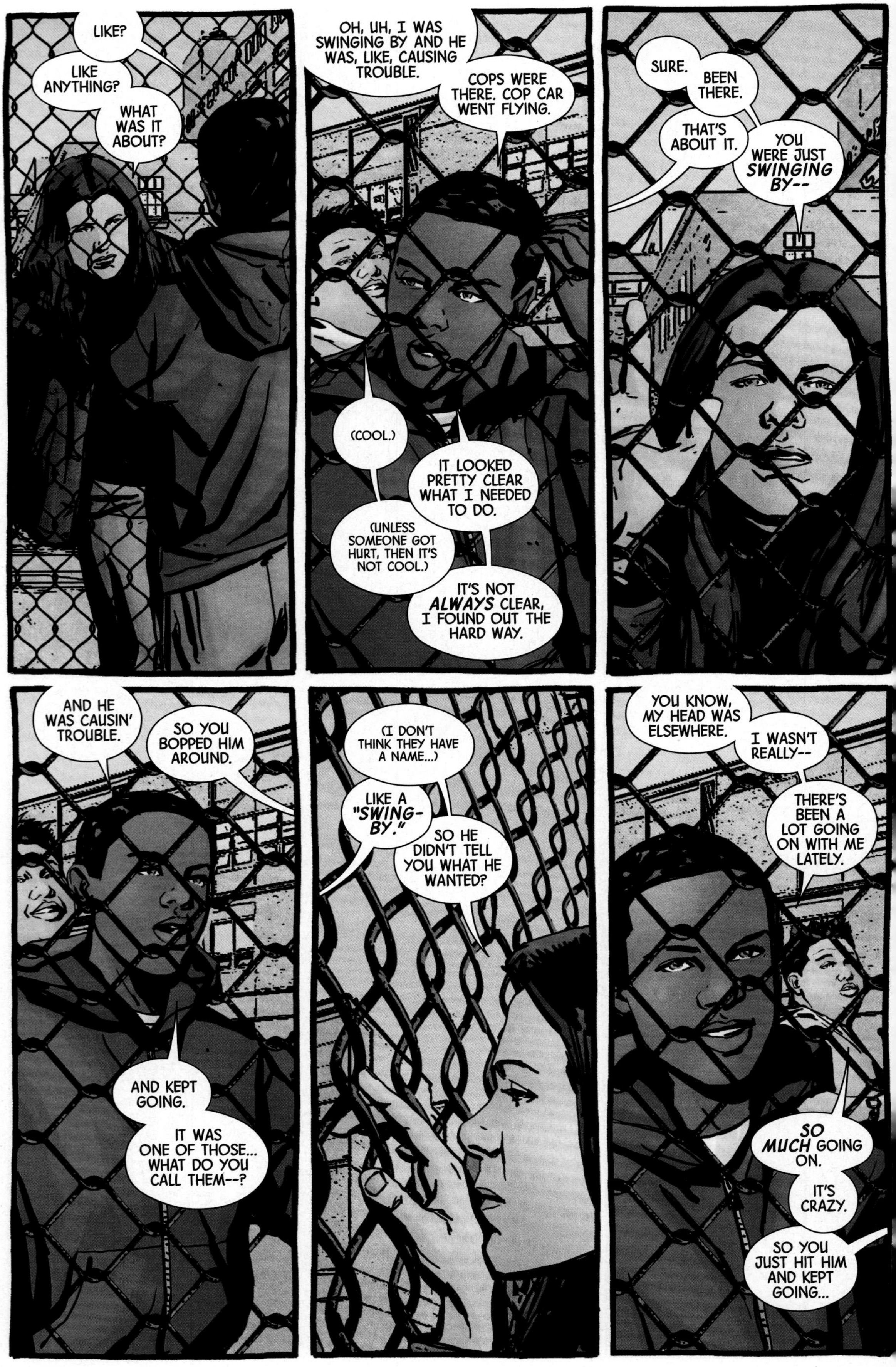
LIKE?
LIKE ANYTHING?
WHAT WAS IT ABOUT?
OH, UH, I WAS SWINGING BY AND HE WAS, LIKE, CAUSING TROUBLE.
COPS WERE THERE. COP CAR WENT FLYING.
(COOL.)
IT LOOKED PRETTY CLEAR WHAT I NEEDED TO DO.
(UNLESS SOMEONE GOT HURT, THEN IT'S NOT COOL.)
IT'S NOT ALWAYS CLEAR, I FOUND OUT THE HARD WAY.
SURE.
BEEN THERE.
THAT'S ABOUT IT.
YOU WERE JUST SWINGING BY--
AND HE WAS CAUSIN' TROUBLE.
SO YOU BOPPED HIM AROUND.
AND KEPT GOING.
IT WAS ONE OF THOSE... WHAT DO YOU CALL THEM--?
(I DON'T THINK THEY HAVE A NAME...)
LIKE A "SWING-BY."
SO HE DIDN'T TELL YOU WHAT HE WANTED?
YOU KNOW, MY HEAD WAS ELSEWHERE.
I WASN'T REALLY--
THERE'S BEEN A LOT GOING ON WITH ME LATELY.
SO MUCH GOING ON.
IT'S CRAZY.
SO YOU JUST HIT HIM AND KEPT GOING...

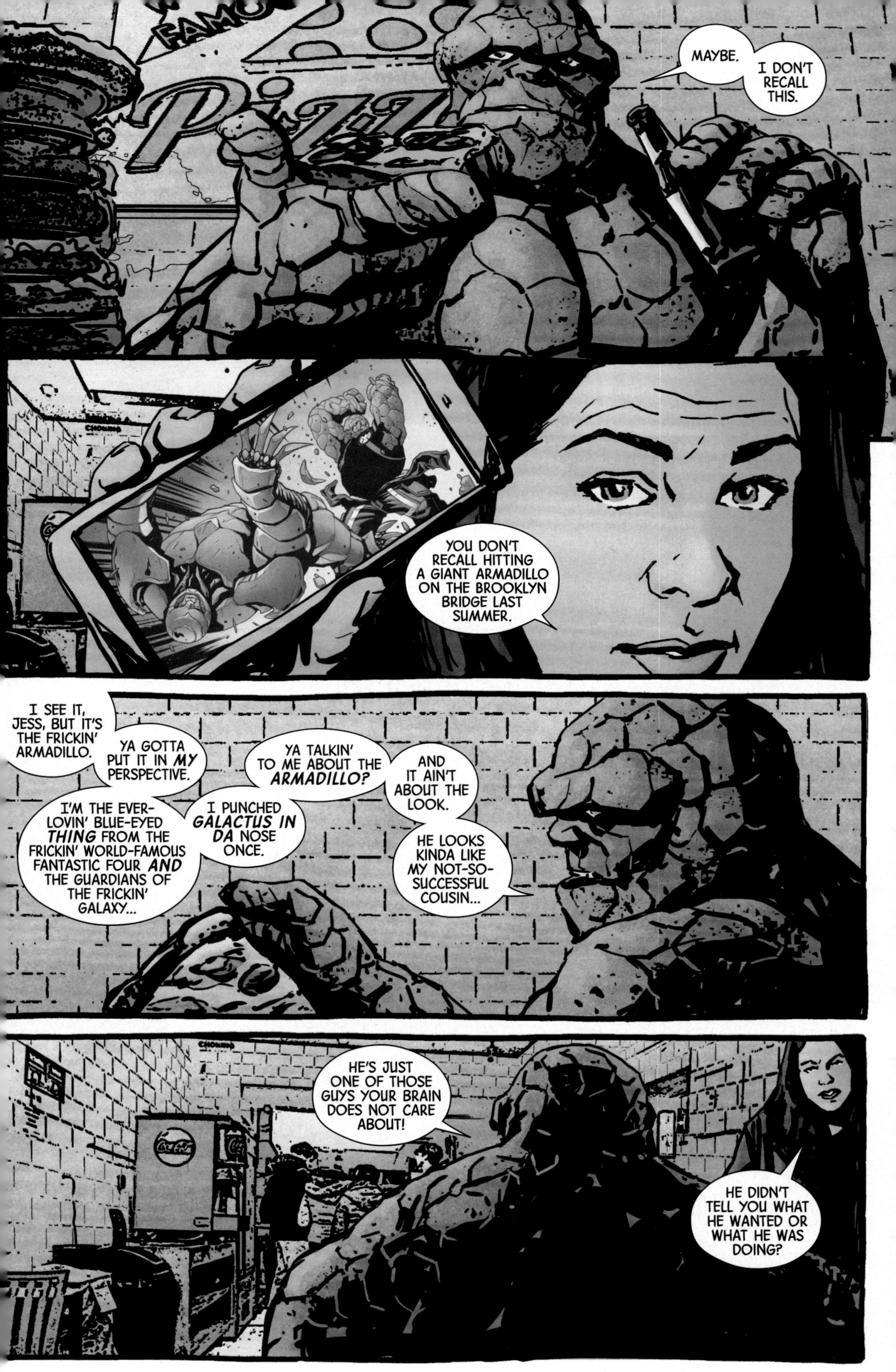
MAYBE.
I DON'T RECALL THIS.
YOU DON'T RECALL HITTING A GIANT ARMADILLO ON THE BROOKLYN BRIDGE LAST SUMMER.
I SEE IT, JESS, BUT IT'S THE FRICKIN' ARMADILLO.
YA GOTTA PUT IT IN MY PERSPECTIVE.
I'M THE EVER-LOVIN' BLUE-EYED THING FROM THE FRICKIN' WORLD-FAMOUS FANTASTIC FOUR AND THE GUARDIANS OF THE FRICKIN' GALAXY...
I PUNCHED GALACTUS IN DA NOSE ONCE.
YA TALKIN' TO ME ABOUT THE ARMADILLO?
AND IT AIN'T ABOUT THE LOOK.
HE LOOKS KINDA LIKE MY NOT-SO-SUCCESSFUL COUSIN...
HE'S JUST ONE OF THOSE GUYS YOUR BRAIN DOES NOT CARE ABOUT!
HE DIDN'T TELL YOU WHAT HE WANTED OR WHAT HE WAS DOING?

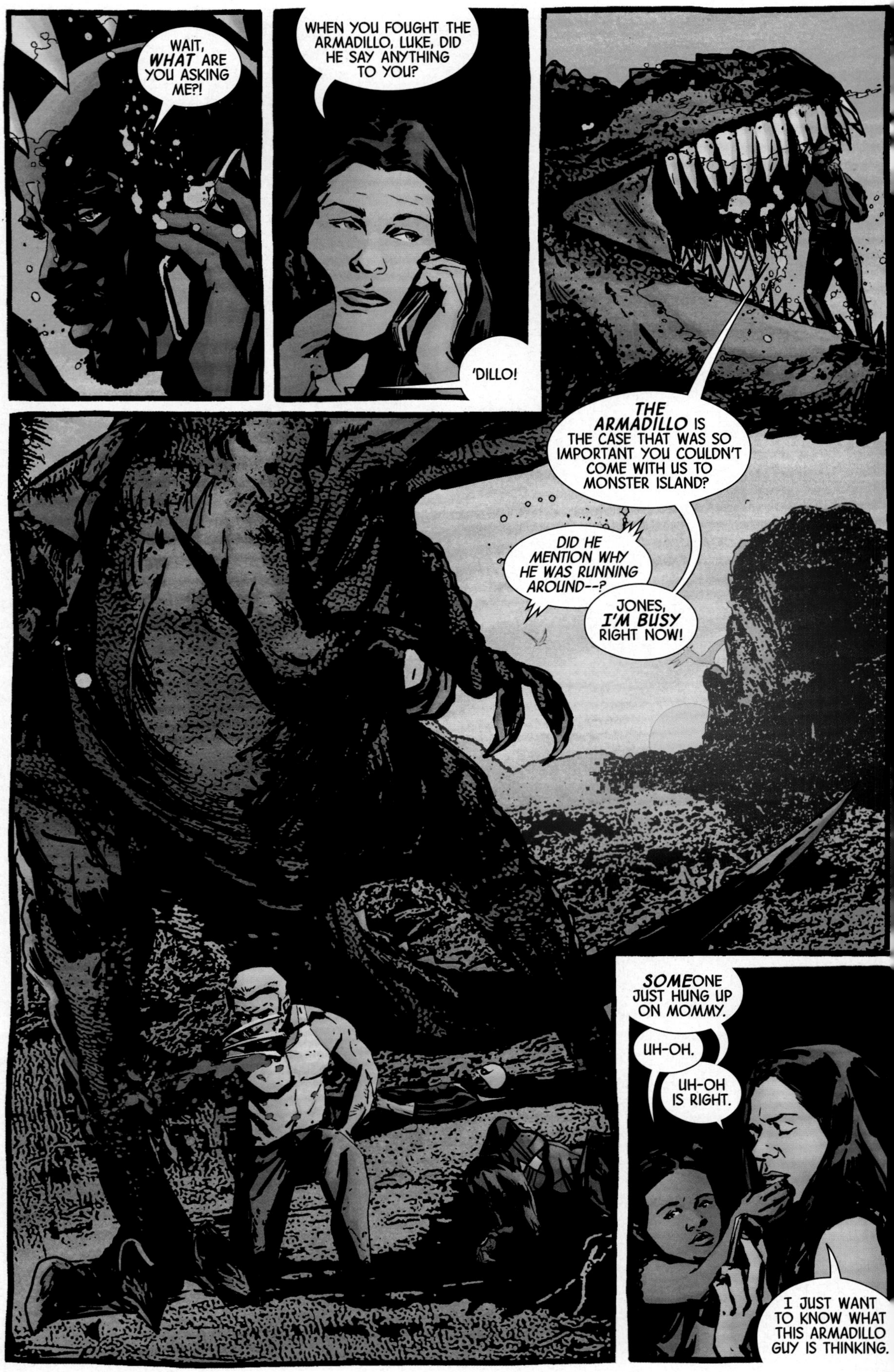
WAIT, WHAT ARE YOU ASKING ME?!
WHEN YOU FOUGHT THE ARMADILLO, LUKE, DID HE SAY ANYTHING TO YOU?
'DILLO!
THE ARMADILLO IS THE CASE THAT WAS SO IMPORTANT YOU COULDN'T COME WITH US TO MONSTER ISLAND?
DID HE MENTION WHY HE WAS RUNNING AROUND--?
JONES, I'M BUSY RIGHT NOW!
SOMEONE JUST HUNG UP ON MOMMY.
UH-OH.
UH-OH IS RIGHT.
I JUST WANT TO KNOW WHAT THIS ARMADILLO GUY IS THINKING.

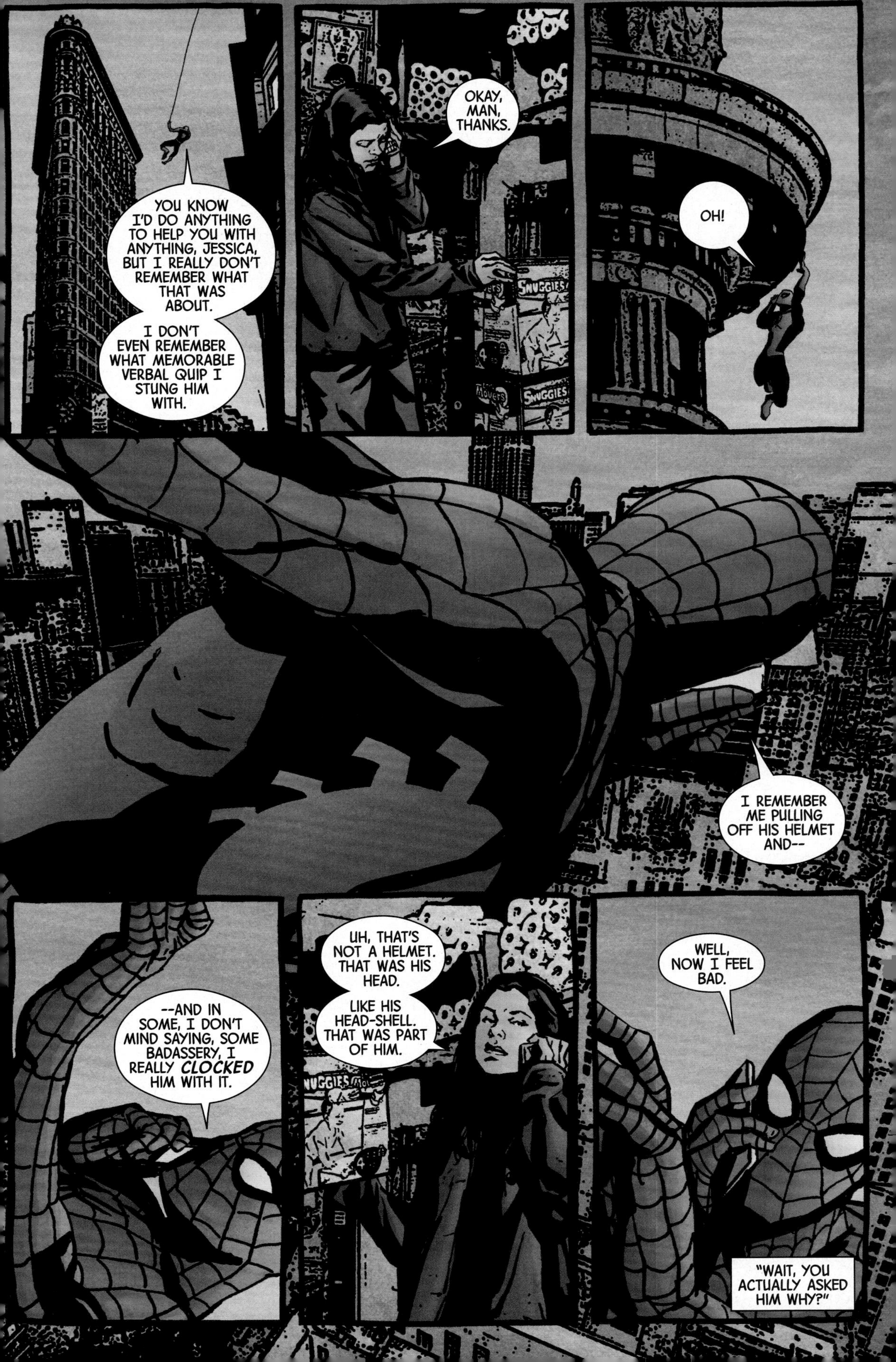
YOU KNOW I'D DO ANYTHING TO HELP YOU WITH ANYTHING, JESSICA, BUT I REALLY DON'T REMEMBER WHAT THAT WAS ABOUT.
I DON'T EVEN REMEMBER WHAT MEMORABLE VERBAL QUIP I STUNG HIM WITH.
OKAY, MAN, THANKS.
SNUGGIES
OH!
I REMEMBER ME PULLING OFF HIS HELMET AND--
--AND IN SOME, I DON'T MIND SAYING, SOME BADASSERY, I REALLY *CLOCKED* HIM WITH IT.
UH, THAT'S NOT A HELMET. THAT WAS HIS HEAD.
LIKE HIS HEAD-SHELL. THAT WAS PART OF HIM.
WELL, NOW I FEEL BAD.
"WAIT, YOU ACTUALLY ASKED HIM WHY?"

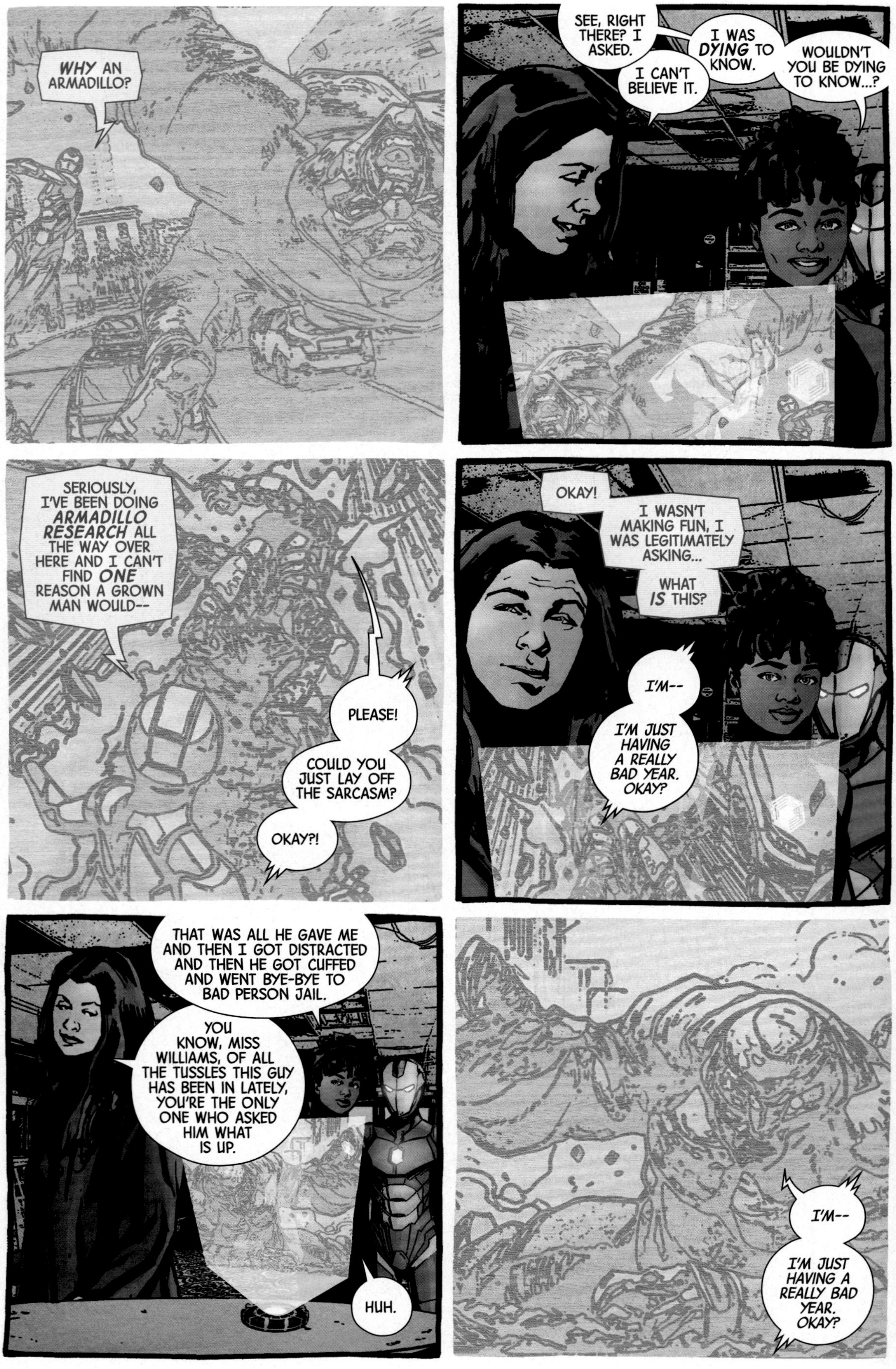

WHY AN ARMADILLO?
SEE, RIGHT THERE? I ASKED.
I CAN'T BELIEVE IT.
I WAS DYING TO KNOW.
WOULDN'T YOU BE DYING TO KNOW...?
SERIOUSLY, I'VE BEEN DOING ARMADILLO RESEARCH ALL THE WAY OVER HERE AND I CAN'T FIND ONE REASON A GROWN MAN WOULD--
PLEASE!
COULD YOU JUST LAY OFF THE SARCASM?
OKAY?!
OKAY!
I WASN'T MAKING FUN, I WAS LEGITIMATELY ASKING...
WHAT IS THIS?
I'M--
I'M JUST HAVING A REALLY BAD YEAR. OKAY?
THAT WAS ALL HE GAVE ME AND THEN I GOT DISTRACTED AND THEN HE GOT CUFFED AND WENT BYE-BYE TO BAD PERSON JAIL.
YOU KNOW, MISS WILLIAMS, OF ALL THE TUSSLES THIS GUY HAS BEEN IN LATELY, YOU'RE THE ONLY ONE WHO ASKED HIM WHAT IS UP.
HUH.
I'M--
I'M JUST HAVING A REALLY BAD YEAR. OKAY?

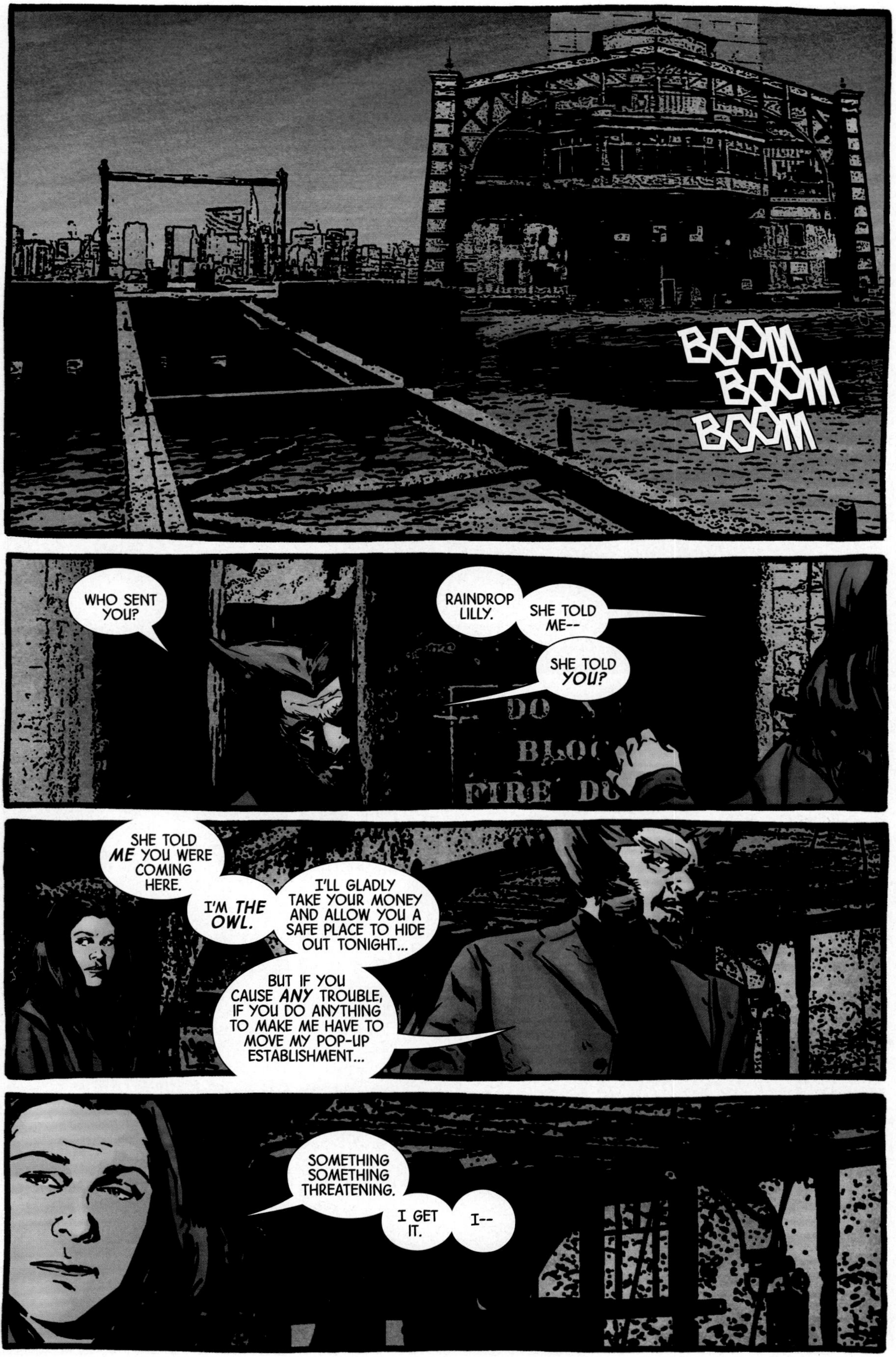
BOOM BOOM BOOM
WHO SENT YOU?
RAINDROP LILLY.
SHE TOLD ME--
SHE TOLD YOU?
DO
BLOC
FIRE DU
SHE TOLD ME YOU WERE COMING HERE.
I'M THE OWL.
I'LL GLADLY TAKE YOUR MONEY AND ALLOW YOU A SAFE PLACE TO HIDE OUT TONIGHT...
BUT IF YOU CAUSE ANY TROUBLE, IF YOU DO ANYTHING TO MAKE ME HAVE TO MOVE MY POP-UP ESTABLISHMENT...
SOMETHING SOMETHING THREATENING.
I GET IT.
I--

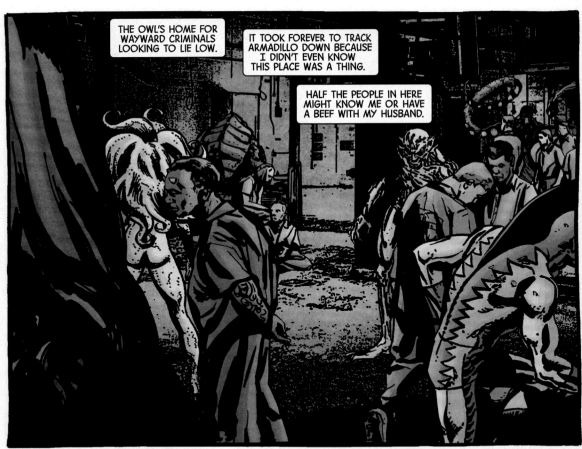

THE OWL'S HOME FOR WAYWARD CRIMINALS LOOKING TO LIE LOW.

IT TOOK FOREVER TO TRACK ARMADILLO DOWN BECAUSE I DIDN'T EVEN KNOW THIS PLACE WAS A THING.

HALF THE PEOPLE IN HERE MIGHT KNOW ME OR HAVE A BEEF WITH MY HUSBAND.

I'M SURE THEY *ALL* HAVE A BEEF WITH MY HUSBAND.

BUT NOW I SEE MOST OF THEM ARE SO STRUNG OUT THEY DON'T EVEN SEE ME.

M'NOT ASLEEP.

GOOD. I'M JESSICA JONES.

DA PRIVATE EYE?

I HEARD A'YA.

YEAH.

GUESS WHO HIRED ME?

AH, DAISY.

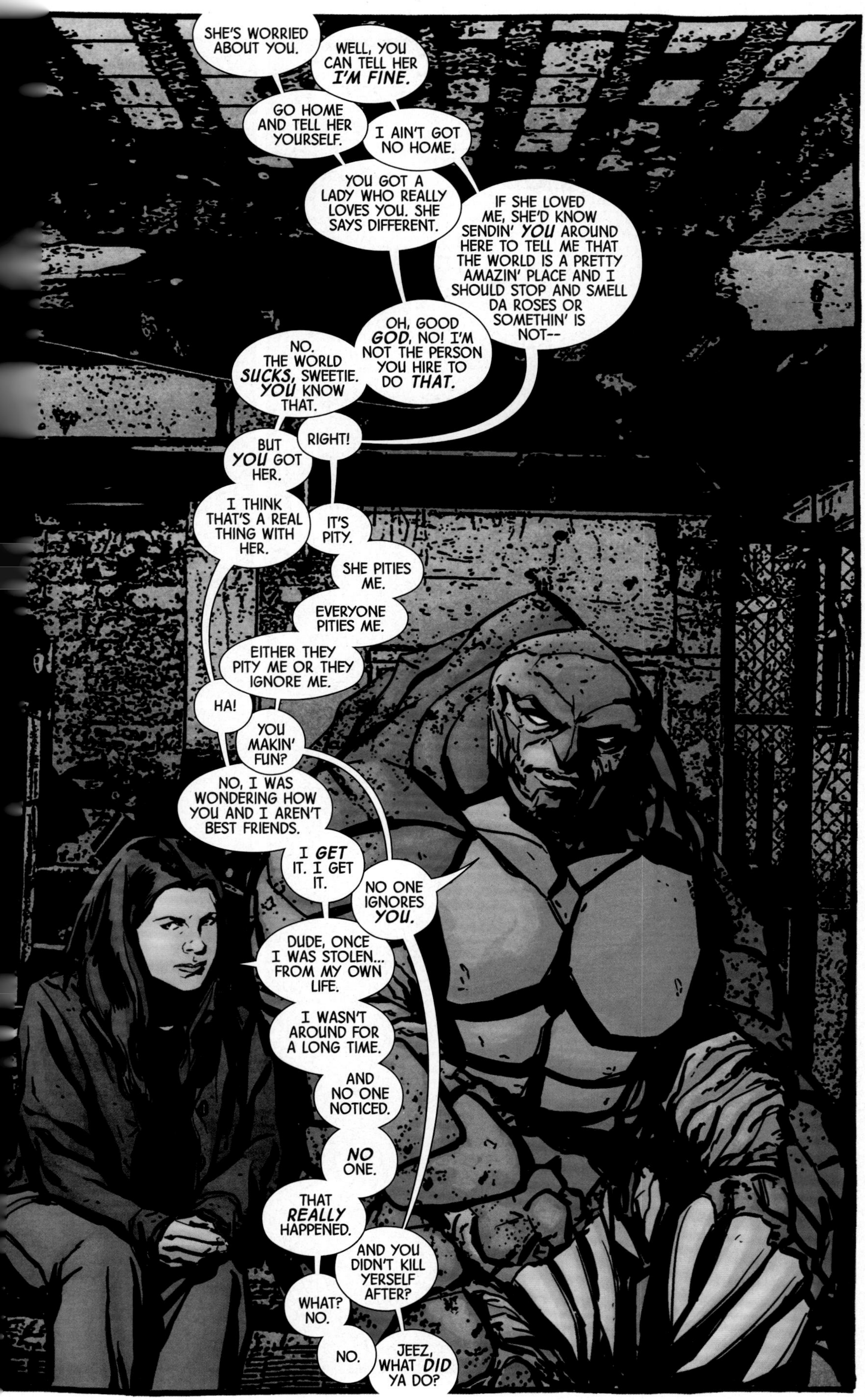
SHE'S WORRIED ABOUT YOU.
WELL, YOU CAN TELL HER I'M FINE.
GO HOME AND TELL HER YOURSELF.
I AIN'T GOT NO HOME.
YOU GOT A LADY WHO REALLY LOVES YOU. SHE SAYS DIFFERENT.
IF SHE LOVED ME, SHE'D KNOW SENDIN' YOU AROUND HERE TO TELL ME THAT THE WORLD IS A PRETTY AMAZIN' PLACE AND I SHOULD STOP AND SMELL DA ROSES OR SOMETHIN' IS NOT--
OH, GOOD GOD, NO! I'M NOT THE PERSON YOU HIRE TO DO THAT.
NO. THE WORLD SUCKS, SWEETIE. YOU KNOW THAT.
RIGHT!
BUT YOU GOT HER.
I THINK THAT'S A REAL THING WITH HER.
IT'S PITY.
SHE PITIES ME.
EVERYONE PITIES ME.
EITHER THEY PITY ME OR THEY IGNORE ME.
HA!
YOU MAKIN' FUN?
NO, I WAS WONDERING HOW YOU AND I AREN'T BEST FRIENDS.
I GET IT. I GET IT.
NO ONE IGNORES YOU.
DUDE, ONCE I WAS STOLEN... FROM MY OWN LIFE.
I WASN'T AROUND FOR A LONG TIME.
AND NO ONE NOTICED.
NO ONE.
THAT REALLY HAPPENED.
AND YOU DIDN'T KILL YERSELF AFTER?
WHAT? NO.
NO.
JEEZ, WHAT DID YA DO?

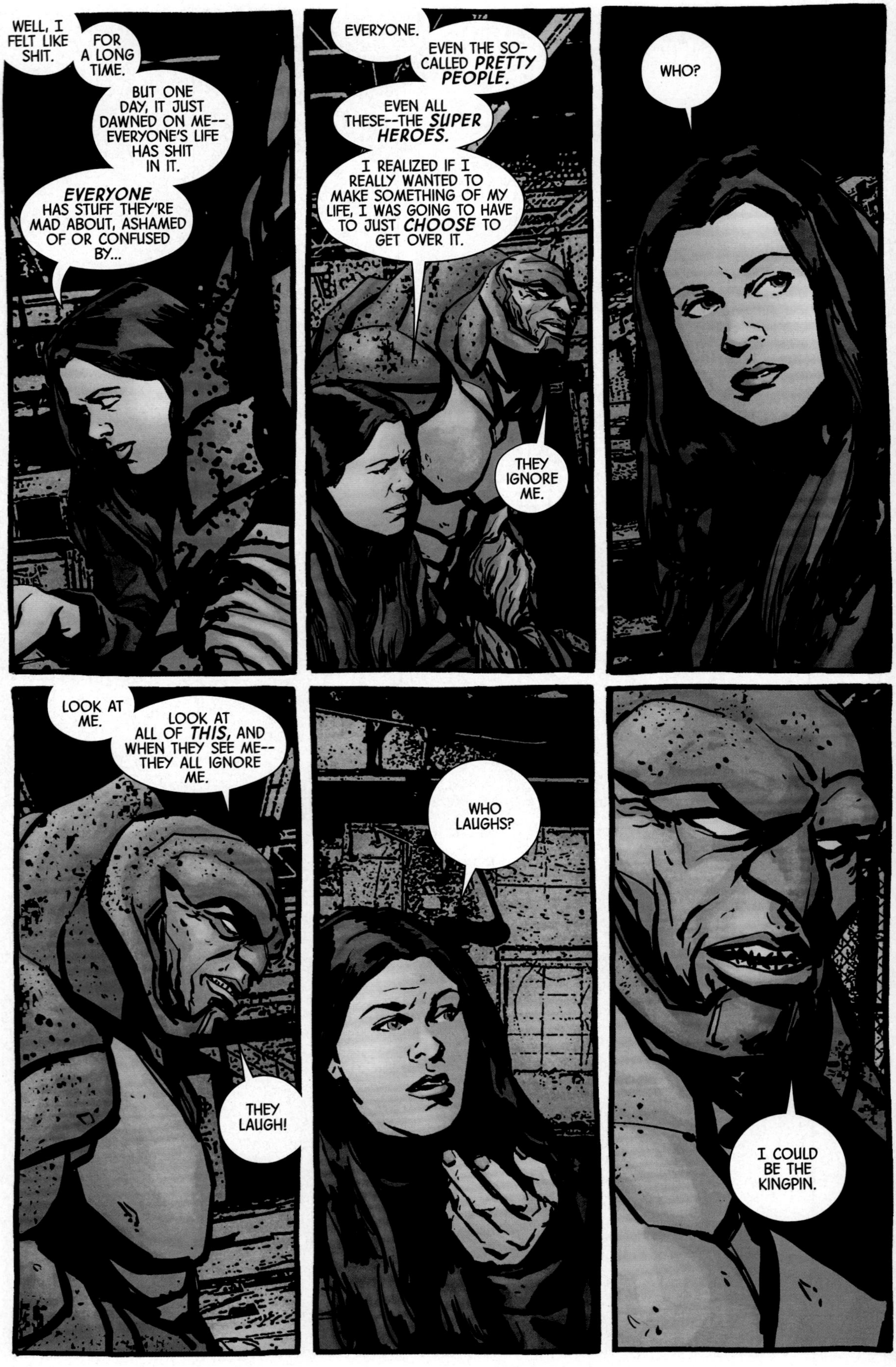

WELL, I FELT LIKE SHIT.
FOR A LONG TIME.
BUT ONE DAY, IT JUST DAWNED ON ME-- EVERYONE'S LIFE HAS SHIT IN IT.
EVERYONE HAS STUFF THEY'RE MAD ABOUT, ASHAMED OF OR CONFUSED BY...
EVERYONE.
EVEN THE SO-CALLED PRETTY PEOPLE.
EVEN ALL THESE--THE SUPER HEROES.
I REALIZED IF I REALLY WANTED TO MAKE SOMETHING OF MY LIFE, I WAS GOING TO HAVE TO JUST CHOOSE TO GET OVER IT.
THEY IGNORE ME.
WHO?
LOOK AT ME.
LOOK AT ALL OF THIS, AND WHEN THEY SEE ME-- THEY ALL IGNORE ME.
THEY LAUGH!
WHO LAUGHS?
I COULD BE THE KINGPIN.

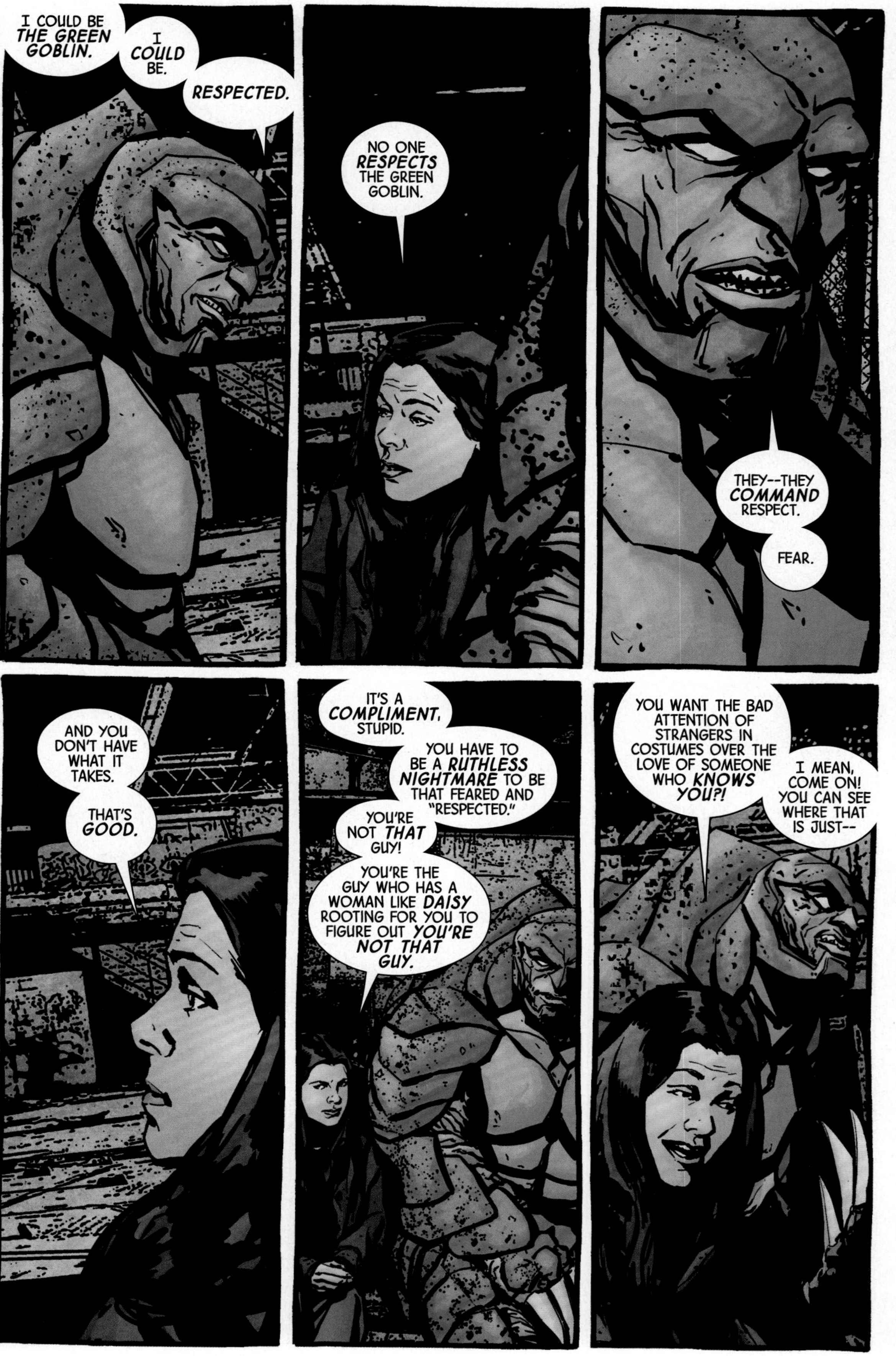
I COULD BE THE GREEN GOBLIN.
I COULD BE.
RESPECTED.
NO ONE RESPECTS THE GREEN GOBLIN.
THEY--THEY COMMAND RESPECT.
FEAR.
AND YOU DON'T HAVE WHAT IT TAKES.
THAT'S GOOD.
IT'S A COMPLIMENT, STUPID.
YOU HAVE TO BE A RUTHLESS NIGHTMARE TO BE THAT FEARED AND "RESPECTED."
YOU'RE NOT THAT GUY!
YOU'RE THE GUY WHO HAS A WOMAN LIKE DAISY ROOTING FOR YOU TO FIGURE OUT YOU'RE NOT THAT GUY.
YOU WANT THE BAD ATTENTION OF STRANGERS IN COSTUMES OVER THE LOVE OF SOMEONE WHO KNOWS YOU?!
I MEAN, COME ON! YOU CAN SEE WHERE THAT IS JUST--

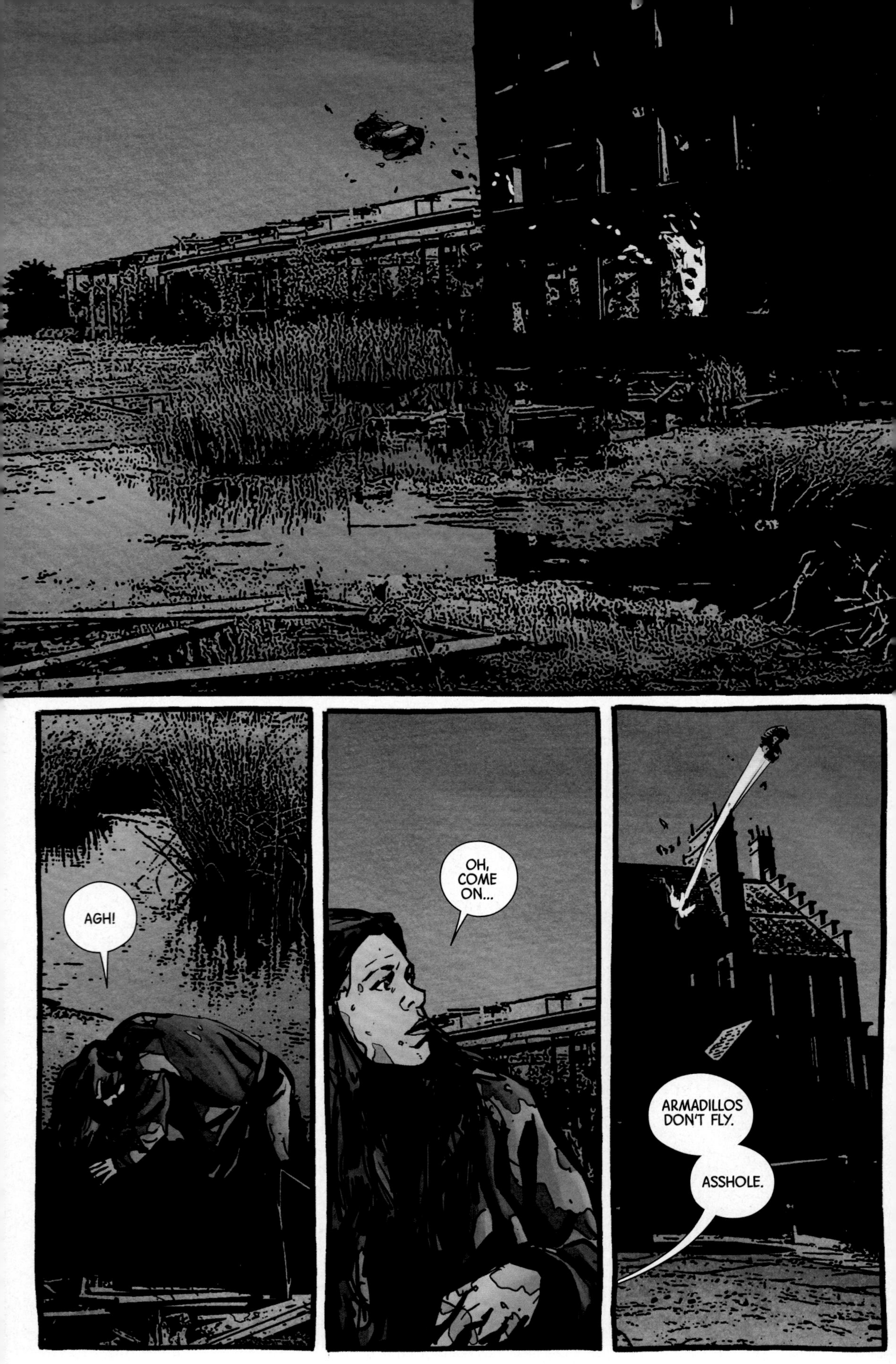
AGH!
OH, COME ON...
ARMADILLOS DON'T FLY.
ASSHOLE.

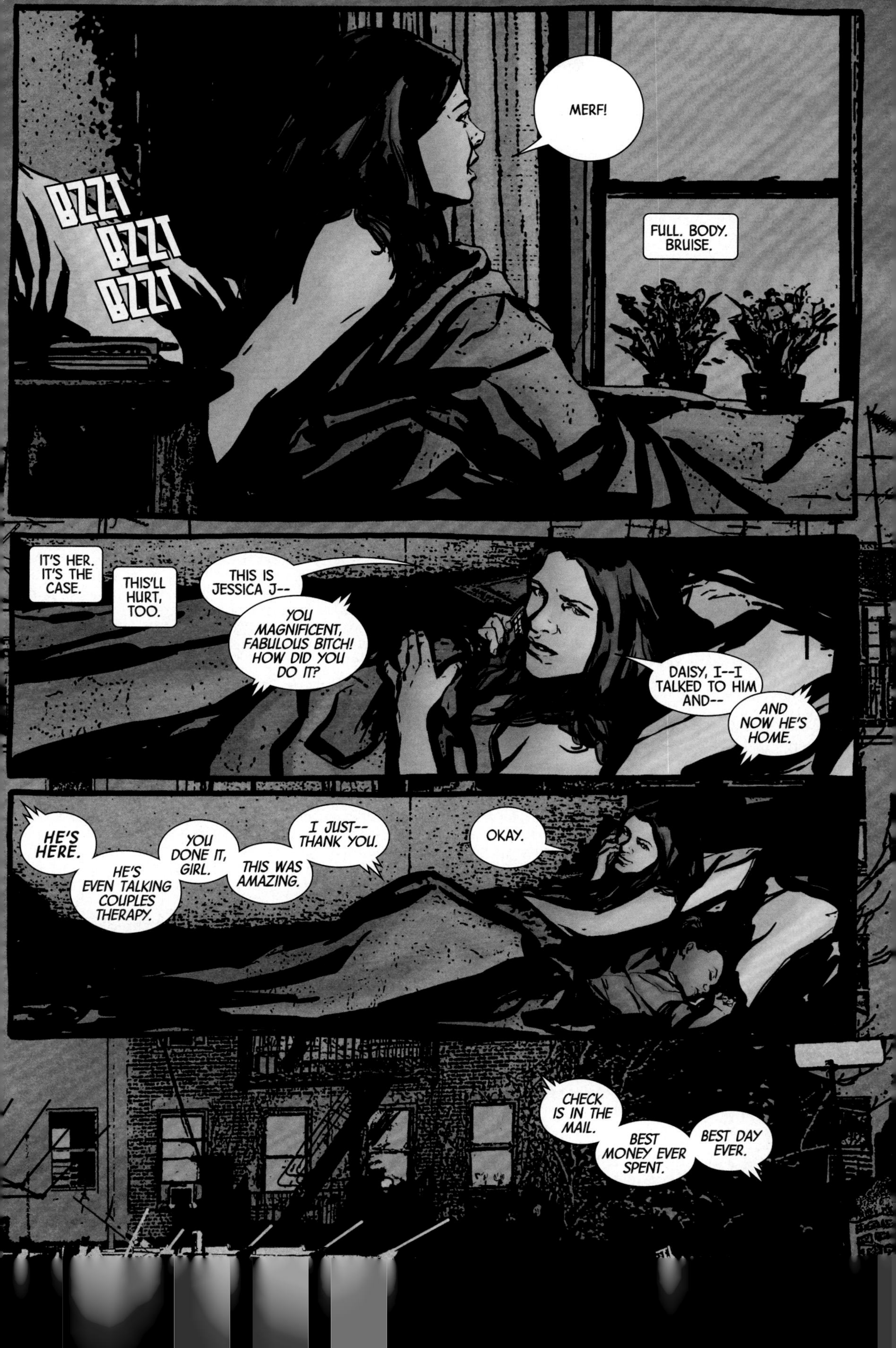
BZZT
BZZT
BZZT
MERF!
FULL. BODY. BRUISE.
IT'S HER. IT'S THE CASE.
THIS'LL HURT, TOO.
THIS IS JESSICA J--
YOU MAGNIFICENT, FABULOUS BITCH! HOW DID YOU DO IT?
DAISY, I--I TALKED TO HIM AND--
AND NOW HE'S HOME.
HE'S HERE.
HE'S EVEN TALKING COUPLES THERAPY.
YOU DONE IT, GIRL.
THIS WAS AMAZING.
I JUST-- THANK YOU.
OKAY.
CHECK IS IN THE MAIL.
BEST MONEY EVER SPENT.
BEST DAY EVER.

Goodbye,

JESSICA JONES

Not words I've ever wanted to say.

But here we are. The end of the road, once again.

Last time, many years ago, we ended the Jessica Jones series ALIAS because we had come to the natural conclusion of that particular story. But no one was going anywhere. Mike had stuff to do. Jessica came with me to other series. As she matured into a real part of the Marvel Universe, the TV gods came and made her a STAR!

TV made Jessica Jones a pop-culture totem. Crazy, right? Was anything about this material screaming, "Love me! Make me a star! I want to be popular"? Yeah, I haven't wrapped my head around it completely either.

When did I know Jessica had ascended past anything any comic book creator ever even wished for? A couple of years ago, JESSICA JONES cover artist David Mack and I were having lunch at the Grove food court in L.A. (Aren't we fancy?) Three women were sitting at the table next to us talking very animatedly about Jessica Jones. As if she were a real person. Just people, strangers, not comics folk (you can tell :)) talking about Jessica as if she were a real person. Like you talk about your fave character on your fave show. These women just happened to be sitting next to two out of the three people who help make her. David and I just stared at each other and listened, thinking about how we've been friends for so many years and have worked on so many projects together. This was so surreal.

Oh, yeah! There was also the time I wasn't home banging my head against the keyboard but instead was on stage at the Peabodys, with the show's cast and creator, accepting our PEABODY AWARD as David Letterman, Steve Martin, Jon Stewart and some of my other comedy god-heroes happened to be in the audience clapping in approval.

What? The comic with the naughty words?

Then there were the letters. The hundreds, then thousands, of notes, tweets, blogs and personal emails about what Jessica has meant to so many people getting over their actual, real-life, horrible shit. It sounds so trite in print but I love each and every one of you. You have no idea how you have inspired me. No idea.

Michael and I came back to Jessica because we were both empowered by her success in the world and felt individually challenged by the question of whether we were capable of accomplishing it again.

We also knew that this would be a shorter run than last time. I basically told Michael that when he was ready to go, I will go with him. We knew this was going to be our last issue long before I knew this would be one of my last comics that I would be writing for Marvel.

Michael and I are leaving to pursue another publishing venture together, so this very well may be goodbye to Jessica forever. It might really be. That's why I chose this as the last story.

I wanted to give Jessica one perfect day. Not a perfect day for you or me, but a perfect day for her. A case that challenges her. A case she solves. A case only she could have solved. All while maintaining all her shit. A perfect "her" day. I had one recently. One for me. A perfect me day. They are so rare. I thought, that is what I owe Jessica. One perfect day.

And all the while paying off my most loyal readers with the chance to go back and reread how I have planted seeds for this story for years in all my books. One last of the kinds of story tricks you can pull when you're under exclusive contract like I was for so many years.

Now, I know enough about life and pop culture and show business to never say never, but at this moment in time, and after having survived a couple of near-death experiences this year, I seem to need to treat this with some pragmatic finality. Can you imagine a phrase less emotional than "pragmatic finality"? :) The words are in direct contrast to how I feel.

How I feel is overwhelmingly proud of the quality of work that Michael Gaydos and Matt Hollingsworth did in the last couple of issues. I think every issue of this particular run is outstanding, but the last couple of issues — which may be empowered by the fact that Michael knew that he was leaving as well — have been subtly exceptional. Michael's artwork may not be as flashy as some, but the soulfulness and the layers of humanity that Mike brings to every single character is perfection to me. There are only a few comic artists working today capable of the level of subtle character acting that Michael accomplishes in every page. It is an honor to write for him.

As I told the story many times, Michael and I actually went to college

together, but we weren't actually friends. Or close. He was better and more successful than me and I was a miserable prick about it. He didn't know I felt this way because he didn't know me and was off being better than me. :)

Now, as we close this chapter in our lives and enter another equally exciting one, I can't help but be charmed by the fact that I have somehow bamboozled this man, who haunted me in college, to partner with me to create work I'm so immensely proud of.

And, listen, when an artist or writer tells you they are proud of something, you should know that they are always, and I mean always, pushing past a natural desire to complain and nitpick or tell you what's wrong with it. It's an effort to isolate the kernel of pride. Pride is hard for creative people on a day-to-day basis. You know, unless they're a sociopath like Mark Millar. :)

I am very deeply proud of Jessica Jones. Not of MY work but of what blossomed out of it. The work of my collaborators, the work of my editors and peers, the work of Melissa Rosenberg and the *Jessica Jones* TV writers' room and even the makers of the clever and excellent MERCHANDISE that I remain stunned by.

I am very proud of this. This collaboration. With Mike. With Matt. With Tom. With Cory. With Alanna. With you.

Jessica's new curators have reached out to me and I have loved what I have heard. I will be buying and reading each comic as Jessica and family are taken to places I haven't even thought of. Unless I still get them for free, then woo-hoo! (But probably don't. :))

And lastly to Joe Quesada. Jessica exists because Joe told me to bring a crime book to Marvel. The end. No Joe, no Jessica. Or Miles Morales for that matter.

Michael and I will see you this summer with our brand-new creation *Pearl*. We have challenged ourselves to come up with a character even more psychically complex than Jessica. I hope you check her crazy ride out, too.

Until the inevitable Marvel/DC crossover where Jessica has to beat the hell out of one of the Batgirls or something, I thank you and I love you.

Goodbye.
BENDIS

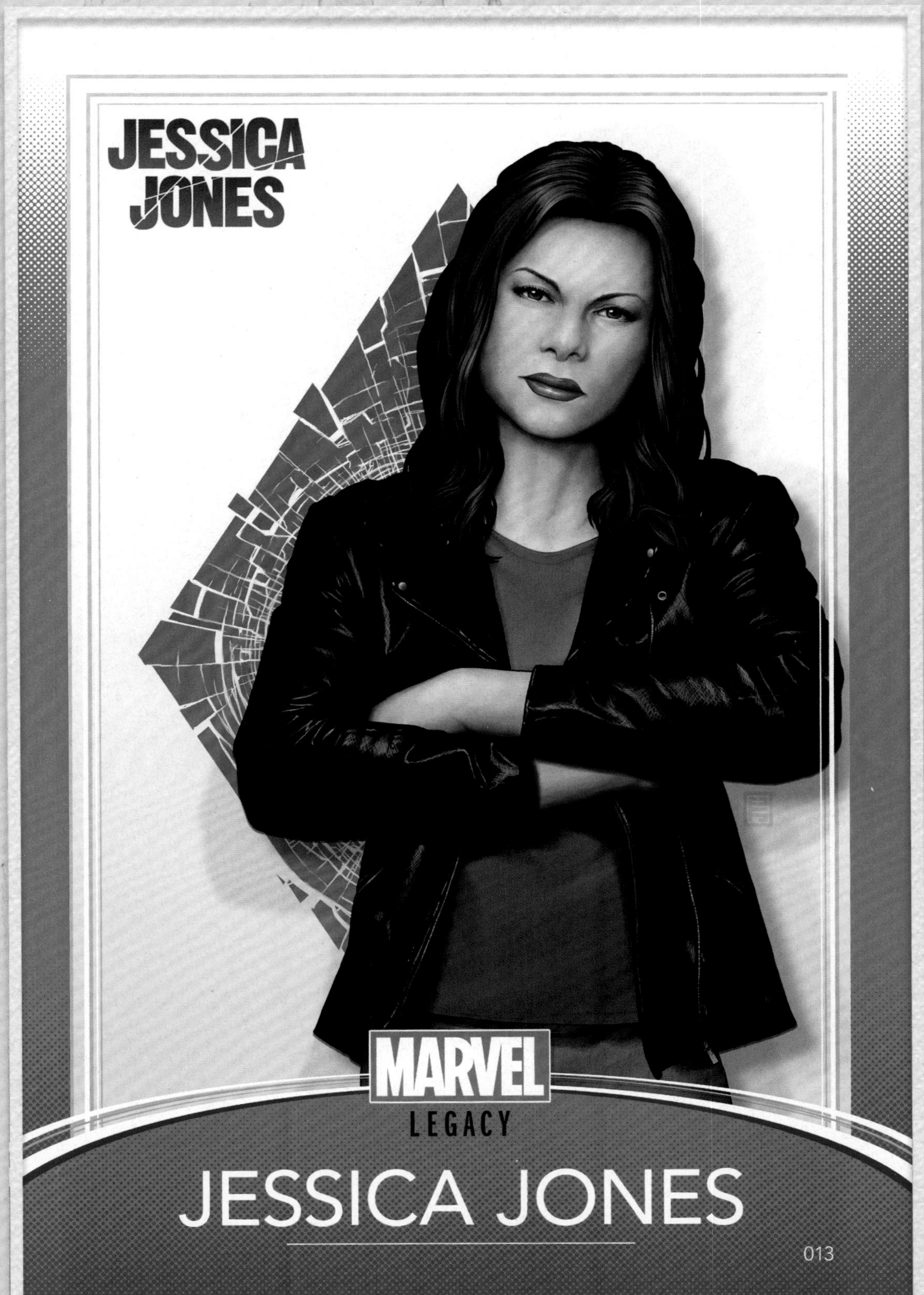
JESSICA
JONES
MARVEL
LEGACY
JESSICA JONES
013

#13 Trading Card variant by **John Tyler Christopher**

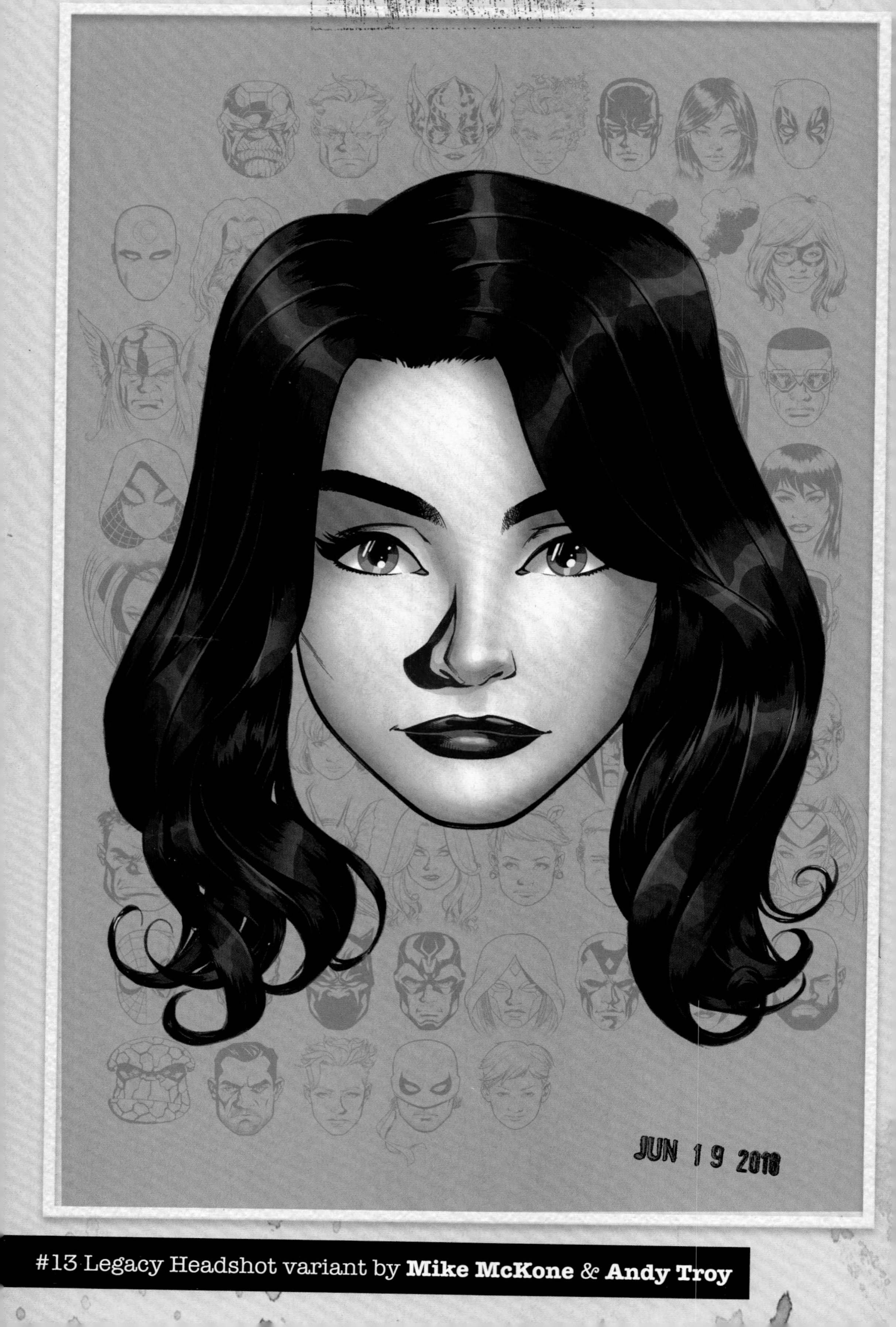

#13 Legacy Headshot variant by **Mike McKone** & **Andy Troy**